T0318781

"The book is very interesting starting from the idea itself to the well cited information in each chapter. It is straightforward, simple language, systematic in its presentation and at the same time eligible to be used for all levels of learning: undergrad/grad/researchers, etc., covered most of the important points in each topic, cleared out the confusion between the different laws (Agency law, Trust law and Corporate law ...) and the difference between the nature of the firm and the theory of the firm ... complete and well presented."

— *Dina Rady*, Ph.D., American University and
George Washington University

Economics, Capitalism, and Corporations

This book is a continuation of *Corporate Law and the Theory of the Firm: Reconstructing Corporations, Shareholders, Directors, Owners, and Investors.* The author extends his analysis of contract law, property law, agency law, trust law, and corporate statutory law and applies that analysis to defy conventional concepts and theories in economics, finance, investment, and accounting and expose the artificial boundaries established by decades of research founded on indefensible assumptions and fallacious conclusions.

Using the Humpty Dumpty principle, where words mean what the authors want them to mean, economists have created "strange new worlds" where contract law, property law, agency law, and corporate statutory law no longer apply.

The author dismantles the theory of the firm by proving that the theory of the firm willfully and intentionally ignores fundamental contract law, property law, agency law, and corporate statutory law. Contrary to the theory of the firm, shareholders do not own corporations, directors are not agents of shareholders, and shareholders are not investors in corporations.

The author proves that by property law and corporate law, capital is not privately owned by capitalists but by corporations. Entire economic and social systems have been constructed that have no basis in law. With the advent of publicly traded corporations, the capital is there, but both capitalists and capitalism have been rendered extinct.

This book will appeal to researchers and graduate and upper-level undergraduate students in economics, finance, accounting, law, and sociology, as well as legal scholars, attorneys, and accountants.

Wm. Dennis Huber received a DBA in international business, accounting, finance, and economics from the University of Sarasota, Florida; a JD, an MBA in accounting and finance, an MA in economics, an Ed.M and an MS in public policy, and a BA in sociology and psychology from the State University of New York at Buffalo. He also has an LL.M in homeland and national security law from the Western Michigan University Thomas M. Cooley School of Law. He is a certified public accountant and admitted to the New York Bar. He has taught at universities in the U.S., Canada, Mexico, and the Middle East.

Routledge Studies in the Economics of Legal Relationships

Sponsored by Michigan State University College of Law
Series Editors:
Nicholas Mercuro, Michigan State University College of Law
Michael D. Kaplowitz, Michigan State University

For a full list of titles in this series please visit https://www.routledge.com/The-Economics-of-Legal-Relationships/book-series/ELR.

Law and Economics
Philosophical issues and fundamental questions
Edited by Aristides N. Hatzis and Nicholas Mercuro

Public Procurement Policy
Edited by Gustavo Piga and Tünde Tatrai

Legal Origins and the Efficiency Dilemma
Nuno Garoupa, Carlos Gómez Ligüerre and Lela Mélon

Law and Economics of Public Procurement Reforms
Edited by Gustavo Piga and Tünde Tátrai

Law and Economics as Interdisciplinary Exchange
Philosophical, Methodological and Historical Perspectives
Péter Cserne and Magdalena Małecka

Extraterritoriality and International Bribery
A Collective Action Perspective
Branislav Hock

Economic Analysis of Property Law Cases
Boudewijn R. A. Bouckaert

Corporate Law and the Theory of the Firm
Reconstructing Corporations, Shareholders, Directors, Owners, and Investors
Wm. Dennis Huber

Economics, Capitalism, and Corporations
Contradictions of Corporate Law, Economics, and the Theory of the Firm
Wm. Dennis Huber

Economics, Capitalism, and Corporations

Contradictions of Corporate Law,
Economics, and the Theory of the Firm

Wm. Dennis Huber

Routledge
Taylor & Francis Group

LONDON AND NEW YORK

First published 2021
by Routledge
2 Park Square, Milton Park, Abingdon, Oxon OX14 4RN

and by Routledge
52 Vanderbilt Avenue, New York, NY 10017

Routledge is an imprint of the Taylor & Francis Group, an informa business

© 2021 Wm. Dennis Huber

The right of Wm. Dennis Huber to be identified as author of this work has
been asserted by him in accordance with sections 77 and 78 of the
Copyright, Designs and Patents Act 1988.

British Library Cataloguing in Publication Data
A catalogue record for this book is available from the British Library

Library of Congress Cataloging-in-Publication Data
Names: Huber, Wm. Dennis (William Dennis), 1951- author. | Huber, Wm.
    Dennis (William Dennis), 1951- Corporate law and the theory of the firm.
Title: Economics, capitalism, and corporations : contradictions of corporate
    law, economics, and the theory of the firm / Wm. Dennis Huber.
Description: Milton Park, Abingdon, Oxon ; New York, NY : Routledge,
    2020. | Series: Routledge studies in the economics of legal relationships |
    Includes bibliographical references and index.
Identifiers: LCCN 2020031967 (print) | LCCN 2020031968 (ebook) | ISBN
    9780367895563 (hardback) | ISBN 9781003019794 (ebook)
Subjects: LCSH: Corporation law–United States. | Business enterprises–Law
    and legislation–United States. | Corporation law–Economic aspects–
    United States. | Corporation law. | Corporation law–Economic aspects. |
    Capitalism.
Classification: LCC KF1414 .H835 2020 (print) | LCC KF1414 (ebook) |
    DDC 346.73/066–dc23
LC record available at https://lccn.loc.gov/2020031967
LC ebook record available at https://lccn.loc.gov/2020031968

ISBN: 978-0-367-89556-3 (hbk)
ISBN: 978-1-003-01979-4 (ebk)

Typeset in Times New Roman
by Taylor & Francis Books

This book is dedicated to Vivian, Jennifer, and Justin.

Contents

Epilogue   195

Illustrations

Figures

Tables

Other publications by this author

References

PCAOB sanctions, sanction risk, sanction risk premiums, and public policy: Theoretical framework and a call for research. *Journal of Accounting, Ethics and Public Policy*, 14 (3), 647–663. (2013). https://papers.ssrn.com/sol3/papers.cfm?abstract_id=2307559.

The history of the decline and fall of the American accounting profession. *International Journal of Economics and Accounting*, 4 (4), 365–388. (2014). https://papers.ssrn.com/sol3/papers.cfm?abstract_id=2260594.

The structure of the public accounting industry: Why existing market models fail. *Journal of Theoretical Accounting Research*, 10 (2). 43–67. (2015). https://papers.ssrn.com/sol3/papers.cfm?abstract_id=2326297.

The research-publication complex and the construct shift in accounting research. *International Journal of Critical Accounting*, 7 (1), 1–48. (2016). https://papers.ssrn.com/sol3/papers.cfm?abstract_id=2360378.

On the hegemony of financial accounting research: A survey of accounting research seen from a global perspective. *Journal of Theoretical Accounting Research*, 11 (1), 14–29. (2016). https://papers.ssrn.com/sol3/papers.cfm?abstract_id=2444245.

Public accounting and the myth of the public interest. *Journal of Accounting, Ethics and Public Policy*, 16 (2), 251–272. (2014). https://papers.ssrn.com/sol3/papers.cfm?abstract_id=2640375.

Guardians of the galaxy: Public accounting and the public interest. *International Journal of Critical Accounting: Special Issue on the Research Endeavours of Tony Lowe*, 7(5/6), 466–476. (2017). https://papers.ssrn.com/sol3/papers.cfm?abstract_id=2596373.

The SEC's ultra vires recognition of the FASB as a standard-setting body. *Richmond Journal of Law & the Public Interest*, 19 (2), 120–152. (2016). https://papers.ssrn.com/sol3/papers.cfm?abstract_id=2662634.

Deep impact: Impact factors and accounting research. *International Journal of Critical Accounting*, 8 (1), 56–67. (2016). https://papers.ssrn.com/sol3/papers.cfm?abstract_id=2441340.

Accounting research productivity: More heat than light? *Journal of Theoretical Accounting Research*, 11 (2), 28–62. (2016). https://papers.ssrn.com/sol3/papers.cfm?abstract_id=2444543.

The myth of protecting the public interest: The case of the missing mandate in federal securities laws. *Journal of Business & Securities Law*, 16 (2), 401–423. (2016). https://papers.ssrn.com/sol3/papers.cfm?abstract_id=2605301.

Can a not-for-profit membership corporation be created as a "shell" corporation? *Liberty University Law Review*, 11 (1), 1–32. (2017). https://papers.ssrn.com/sol3/papers.cfm?abstract_id=2361909.

On neo-colonialism and the colonization of accounting research. *International Journal of Critical Accounting*, 9 (1), 18–41. (2017). https://papers.ssrn.com/sol3/papers.cfm?abstract_id=2548742.

Law, language, and corporatehood: Corporations and the U.S. Constitution. *International Journal for the Rule of Law, Courtroom Procedures, Judicial Linguistics & Legal English*, 1 (2), 78–110. (2018). https://papers.ssrn.com/sol3/papers.cfm?abstract_id=2835563.

Irreconcilable differences? The FASB's Conceptual Framework and the public interest. *International Journal of Critical Accounting*, 9 (5/6), 514–523. (2018). https://papers.ssrn.com/sol3/papers.cfm?abstract_id=2789907.

The Supreme Court's subversion of the constitutional process and the creation of persons ex nihilo. *International Journal for the Rule of Law, Courtroom Procedures, Judicial Linguistics & Legal English*, 2 (1), 53–72. (2018). https://papers.ssrn.com/sol3/papers.cfm?abstract_id=2841825.

The FASB's sabotage of Congressional policy and federal securities laws. *Journal of Accounting, Ethics, and Public Policy*, 20 (1): 31–75. (2019). https://papers.ssrn.com/sol3/papers.cfm?abstract_id=2841825.

The FASB's Conceptual Framework: A case of the Emperor's New Clothes. *Journal of Accounting, Ethics & Public Policy*, 21 (1), 77–114. (2020). https://papers.ssrn.com/sol3/papers.cfm?abstract_id=3400769.

Social/Critical/Emancipatory accounting research: Its failure and prospects for redemption. In *Accounting, accountability and society*, Del Baldo, Baldarelli, Dillard, Ciambotti (Eds.), London: Springer. (2020).

Corporate law and the theory of the firm: Reconstructing corporations, shareholders, directors, owners, and investors. New York: Routledge. (2020).

Acknowledgments

Thanks to Dr. Dina Rady, Dr. Stephen Errol Blythe, and Dr. Bob McGee.

Thanks to Kristina Abbots and Christiana Mandizha and the production staff at Routledge.

Thanks to Vivian for proofreading portions and making helpful suggestions.

Prologue

This book is an extension of *Corporate Law and the Theory of the Firm: Reconstructing Corporations, Shareholders, Directors, Owners, and Investors,* which was an exposé of the contradictions of contract law, property law, agency law, trust law, and corporate law and from which some portions of this book are adopted and summarized with permission. This book delves much more deeply into the contradictions between corporate law and the economic theory of the firm and expands the analysis into the contradictions between corporate law and economics, finance, and accounting. It reveals how the term, and therefore the concept, of "capital" has been distorted and how "capitalist" and "capitalism" as a social system have been twisted and perverted.

The book begins with a brief review of corporate law and its contradictions, including property law and agency law, in order to establish the context and provide a foundation for an analysis of corporations and economic considerations, finance considerations, investment considerations, and accounting considerations.

Jensen and Meckling's (1976) *Theory of the Firm: Managerial Behavior, Agency Costs and Ownership Structure* is considered the classic on the "theory of the firm." Jensen and Meckling attempt to "integrate elements from the theory of agency, the theory of property rights and the theory of finance to develop a theory of the ownership structure of the firm" (p. 305). While it was successful in launching an entirely new branch of literature on the economic theory of the firm, it was an abject failure in achieving its objective. It did not integrate elements from the theory of agency with the theory of property rights and the theory of finance to develop a theory of the ownership structure of the firm because it not only ignored but made assumptions contradicted by corporate law, property law, and agency law.

Their approach was backwards. They (attempt to) use the theory of agency, the theory of property rights, and the theory of finance to develop a theory of the ownership structure of the firm rather than establishing the legal ownership structure of the firm as determined by agency law and property law to develop an economic theory of the firm. Property law determines the ownership of the firm, and agency law determines the relationship of directors and shareholders. It is only after the legal ownership structure of the firm and the relationship of corporations, directors, and shareholders are determined that the economic and finance theory of firm can be developed. But Jensen and Meckling completely ignored an analysis of property law and agency law, choosing rather to rest on invalid assumptions and unjustified conclusions about the relationship of property law and agency law to corporations.

Jensen and Meckling's *Theory of the Firm*, along with Fama and Jensen's 1983 *Separation of Ownership and Control*, laid the groundwork of the economic "theory of the firm." The economic "theory of the firm" is grounded in agency theory, which is a function of Berle and Mean's theory of the separation of ownership and control in corporations. The separation of ownership and control takes as an axiom that shareholders are owners of the corporation. Thus, corporate ownership necessarily determines the economic theory of the firm. But since shareholders do not own the corporation, there are no owners to be separated from. If shareholders do not own the corporation, directors are not their agents. Therefore, there can be no agency theory of the firm or agency costs on which the theory of the firm is grounded and the entire economic "theory of the firm" falls apart. The entire economic theory of the firm stands or falls on whether shareholders own the corporation. It is inexplicable how Jensen and Meckling and Fama and Jensen—and those who followed them—were able to create an entire body of literature on the theory of the firm based on agency costs without even acknowledging the requirements of agency law. Referring to directors as agents of shareholders is legally incorrect and misleading economically.

As taught in every introductory economics textbook, economics is the study of the allocation of scarce resources. The allocation of scarce resources is a function of the legal structure of society (Banner, 2011), which is therefore necessarily a function of corporate law since corporate law determines the economics of the corporation which in turn determines the allocation of scarce resources.

Virtually all textbooks used in the first course in accounting, typically called "Principles of Accounting" or "Introductory Accounting," include chapters dedicated to various parts of a corporate balance sheet beginning with the familiar equation assets equals liabilities plus equity, further divided into current assets, long-term assets, current liabilities, long-term liabilities (relevant here, bonds), and equity. Equity is then divided into common stock, preferred stock, and retained earnings. Equity is simply the net assets—that is, total assets minus liabilities equals net assets.

The equity section is universally referred to as "Shareholders' Equity" or "Owners' [plural] Equity." Referring to corporate equity as shareholders' equity is a perversion of property law and corporate law. If there are no owners of a corporation it cannot be "owners' equity" or "shareholders' equity." The corporation owns the total assets, therefore by law it owns the net assets. The equity of a corporation is not the *shareholders'* equity. It is the *corporation's* equity and is so recognized by at least a few courts (e.g., *Rhode Island Hospital Trust Co. v. Doughton*[1]). This fundamental misconception of ownership of the corporation's equity is at once the cause and result of the erroneous construction of "capital," "capitalist," and "capitalism."

Financial capital and capital resources of production (physical assets) have been used interchangeably as if they are equivalent or worse, a case of the Humpty Dumpty principle—"When I use a word … it means just what I choose it to mean—neither more nor less."[2] Shareholders of corporations whose shares are traded in the market are considered to be capitalists, while those same corporations (or their directors, officers, or managers) are referred to as entrepreneurs.

Furthermore, entire social systems have been constructed on concepts of "capital," "capitalist," and "capitalism" that are not legally, historically, economically, or sociologically valid. Capitalism as a social and economic system is said to be a function of the laws of private property while at the same time it is said to be based on the private, as opposed to government, ownership of the means of production. Refusing to interpret capital, capitalist, and capitalism within the parameters of corporate and property law corrupts the meaning of capital, capitalist, and capitalism.

Ownership of capital, whether financial or physical, as determined by property law and corporate law is ignored, imputed to shareholders rather than the corporation. As a matter of corporate law and private property law, shareholders do not own either the financial capital or the means of production. Therefore, shareholders are not and cannot be capitalists, and corporations (or their directors, officers, or managers) cannot be entrepreneurs and therefore cannot be capitalists.

The purposes of this book is first to identify the more outrageously invalid assumptions and conclusions of the theory of the firm as substantiated by corporate law, property law, and agency law.

Second, it is to expose the blatant contradictions concerning the use of the terms "capital" and as a consequence "capitalist" and "capitalism" by examining the underlying theories and concepts of what constitutes capital, who are capitalists, and how capital and capitalist are related to capitalism.

Third, it is to reveal the discrepancies between judicial opinions, and corporate law, economics, finance, investment, and accounting which are the result of failing to use terms consistently across fields and disciplines thus isolating each field and discipline from other fields and disciplines. "Capital," for example, is used inconsistently, and therefore contradictorily, in economics, finance, and accounting.

Fourth, it is to discover a common denominator between economics, finance, investment, and accounting that will serve to dismantle the artificial boundaries established by decades of research founded on indefensible assumptions and fallacious conclusions.

Before the critics say I neglected to include this work or omitted that author, I plead guilty. There are literally multiple dozens of books and research papers in law reviews, economic journals, and accounting journals that I could have included here but have not. First, there are space limitations to contend with, but more important, it is not necessary to include all of them, or even more of them. The arguments I make herein are sufficiently supported by a representative sample. Citing additional authors, books or articles or cases would not make the arguments presented herein more truthful or more persuasive.

Notes on limitations and usage of terms

1   The "firm" and the "corporation" are sometimes considered identical in the literature, but other times they are considered different. Robé (2011) explains the use of the terms as follows:

> The notions of 'firm' and 'corporation' are very often confused in the literature on the theory of the firm. In this paper ... the corporation is a legal entity entitled to operate in the legal system and in particular to own assets, to enter into contracts and to incur liabilities ... . The firm is the economic activity developed as a consequence of the cluster of contracts connecting the corporation owning these assets to various holders of resources required in the firm's operations.
>
> (p. 1)

I consider "corporations," "firms," and "enterprises" to be identical unless otherwise stated. That is, I intentionally use the terms "corporation," "firm," and "enterprise" interchangeably since the legal entity, the corporation, and its economic activities, the firm or enterprise, are inseparable when analyzing the contradictions of law and economics. Furthermore, there can be no firm unless there is first a corporation. There are times and contexts when the terms "firm," "corporation," or "enterprise" should be used to mean different things, but not for the purposes of this book. There are also theories of the firm other than economic based theories (e.g., behavioral theories, organizational theories, management theories; Walker, 2016). Fifty years ago, a survey found "at least 21 different 'concepts of the firm' in the literature of business and economics" (Orts, 2013). However, they are not relevant to the purpose of this book.

2   I sometimes use the term "publicly traded corporation" because that is the conventional parlance in legal, economic, and accounting research. However, it is a misnomer. It is not the corporation that is publicly traded, but the shares of the corporation that are publicly traded in the market (e.g., the New York Stock Exchange), and the reader should bear this in mind when seeing that term. Most of the time I use the lengthier, but more accurate, term "corporation whose shares are traded in the market."

Notes on style

1   As with *Corporate Law and the Theory of the Firm: Reconstructing Corporations, Shareholders, Directors, Owners, and Investors*, I endeavor to maintain a "Goldilocks" approach. That is, while there is a core of lawyers, judges, and legal scholars who have training in economics, and likewise a small cadre of economists and economics researchers who have training in law, there are many lawyers, judges, and legal scholars who have insufficient training in economics and many economists and economics researchers who have no training in law. Thus, while it is not written as a legal brief trying to convince a judge or a law review article debating the finer points of law, my goal is to present a work that is sufficiently technical and accurate from a legal perspective to be meaningful to law students, lawyers, and judges but not so technical as to be irrelevant to economists and economics researchers. At the same time, although there are no charts, graphs, statistics, or econometrics (or even any equations other than assets = liabilities + equity or the financial asset pricing model) that is the mainstay of economists, my aim is to make this work sufficiently technical and accurate from an economics perspective to be meaningful to economists and economics researchers but not so technical as to make it irrelevant to law students, lawyers, and judges. A challenge at the very least, and I apologize in advance if I fall short in achieving that goal.

2   There is significant overlap between and among the fields and disciplines of corporate law, economics, finance, accounting, history, and sociology. There is, therefore, a significant amount of cross-referencing within and between the chapters in this book. What may appear as repetition, however, is not actually repetition. It is an examination of theories and principles from different perspectives, which is necessary since I am examining each factor not only in isolation but in relation to all the others, like a polygon. Oddly, in spite of the overlap, the fields and disciplines remain essentially isolated with no attempt to find a common denominator that cuts across fields and disciplines.

Notes

1   Rhode Island Hospital Trust Co. v. Doughton, 270 U.S. 69, 81, 46 S.Ct. 256 70, L. Ed. 475 (1926).
2   Lewis Carroll, *Alice Through the Looking-Glass*, 1871.

Bibliography

Cases

Rhode Island Hospital Trust Co. v. Doughton, 270 U.S. 69, 81, 46 S.Ct. 256 70, L.Ed. 475 (1926).

Authors

Banner, S. (2011). *American property: A history of how, why, and what we own.* Cambridge, MA: Harvard University Press.

Fama, E.F., & Jensen, M.C. (1983). Separation of ownership and control. *Journal of Law Economics*, 26 (2), 301–326. doi:10.1086/467037.

Jensen, M.C., & Meckling, W.H. (1976). Theory of the firm: Managerial behavior, agency costs and ownership structure. *Journal of Financial Economics*, 3, 305–360. doi:10.1016/0304-405X(76)90026-X.

Orts, E.W. (2013). *Business persons: A legal theory of the firm.* London: Oxford University Press..

Robé, J.-P. (2011). The legal structure of the firm. *Accounting, Economics, and Law—A Convivium*, 1 (1), 1–85. doi:10.2202/2152-2820.1001.

Walker, P. (2016). *The theory of the firm: An overview of the economic mainstream.* London: Routledge.

1 Review of corporations and corporate law, contract law, property law, agency law, and trust law[1]

Introduction

Economics, as defined by every introductory economics textbook, is the science of the allocation of scarce resources. Property in its various forms constitutes resources to the owner of those resources. The legal structure of society determines who owns the resources (e.g., private persons, government, or "the people"), which resources are allocated and controlled (e.g., labor or capital), and how the resources are allocated and controlled (by the market or centrally planned by the government).

Corporations are powerful economic forces in the global economy. Understanding corporate law is therefore important since corporate law determines the ownership and legal structure of corporations, and the ownership and legal structure of the corporation determines the economics of the corporation and consequently the allocation of scarce resources.

In this chapter I review corporations and corporate law and how contract law, property law, agency law, and trust law apply to corporations and shareholders in order to establish the foundation for the analysis of *Economics, Capitalism, and Corporations: Contradictions of Corporate Law, Economics, and the Theory of the Firm*. While this chapter is not intended to be as comprehensive a review of corporations and corporate law as presented in *Corporate Law and the Theory of the Firm: Reconstructing Corporations, Shareholders, Directors, Owners, and Investors*, it is sufficient to sustain my argument that shareholders do not own corporations, that shareholders are not investors in corporations, and directors are not agents of shareholders thus obliterating any validity for the theory of the firm. Readers who are interested in learning more about contract law, property law, agency law, trust law, and corporate law in greater depth are referred to that work.

Economists either downplay or reject outright the role of the law in defining the firm (Masten, 1993). But understanding contract law, property law, agency law, trust law, and corporate law and their contradictions is important since the allocation of scarce resources is a function of the legal structure of society (Banner, 2011). Corporate law determines the ownership and legal structure of the corporation, and the legal structure of the corporation determines the economics of the corporation and therefore the allocation of scarce resources. Understanding the ownership of a corporation is necessary for a proper understanding of the nature of the corporation and an important consideration in the allocation of resources and rights in the corporation (Velasco, 2010).

The economic theory of the firm is founded primarily on the theory of separation of ownership and control of corporations. According to the theory, since there is a separation of ownership and control shareholders hire directors as their agents creating, as a result, agency costs.

Proponents of the theory of the firm make a distinction between the "corporation" as a legal entity and the "firm" as an economic entity and therefore between legal agents and economic agents. But that is a false dichotomy. The fact that one person, a principal, hires another person to be an "economic agent," i.e., to represent her in an economic transaction, necessarily and automatically makes the economic agent a legal agent. An agent cannot be an economic agent unless they are first a legal agent: i.e., that complies with the laws of agency.

Corporations: creation, governance and operations, and ownership and control

Creation of corporations

Corporations can only be created by state corporation statutes. Corporate governance and operations are also controlled by state corporation statutes.

The Delaware General Corporation Law sets forth the requirements for creating a corporation:

> Any person, partnership, association or corporation, singly or jointly with others, and without regard to such person's or entity's residence, domicile or state of incorporation, may incorporate or organize a corporation under this chapter by filing with the Division of Corporations in the Department of State a certificate of incorporation which shall be executed, acknowledged and filed in accordance with § 103 of this title.[2]

The New York Business Corporation Law, on the other hand, limits the formation of a corporation to natural, not artificial, legal, or fictitious persons: "Incorporators. One or more natural persons of the age of eighteen years or over may act as incorporators of a corporation to be formed under this chapter."[3]

In all jurisdictions, corporations begin their existence and operation when the articles of incorporation are filed with the secretary (or department) of state, not when shares are issued or assets transferred to the corporation.

In Delaware, once the certificate of incorporation is filed in accordance with the Delaware General Corporation Law, the corporation begins its existence:

Upon the filing with the Secretary of State of the certificate of incorporation, executed and acknowledged in accordance with § 103 of this title, the incorporator or incorporators who signed the certificate, and such incorporator's or incorporators' successors and assigns, shall, from the date of such filing, be and constitute a body corporate, by the name set forth in the certificate, subject to § 103(d) of this title and subject to dissolution or other termination of its existence as provided in this chapter.[4]

The New York Business Corporation Law is more emphatic: "Upon the filing of the certificate of incorporation by the department of state, the corporate existence shall begin ... ."[5]

It is important to note that upon creation the corporation exists without assets, without shares, and without shareholders. Significantly, the corporation begins its existence and the governance structure is in place prior to the election of the directors by the shareholders. There are in fact no shares outstanding at this time so there are no shareholders to elect the directors.[6] The duties of directors to the corporation begin at the time the directors are named in the articles of incorporation and filed or when they are appointed by the incorporators.

Governance and operations of corporations

Corporate governance must first be in accordance with corporate statutory law. Common law only enters into the interpretation of corporate governance when statutory law is ambiguous or silent.

Corporate governance is the foundation of the economic "theory of the firm" since corporate governance addresses the theory of "separation of ownership and control" and "agency theory." As a prelude to the corporate governance and theory of the firm, the statutory and common law requirements of corporate governance must be examined.

Corporate governance in statutory law

The Delaware General Corporation Law provides that "The business and affairs of every corporation organized under this chapter shall be managed by or under the direction of a board of directors."[7] "Managed by or under the direction of a board of directors" necessarily includes decisions on how to allocate corporate resources.

In New York, "the business of a corporation shall be managed under the direction of its board of directors ... ."[8]

In Delaware, if shareholders' voting rights are not denied, after incorporation and the directors are either named in the articles of incorporation or elected by the incorporators, "Directors shall be elected by a plurality of the votes" present at an annual meeting.[9]

In New York, initial directors are not named in the certificate of incorporation. If shareholders' voting rights are not denied, after the articles of incorporation are filed, "an organization meeting of the incorporator or incorporators shall be held within or without this state, for the purpose of ... electing directors to hold office until the first annual meeting of shareholders ... ."[10]

Note that under the Delaware General Corporation Law[11] and the New York Business Corporation Law[12] after the certificate of incorporation is filed, if directors are not named in the certificate of incorporation, the incorporators must hold an organizational meeting to elect directors until the first annual meeting of shareholders is held at which time the shareholders elect directors. Either way, the corporation has begun its existence and operations, and it is important to understand at this point that whether the directors are named in the articles of incorporation or are appointed by the incorporators, it is the unelected directors who are in control of, and govern and manage, the corporation, prior to the existence of shareholders. For example, in Delaware,

> If the persons who are to serve as directors until the first annual meeting of stockholders have not been named in the certificate of incorporation, the incorporator or incorporators, until the directors are elected, shall manage the affairs of the corporation and may do whatever is necessary and proper to perfect the organization of the corporation, including the adoption of the original bylaws of the corporation and the election of directors.[13]

That undeniably demonstrates that the corporation is operational and corporate governance is in place prior to shareholders owning shares, and therefore directors are not agents of shareholders since there are no shareholders.

In order for there to be shareholders, the initial directors must issue shares, Shareholders must pay for the shares the price determined by the directors in an arm's length transaction. When shareholders purchase shares in an IPO ("initial public offering"), they are not purchasing x/n% of the corporation or x/n% of the assets of the corporation. They are purchasing x/n% of the shares issued by the corporation where x is the number of shares they purchase and n is the total number of shares issued. They are purchasing a set of rights as determined by the articles of incorporation and the terms of the class of stock which they are purchasing.

In addition to the cash paid when purchasing shares issued in an initial public offering (IPO), consideration can include a surrender of rights. That is, in addition to the cash paid, shareholders surrender their rights to decide how to allocate their assets (cash) in exchange for obtaining other rights (e.g., right to vote) and a set of expectations.

In all jurisdictions, as with corporate existence, corporate operations begin when the articles of incorporation are filed with the secretary (or department) of state, not when assets are transferred to the corporation. Indeed, the corporation cannot issue shares and assets cannot be transferred to the corporation unless there are directors and it has begun operations. (See Huber, 2017, for a novel argument that a not-for-profit corporation never began operations even though there were directors because no assets were transferred to the corporation.)

The initial directors must issue shares. While shares and shareholders are not necessary to begin operations, issuing shares is necessary in order to receive financial capital which shareholders provide when they purchase stock in an IPO. Prior to stock being issued, the corporation could borrow money, or a least arrange to borrow money once shares are issued. It can also sign contracts.

Only the directors may issue stock on behalf of the corporation. Under the Delaware General Corporation Law the initial board of directors, who have not been elected by shareholders, "may authorize capital stock to be issued for consideration consisting of cash, any tangible or intangible property or any benefit to the corporation, or any combination thereof."[14] The shares issued by the corporation need not be evidenced by a certificate (i.e., a piece of paper).[15]

> Every corporation may issue 1 or more classes of stock or 1 or more series of stock within any class thereof, any or all of which classes may be of stock with par value or stock without par value and which classes or series may have such voting powers, full or limited, or no voting powers, and such designations, preferences and relative, participating, optional or other special rights, and qualifications, limitations or restrictions thereof, as shall be stated and expressed in the certificate of incorporation or of any amendment thereto, or in the resolution or resolutions providing for the issue of such stock adopted by the board of directors pursuant to authority expressly vested in it by the provisions of its certificate of incorporation.[16]
>
> The consideration, as determined pursuant to § 153(a) and (b) of this title, for subscriptions to, or the purchase of, the capital stock to be issued by a corporation shall be paid in such form and in such manner as the board of directors shall determine … . The board of directors may determine the amount of consideration for which shares may be issued by setting a minimum amount of consideration …[17]

The New York Business Corporation Law contains similar provisions:

> Consideration for the issue of shares shall consist of money or other property, tangible or intangible; labor or services actually received by or performed for the corporation or for its benefit or in its formation or reorganization; a binding obligation to pay the purchase price or the subscription price in cash or other property … .[18]

Corporate rights are extremely broad. First, a corporation has the right to sue and be sued as a corporation; i.e., as an entity in the name of the corporation.

The Delaware General Corporation Law provides that

> Every corporation created under this chapter shall have power to ... [s]ue and be sued in all courts and participate, as a party or otherwise, in any judicial, administrative, arbitrative or other proceeding, in its corporate name ... .[19]

Thus, e.g., if a corporation sustains economic damages, it is the corporation that must bring the action to recover damages, not the shareholders. If the corporation causes injury, the injured party must sue the corporation, not the shareholders.

Furthermore, if a director causes the injury, the plaintiff must sue the corporation as the principal, not the shareholders as principals, which would be the case if directors were agents of the shareholders since principals are responsible for the acts of their agents.

New York grants similar rights:

> Each corporation, subject to any limitations provided in this chapter or any other statute of this state or its certificate of incorporation, shall have power in furtherance of its corporate purposes ... . (2) To sue and be sued in all courts and to participate in actions and proceedings, whether judicial, administrative, arbitrative or otherwise, in like cases *as natural persons* [emphasis added].[20]

In addition to the right to sue and be sued, corporations have very expansive powers. The Delaware General Corporation Law grants that

> In addition to the powers enumerated in § 122 of this title, every corporation, its officers, directors and stockholders shall possess and may exercise all the powers and privileges granted by this chapter or by any other law or by its certificate of incorporation, together with any powers incidental thereto, so far as such powers and privileges are necessary or convenient to the conduct, promotion or attainment of the business or purposes set forth in its certificate of incorporation.[21]

The powers of a Delaware corporation are not unlimited, however: "Every corporation shall be governed by the provisions and be subject to the restrictions and liabilities contained in this chapter."[22]

In New York, corporations shall "have and exercise all powers necessary or convenient to effect any or all of the purposes for which the corporation is formed."[23]

Property and property rights

Corporations and property rights will be discussed in greater detail below. The Delaware General Corporation Law is explicit in explaining the rights of a corporation in relationship to property:

> Every corporation created under this chapter shall have power to ... *Purchase*, receive, take by grant, gift, devise, bequest or otherwise, lease, or otherwise acquire, *own*, hold, improve, employ, use and otherwise deal in and with real or personal property, or any interest therein, wherever situated, and to *sell*, convey, lease, exchange, transfer or otherwise dispose of, or mortgage or pledge, *all or any of its property and ass*ets, or any interest therein, wherever situated [emphasis added].[24]

The New York Business Corporation Law provides that

> Each corporation ... shall have power in furtherance of its corporate purposes ... (4) To *purchase*, receive, take by grant, gift, devise, bequest or otherwise, lease, or otherwise acquire, *own*, hold, improve, employ, use and otherwise deal in and with, real or personal property, or any interest therein, wherever situated; (5) To *sell*, convey, lease, exchange, transfer or otherwise dispose of, or mortgage or pledge, or create a security interest in, all or any of its property, or any interest therein, wherever situated; (6) To *purchase*, take, receive, subscribe for, or otherwise acquire, own, hold, vote, employ, sell, lend, lease, exchange, transfer, or otherwise dispose of, mortgage, pledge, use and otherwise deal in and with, bonds and other obligations, shares, or other securities or interests issued by others, whether engaged in similar or different business, governmental, or other activities; (7) To *make contracts*, give guarantees and incur liabilities, borrow money at such rates of interest as the corporation may determine, issue its notes, bonds and other obligations, and secure any of its obligations by mortgage or pledge of all or any of its property or any interest therein, wherever situated; (8) To lend money, invest and reinvest its funds, and take and hold real and personal property as security for the payment of funds so loaned or invested [emphasis added].[25]

Thus, by statutory law, corporations own corporate property. Shareholders are explicitly excluded from owning corporate property and are thus explicitly excluded from making decisions about corporate property or its uses and allocation, in particular, its financial capital or productive capital.

Ownership and control of corporations

Since the theory of the firm rests on the separation of ownership and control, understanding the legal basis of ownership and control of corporations is necessary before examining the economic implications of ownership and control, and the separation of ownership and control

Corporate governance and control is dictated by state corporation statutes as interpreted by common law if the statutes are silent or ambiguous. The Delaware General Corporation Law states, "Every corporation shall be governed by the provisions and be subject to the restrictions and liabilities contained in this chapter."[26]

Jensen & Meckling (1976) boldly declare:

> Since the relationship between the stockholders and manager of a corporation *fit the definition of a pure agency relationship* it should be no surprise to discover that the issues associated with the 'separation of ownership and control' in the modern diffuse ownership corporation are intimately associated with the general problem of agency. We show below that an explanation of why and how the *agency costs generated by the corporate form are born leads to a theory of the ownership (or capital) structure of the firm.*
>
> (p. 309, emphases added)

They first define the relationship between the stockholders and directors of a corporation as a "pure agency relationship." It is only then that they generate a theory of ownership. In other words, it is backwards. As Masten (1993) tells us, it is the law that defines the ownership of the firm, and therefore, "ownership itself is a condition sustained by legal rules and remedies."

If directors are agents of shareholders, that necessarily means that shareholders have conferred upon directors the authority to act as their agents. But shareholders do not confer power on directors. A century ago the New York Court of Appeals[27] ruled in *Mason v. Curtis,*[28] "The stockholders do not confer, nor can they revoke those powers. They are derivative only in the sense of being received from the state in the act of incorporation."[29] (See also Suojanen, 1954).

The modern economic "theory of firm" is a product of the theory of the "separation of ownership and control," aka "agency theory," which is considered by many to begin with Berle and Means' 1932 classic, *The Modern Corporation and Private Property.* For more than eighty years the "master problem for research" for legal scholarship on corporate law has focused on the separation of ownership and control (Reich-Graefe, 2011). The theory of separation of ownership and control concept evolved into the theory of the firm as espoused by economists.

As a preface, it should be noted that first, state incorporation statutes do not say that shareholders are the owners of the corporation. That shareholders are considered the owners of the corporation is a consequence of common law.

Arthur Levitt, Jr., former chairman of the Securities Exchange Commission, asserts, "*The principle that shareholders own the companies in which they invest*—and are the ultimate bosses of those running them—*is central to modern capitalism*" (Levitt, 2008, emphases added).[30]

It is both amusing and sad that Friedman (1970) assails discussions of the "social responsibilities of business" for its "notable ... analytical looseness and lack of rigor" when he himself offered neither analysis nor rigor. Says Friedman,

> In a free-enterprise, private-property system, a corporate executive is an employee of the owners of the business. He has direct responsibility to his employers. That responsibility is to conduct the business in accordance with their desires.

By "corporate executive is an employee of the owners of the business" Friedman means "directors are employees of the owners of the business," as proven by his statement, "The whole justification for permitting the corporate executive to be selected by the stockholders is that the executive is an agent serving the interests of his principal." Only directors can be selected by shareholders. However, corporate executives, as he uses the term, are not employees (i.e., agents) of the owners of the business, by which he means shareholders, because shareholders do not own the corporation.

State incorporation statutes do not confer upon directors the status or position of agent (or trustee), nor does it confer upon shareholders the status or position of principal (or grantor or beneficial owner). That has merely been inferred by courts and legal and economic scholars.

Berle and Means (1991) state in reference to shareholders and directors, "whenever one man or group of men trust another man or group with the management of property the second group became fiduciaries" (p. 295). But that is incorrect for at least two reasons. First, shareholders do not entrust directors with the management of their property (assumed to mean cash). Shareholders simply enter into a contract (Stout, 2012). They purchase shares for consideration in an amount determined by the directors in an arm's length transaction. When you purchase a bond from a corporation you are not entrusting the directors of the corporation to "manage your money" as a fiduciary. You are simply entering into a contract. The same reasoning applies to purchasing shares. There is no legal justification for thinking a shareholder is entrusting her money to the corporation's directors when purchasing shares.

Second, once a shareholder purchases shares in an IPO the money is no longer hers. It now belongs to the corporation. The corporation holds legal title to and becomes the sole legal owner of all assets, total and net, including the financial capital it received from issuing the shares (Berle & Means, 1991). The purchase of shares does not magically transform a shareholder into an owner of the corporation, whether actual, beneficial, or residual. She is only an owner of the shares, not of the corporation.

The fiduciary duty said to be owed by directors to shareholders rests on two separate but mutually exclusive legal theories—directors are agents of shareholders, and directors are trustees of shareholders. There can be no fiduciary duty unless one of the legal theories applies to the exclusion of the other. However, if directors are neither agents nor trustees, they do not and cannot owe a fiduciary duty to shareholders,

The first theory is that directors are agents of shareholders. A multitude of judicial opinions have ruled that directors are agents of corporations. If directors are agents of shareholders then a fiduciary duty naturally attaches to directors based on common law principles. But, if directors are agents of shareholders, then shareholders are the principals of directors, which would make shareholders liable for the acts of the directors as their agents. Furthermore, while the fiduciary and principal-agent relationship are powerful metaphors, they misrepresent the realities of the shareholder-director relationship since shareholders are not owners of corporations, principals to directors, or individuals dependent on fiduciaries (Green, 1993).

The second theory which is said to create a fiduciary duty owed by directors to shareholders is found in trust law, as several judicial opinions have ruled. In a trust relationship the trustee takes legal title to administer the trust for the benefit of the beneficial owner (the beneficiary). Directors are said to be the trustees and shareholders are said to be beneficial owners. But directors do not take legal title to any property.

Shepherd (1981) emphasizes the fact that "The whole purpose of a trustee's existence is to administer property on behalf of another," which is the precisely the reason why directors cannot be trustees. In order to administer property on behalf of another the trustee must hold legal title to the property, an absolute requirement. Since directors do not have legal title to the corporation or the corporation's property directors cannot be trustees of either the corporation or the shareholders.

If shareholders do not own the corporation and directors are not agents of shareholders, Friedman's thesis, like the economic theory of the firm, disintegrates into nothing more than dust in the wind.

Directors' duties

By statute, directors have duties to the corporation. By common law they have duties to shareholders. The duties to shareholders are contrary to the duties to the corporation. It is of the utmost importance here to understand that the fact that directors have duties to the corporation (and to shareholders) absolutely precludes directors from being capitalists or entrepreneurs.

The primary duty, as well as right, of directors (in particular the initial directors) is to issue shares in accordance with the articles of incorporation. While issuing shares is not a duty imposed on directors by the Delaware General Corporation Law or the New York Business Corporation Law, the corporation can operate prior to shares being issued (which in fact the Delaware General Corporation Law specifically requires), the corporation must issue shares in order to receive financial capital which is necessary for the corporation to fulfill its purpose as stated in the articles of incorporation. Thus, the directors have an implicit duty to issue shares.

Directors' duties begin at the time initial directors are named, whether in the articles of incorporation, as in Delaware, or by the incorporators in an organization meeting, as in New York. Their duties do not begin when the shares are issued. Issuing shares is part of their duties.

Directors' have a fiduciary duty to the corporation. On that there is no disagreement. Whether a director has a fiduciary duty to shareholders, however, is a hotly contested argument in corporate law.[31] Furthermore, there are conflicting laws regarding what constitutes fiduciary duty.

Many courts have ruled that directors have a fiduciary duty to shareholders because they are agents of shareholders. But making directors agents of shareholders is contrary to the laws of agency. Several court rulings have held that directors have a fiduciary duty to shareholders because they are trustees of shareholders. But if directors have a fiduciary duty to shareholders because they are trustees of shareholders, then they cannot at the same time have a fiduciary duty to the corporation for which they are not trustees. Nor can they have fiduciary duties as agents and at the same time have fiduciary duties as trustees. Such a conflict of interest in a fiduciary duty is expressly prohibited by agency and trust law.

Some courts have held that directors' fiduciary duty includes the duty of loyalty, but statutory law contradicts this.

The duty of loyalty in the Delaware General Corporation Law is absolute. The certificate of incorporation may contain a

> provision eliminating or limiting the personal liability of a director to the corporation or its stockholders for monetary damages for breach of fiduciary duty as a director, provided that such provision shall not eliminate or limit the liability of a director: (i) For any breach of the director's duty of loyalty to the corporation or its stockholders ... .[32]

Two things are important to note here. First, it is of the utmost importance to understand that the fiduciary duty here is merely implied. It is not imposed.

Second, contrary to what several courts have ruled, the duty of loyalty and fiduciary duties are not identical or synonymous. This is seen by the Delaware General Corporation Law's provision permitting eliminating or limiting personal liability of directors for breach of fiduciary duty to be included in the articles of incorporation, but eliminating or limiting personal liability of directors for breach of a duty of loyalty may not be eliminated.

That directors have a fiduciary duty to shareholders is a function of common law (Berle & Means, 1991), a belief started decades, if not centuries, ago which has merely been repeated and reinforced in dozens of authoritative court rulings, a classic example of when something is repeated often enough people will believe it even if it is not true. The courts' rulings that directors have a fiduciary duty to shareholders was not the result of a rigorous analysis of corporate statutes, laws of property, or laws of agency. It was, and continues to be, an unjustified and unjustifiable assumption.

For example, the controlling case in Delaware is *Loft v. Guth*,[33] a 1938 case decided by the Delaware Court of Chancery.[34] In *Loft v. Guth* the Delaware Court of Chancery stated, "It has frequently been said by this court and clearly enunciated by the Supreme Court of this State in *Lofland et al. v. Cahall, Rec'r*,[35] that the directors of a corporation stand in a fiduciary relation to the corporation and its stockholders." Turning to the 1922 case of *Lofland et al. v. Cahall, Rec'r* we see that the Supreme Court of Delaware held that

> [it] would be violative of well settled principles of equity applicable to trustees and ... inconsistent with the fiduciary relation existing between directors and stockholders, to hold that there was an implied agreement on the part of the company to pay the six appellants for the services they claim to have rendered in the organization of the company and in the sale of its capital stock.

That a fiduciary relation exists between directors and stockholders was basically created by judicial fiat. There was never any attempt by either the Delaware Supreme Court or the Delaware Court of Chancery to analyze the relationship of shareholders, corporations, directors, and corporate property, or how a fiduciary duty to shareholders is or could be implemented as explained below.

One problem with the *Loft* ruling, therefore, and one that the court should have known, is that directors cannot be trustees of shareholders under "well settled principles of equity applicable to trustees" because that would be contrary to the laws of trusts. A careful analysis of well settled principles of trust law would have revealed that such a duty cannot exist given the laws of trust, property, and agency.[36] The reasoning of the Court was nothing more than smoke and mirrors. The Delaware General Corporation Law does not make directors trustees of shareholders.

The Delaware Supreme Court revisited the issue in 1998. In *Malone v. Brincat*,[37] the Court ruled

> An underlying premise for the imposition of fiduciary duties is a *separation of legal control from beneficial ownership*. Equitable principles act in those circumstances to protect the beneficiaries who are not in a position to protect themselves. One of the fundamental tenets of Delaware corporate law provides for a separation of control and ownership. The board of directors has the legal responsibility to manage the business of a corporation *for the benefit of its shareholder owners*. Accordingly, fiduciary duties are imposed on the directors of Delaware corporations to regulate their conduct when they discharge that function.

The directors of Delaware corporations stand in a fiduciary relationship not only to the stockholders but also to the corporations upon whose boards they serve. The director's *fiduciary duty to both* the corporation and its shareholders has been characterized by this Court as a triad: due care, good faith, and loyalty [emphasis added].

Note that the court erroneously interpreted fiduciary duty as characterized by the duty of loyalty even though they are not the same under the Delaware General Corporation Law.

By "beneficial owners" the Delaware Supreme Court meant that shareholders are owners of the corporation, which is made explicit by its statement that

One of the fundamental tenets of Delaware corporate law provides for a separation of control and ownership. The board of directors has the legal responsibility to manage the business of a corporation for the *benefit of its shareholder owners.* Accordingly, fiduciary duties are *imposed* on the directors of Delaware corporations ... [emphasis added].

The court did not say how fiduciary duties are imposed on the directors of Delaware corporations. It is certainly not imposed by the Delaware General Corporation Law which must mean it is imposed by the court. But the court is not empowered to impose such a duty contrary to unambiguous statutory law. The Delaware Supreme Court was, simply, wrong.

Another problem with the *Malone* ruling is that Delaware corporate law does not make shareholders the owners of the corporation. It is simply not true that "Delaware corporate law provides for a separation of control and ownership," and nowhere in Delaware General Corporation Law is there any section or paragraph that "provides for a separation of control and ownership." It does not exist. It is an unjustifiable construct created with smoke and mirrors.

In *NACEPF, Inc v. Rob Gheewalla, et al.,*[38] the Delaware Supreme Court ruled, "the *creditors* of a Delaware corporation ... *have no right, as a matter of law,* to assert direct claims for breach of fiduciary duty against the corporation's directors" (emphasis added).

Therefore, consider that normally as a matter of law creditors have no right to vote for directors of a corporation (although sometimes they can). Shareholders do have a right to vote for directors of a corporation (although that right may be denied in the articles of incorporation). Creditors are not referred to as "owners" or "beneficial owners" even though bondholders may be entitled to vote. Thus, the meaning of the *NACEPF* ruling can mean nothing other than that the distinction between creditors who normally have no right to vote for directors of a corporation and are not considered "beneficial owners" and shareholders who normally have the right to vote for directors of a corporation and who are referred to as "beneficial owners" is simply the right to vote. But nothing in the Delaware General Corporation Law confers on shareholders the ownership of the corporation whether with or without voting rights.

Delaware Supreme Court decisions that hold Delaware corporate law makes shareholders the owners of a corporation, that Delaware corporate law provides for the separation of ownership and control, or that Delaware corporate law makes directors agents or trustees of shareholders, have no foundation in the Delaware General Corporation law. If, as Robé (2011, 2019) and others have concluded, shareholders do not own the corporation, the Delaware Supreme Court was, again, wrong. The Delaware Supreme Court expanded and interpreted Delaware corporate law well beyond the plain language of the statute.

Several things must be noted here. First and foremost, this section of the Delaware General Corporation Law does not impose on directors a fiduciary duty to stockholders. Contrary to the court's ruling, nowhere in the entire statute is a fiduciary duty to stockholders imposed on directors.

The duty of directors as defined by the New York Business Corporation Law does not include a fiduciary duty to stockholders or a duty of loyalty *per se*. Instead, the duties of directors seem to incorporate some sense of "corporate social responsibility" (which is beyond the scope of this book). The New York Business Corporation Law is very explicit and comprehensive in defining the duties of directors:

> (a) A director shall perform his duties as a director ... *in good faith* and with that degree of care which an ordinarily prudent person in a like position would use under similar circumstances ... . (b) In taking action, including, without limitation, action which may involve or relate to a change or potential change in the control of the corporation, a director shall be entitled to consider, without limitation, (1) both the long-term and the short-term interests of the corporation and its shareholders and (2) the effects that the corporations [sic] actions may have in the short-term or in the long-term upon any of the following: (i) the prospects for potential growth, development, productivity and profitability of the corporation; (ii) the corporations [sic] current employees; (iii) the corporations [sic] retired employees and other beneficiaries receiving or entitled to receive retirement, welfare or similar benefits from or pursuant to any plan sponsored, or agreement entered into, by the corporation; (iv) the corporations [sic] customers and creditors; and (v) the ability of the corporation to provide, as a going concern, goods, services, employment opportunities and employment benefits and otherwise to contribute to the communities in which it does business. *Nothing in this paragraph shall* create any duties owed by any director to any person or entity to consider or afford any particular weight to any of the foregoing or abrogate any duty of the directors, either statutory or recognized by common law or court decisions. For purposes of this paragraph, '*control*' *shall mean the*

possession, directly or indirectly, of the power to direct or cause the direction of the management and policies of the corporation, whether through the ownership of voting stock, by contract, or otherwise [all emphasis added].[39]

Note that nothing in the paragraph either creates nor abrogates any duty of the directors, whether statutory or recognized by common law or court decisions. Thus, no fiduciary duty between directors and shareholders is created by the statute. Furthermore, if there is a duty created by common law, such a duty is not abrogated. Thus, it is up to the courts to interpret fiduciary duty.

The astute reader can immediately see the problem, a direct result of the director-as-agent-of-shareholders theory. The problem is whether the initial directors are named in the certificate of incorporation or are elected by the incorporators at the organization meeting, the corporation is operational and there are directors prior to shares being issued and prior to there being any shareholders.

A director who owes a fiduciary duty to shareholders, either as an agent or trustee, must fulfill that duty according to the fiduciary duties imposed by agency or trust law. Upon the establishment of a principal-agent relationship, a fiduciary duty of the agent to the principal arises as a matter of law.[40] That is, "an agent has a fiduciary duty to act loyally for the principal's benefit in all matters connected with the agency relationship."[41] This is, of course, the duty the director owes to the corporation. (The Delaware Supreme Court considers directors' fiduciary duty to consist of a "triad" of duties—good faith, loyalty or due care.[42]) But in a trust relationship, "the fiduciary nature of the relationship between the trustee and the beneficiary demands an unusually high standard of ethical or moral conduct." The Supreme Court of Utah has emphasized that "trustees are charged as fiduciaries with one of the *highest duties of care and loyalty known in the law*" (emphasis added).[43]

Directors' duty of loyalty is absolute in the Delaware General Corporation Law. In the Delaware General Corporation Law, a corporation

> *may* contain *a provision eliminating or limiting the personal liability of a director to the corporation or its stockholders* for monetary damages *for breach of fiduciary duty* as a director, provided that such provision *shall not eliminate or limit the liability of a director*: (i) *For any breach of the director's duty of loyalty* to the corporation or its stockholders ... [all emphasis added].[44]

Shareholders' rights

Shareholders have rights, but not all rights are absolute. Some rights may be denied in the articles of incorporation, or in the class of stock issued by the corporation. It is not the corporation that gives the rights to shareholders; it is the shares. The rights are attached to the share and it is the owner of the shares who may exercise those rights, but absolutely no right confers on shareholders any claim against the corporation or its assets.

The most important right is the right to vote, but shareholders' right to vote in Delaware and other jurisdictions may be denied: "*Unless otherwise provided* in the certificate of incorporation and subject to § 213 of this title, each stockholder shall be entitled to 1 vote for each share of capital stock held by such stockholder" (emphasis added).[45]

In New York,

> Every corporation shall have power to create and issue the number of shares stated in its certificate of incorporation. Such shares may be all of one class or may be divided into two or more classes ... . *The certificate of incorporation may deny*, limit or otherwise define the *voting rights* and may limit or otherwise define the dividend or liquidation rights of shares of any class, *but no such denial*, limitation or definition *of voting rights shall be effective unless at the time one or more classes of outstanding shares or bonds, singly or in the aggregate, are entitled to full voting rights*, and no such limitation or definition of dividend or liquidation rights shall be effective unless at the time one or more classes of outstanding shares, singly or in the aggregate, are entitled to unlimited dividend and liquidation rights [all emphasis added].[46]

None of these rights to vote confer on shareholders ownership of the corporation or of corporate property.

Shareholders' right to vote for directors

Shareholders' right to vote for directors is assumed to be absolute. While shareholders' right to vote for directors is common it is not absolute or guaranteed. It is important to recall that directors are not capitalists or entrepreneurs, even if elected by shareholders, as discussed in chapter 8.

In Delaware shareholders' right to vote for directors is not absolute. In Delaware,

> The certificate of incorporation shall set forth ... a statement of the designations and the powers, preferences and rights, and the qualifications, limitations or restrictions thereof, which are permitted by § 151 of this title in respect of any class or classes of stock ... .[47]

Section 151 of the Delaware General Corporation Law states:

> Every corporation may issue 1 or more classes of stock or 1 or more series of stock within any class thereof, any or all of which classes may be of stock with par value or stock without par value and which classes or series may have such voting powers, full or limited, or no voting powers ... .[48]

The New York Business Corporation Law is similar to Delaware's General Corporation Law:

> The certificate of incorporation may set forth any provision, not inconsistent with this chapter or any other statute of this state, relating to the business of the corporation, its affairs, its rights or powers, or the rights or powers of its shareholders, directors or officers including any provision relating to matters which under this chapter are required or permitted to be set forth in the by-laws. It is not necessary to set forth in the certificate of incorporation any of the powers enumerated in this chapter.[49]

The New York Business Corporation Law continues to explain limitations on shareholders' right to vote: "Every shareholder of record shall be entitled at every meeting of shareholders to one vote for every share standing in his name on the record of shareholders, unless otherwise provided in the certificate of incorporation."[50]

In New York

> At each annual meeting of shareholders, directors shall be elected to hold office until the next annual meeting…The certificate of incorporation may provide for the election of one or more directors by the holders of the shares of any class or series, or by the holders of bonds entitled to vote in the election of directors … .[51]

Shareholders' right to protection from creditors

What is referred to as "limited liability" is perhaps the right most well known by the public and is one of the major attractions for people to invest in shares. Yet this is a common misconception. Shareholders have no liability, limited or otherwise. What is really meant by the phrase "limited liability" is "limited risk." Even Posner (2014) had it wrong when he said, "shareholders' liability for corporate debt is limited to the value of his shares" (p. 536). While shareholders may lose the entire value of their shares when the market price falls to zero, the value of their shares cannot be used to satisfy any claims of creditors and they are not liable for any corporate debts. Their risk of loss is limited to the market value of their shares. In the case of corporate liquidation, corporate equity, which is owned by the corporation, not the shareholders, is used to satisfy corporate liabilities.

When a partner is bankrupt, creditors can satisfy their claims against his partnership interest in the partnership because the partners own the partnership. When a shareholder is bankrupt the shareholder's creditors cannot satisfy their claims against the corporation because the shareholder does not own the corporation. Creditors can only satisfy their claims against the shareholder against the shares of the shareholder because the shares are personal property which can be sold to satisfy the shareholder's creditors' claims.

If directors are agents of shareholders, "limited liability" of shareholders is contrary to the laws of agency where third parties have recourse against principals for acts of the agents, thus again negating the applicability of agency law to shareholders and directors. Note also that the corporation, not the shareholders, is liable as a principal for the acts of its directors.

For the most part shareholders are protected from creditors' claims against the corporation. The exception is for unpaid subscriptions to stock. Stockholders are protected from creditors in two situations. One situation is in dissolved corporations, and the other is in normal operations.

In Delaware, in any event, "The aggregate liability of any stockholder of a dissolved corporation for claims against the dissolved corporation shall not exceed the amount distributed to such stockholder in dissolution."[52]

In New York shareholder limited liability is more implied than expressed.[53] But again, shareholders have no liability for claims against the corporation so the Delaware provision, and any similar provision of any state, has no meaning. The value of their shares cannot be used to satisfy any claims of creditors and they are not liable for any corporate debts. The amount distributed to stockholders in a dissolution is the net assets, which are owned by the corporation, not the shareholders.

It is important to note that stockholders in all jurisdictions are liable for purchase of the stock or subscriptions that are not paid in full if the assets of the corporation are otherwise insufficient to satisfy creditors' claims. This is more proof that the purchase of shares is a matter of contract, not of creating a trust. The shareholder of an unpaid balance is liable for payment as a breach of contract, not as a principal of an agent, and certainly not as either a trustor or a beneficial owner. A shareholder is never described as a principal of a corporation, and a corporation is never described as an agent of a shareholder.

Both the Delaware and New York statutes make the unjustified, and unjustifiable, assumption that the corporate equity belongs to the stockholders. This is false.

Furthermore, when the power of a corporation to purchase, own, or sell property is combined with (1) agency law which makes principals liable for the acts of their agents as discussed in chapter 2, and (2) the rights of corporations to sue and be sued, then if directors were agents of shareholders, shareholders would be liable as principals in a law suit for the contracts made by directors.

Shareholders' right to dividends and distributions

In an IPO, everyone pays the same price for a share of stock. If another IPO is issued, the price of a share of stock will most likely be different than the first IPO. Sharing profits by way of dividends is based on the number of shares owned, not on the consideration paid to the corporation in an IPO, and certainly not on the consideration paid in acquiring the shares on an exchange as it is in a partnership. In a partnership, shared profit is normally based on the amount paid into the partnership (assuming no agreement to the contrary), which constitutes the economic interest a partner has in the partnership.

While shareholders have a right to dividends, that right is not absolute. Under Delaware General Corporation Law, "The directors of every corporation, subject to any restrictions contained in its certificate of incorporation, may declare and pay dividends upon the shares of its capital stock ... ."[54] Thus, receiving dividends is merely an expectation.

In New York, "a corporation may declare and pay dividends or make other distributions in cash or its bonds or its property, including the shares or bonds of other corporations, on its outstanding shares."[55]

Shareholders' right to liquidation proceeds

Shareholders have a right to net liquidation proceeds if any, regardless of when they purchased the shares (i.e., in an IPO or in the market). But the net liquidation proceeds are based on number of shares, not on the purchase price of the shares, and not on equity interest. Therefore, each shareholder receives an amount calculated as (net liquidation proceeds ÷ total number of shares * the number of shares owned by the shareholder), which means each shareholder receives a different amount of proceeds based on the proportion of the number of shares they own to the total number of shares outstanding, not on the price paid for the shares.

Shareholders have been referred to as "residual claimants." The term "residual claimant" refers to the theory that shareholders have a claim on net assets after all liabilities are satisfied. While shareholders have a right to receive a distribution of the net assets, if any, they have no claim on either the assets or net assets of the corporation the way a creditor has a claim against the assets of the corporation.

In Delaware, for example, upon dissolution, "any assets remaining after payment of claims and liabilities, shall be distributed to the stockholders."[56] In New York, after paying all liabilities, "The corporation, if authorized at a meeting of shareholders by a majority of the votes of all outstanding shares entitled to vote thereon may sell its remaining assets ... and distribute the same among the shareholders according to their respective rights."[57]

Shareholders can assert no claim against the corporation either during operations or during liquidation. Thus, shareholders are not residual claimants.

It is easily seen that not one of these rights confers an ownership interest in the corporation, its assets, or its net asset. Not one of these rights is a right associated with rights of ownership of the corporation as property of the shareholder the way the rights of partners are associated with the ownership of the partnership as property of the partners.

Berle and Means defined the control of a corporation as the power to select a majority of the board of directors. Stigler and Friedland (1983) maintain that "The majority of the voting stock is the ultimate control over a corporation even if that stock is diffused among many owners."

The Delaware General Corporation Law distinguishes between management and control. According to Delaware General Corporation Law a corporation's business and affairs are to be managed and all corporate powers shall be exercised by or under the direction of the board and all corporate powers are to be exercised under the ultimate direction of the board.[58] Yet, control

> means the possession, directly or indirectly, of the power to direct or cause the direction of the management ... through the ownership of voting stock ... [a] person who is the owner of 20% or more of the outstanding voting stock of any corporation ... shall be presumed to have control of such entity, in the absence of proof by a preponderance of the evidence to the contrary ... .[59]

Note first that this is a rebuttable presumption, but at the same time it does not preclude a less than 20% shareholder from exercising what the statute defines as control. While it is true that not many shareholders of publicly traded corporations own 20% or more of the outstanding stock,[60] the point is, if they do own 20% or more of the outstanding stock and if shareholders own the corporation as the theory of separation and control asserts, the theory of the firm and of separation and control is largely invalidated.

More important, however, is that owning 20% or of the outstanding voting stock, or the majority of voting stock, does not confer on shareholders ownership of the corporation itself. The right of shareholders to vote for directors is a matter of corporate law, the articles of incorporation, and the class of stock. It is not a matter of ownership of the corporation.

But the more egregious fact that economists and legal scholars holding to the theory of separation and control ignore is the inversion of the separation of ownership and control. The theory of the firm rests on the proposition that shareholders own the corporation yet do not control it. In a bit of twisted legal logic, we are confronted here with the situation of a shareholder controlling a corporation she does not own!

Corporations and contract law, property law, agency law, and trust law

Corporations and contract law

The definition of a contract is "an agreement to do, or refrain from doing, a particular thing."[61] But there are additional requirements to create an enforceable contract such as competent parties, offer and acceptance, consideration (mutual promises), mutual agreement, and legal purpose.[62] A contract is not a law. The agreement plus the law makes the contract an enforceable obligation.[63] Contract law is a product of common law,[64] much of which has been codified in the Uniform Commercial Code. Contract law is the foundation for any purchase and sale, and therefore highly relevant to purchasing shares in a corporation since purchasing securities from a corporation is a matter of contract. Furthermore, a basic understanding of contract law is imperative in order to understand the theory of the firm as a "nexus of contracts," which is discussed in chapter 7.

Promises

Promises are the essential feature of a contract (Am Jur 2d, Contracts, §3). A promise may be expressed or implied and may consist of mutual promises or a promise in exchange for an act.[65]

A bilateral contract is a promise in exchange for a promise (Am Jur 2d, Contracts, §8). A unilateral contract is a promise in exchange for an act (Am Jur 2d, Contracts, §8). Purchasing shares from a corporation is a bilateral contract. I promise to give the corporation $20,000 for x# of shares, the corporation promises to give me x# of shares in exchange for $20,000. Of course, the promises and exchange of promises (consideration) is usually (relatively) simultaneous. The purchase of shares is an exchange of promises consisting of a mutual grant of certain rights from the corporation to me and cash being transferred to the corporation by me and an agreement by me to surrender certain rights.

Offer and acceptance—agreement

An enforceable contract requires an agreement between the parties (Am Jur 2d, Contracts, §2). The agreement constitutes an offer by one party and acceptance of the offer by another party (Am Jur 2d, Contracts, §29). A contract of adhesion is found in such things as credit card agreements or terms of service of internet providers. It is one-sided, take it or leave it. The credit card or internet provider offers certain terms. The terms are non-negotiable. You agree to the terms or they do not issue a credit card or provide internet service to you.

Purchases of securities from a corporation is a contract of adhesion. The corporation offers to sell you securities in an initial public offering or "IPO." You agree to accept the terms when you purchase the securities. There is no negotiation.

Consideration

Consideration is essentially a promise given by the promissor if the promise is accepted by the promisee (person to whom the promise is given).[66] Consideration is normally set in terms of property (cash), but consideration can also consist of surrendering rights, or selling your rights.

When issuing securities, directors of a corporation are empowered by statute to determine what is sufficient consideration for the securities. When securities are purchased in the market, the market determines the price of securities. (Note that none of the consideration goes to the corporation when securities are purchased in the market.)

In addition to cash, a purchaser of securities agrees to surrender to the corporation her rights to decide how to allocate the cash she pays for the securities. The corporation purchases her rights to decide how to use the cash it receives to acquire and allocate resources of production by issuing her the stock. The corporation now owns the cash along with the shareholder's rights to decide how to allocate the cash and, by extension, how to acquire and allocate the assets the corporation acquires with the cash received from the shareholder. The shareholder now owns the shares with certain rights attached to the shares such as the right (usually) to vote for directors and the right to liquidation proceeds.

Surrender of rights

Adequate consideration can consist of property, an act, or a return promise. A return promise can be a forbearance to act, or a creation, modification, or destruction of a legal relation.[67] When a person purchases shares from a corporation they are selling their rights to decide how to use the cash paid to the corporation for the shares and how to allocate the resources acquired with the cash paid for the shares. In exchange, the corporation gives the shareholder the right to vote for directors (usually), to vote on mergers (usually), to amend the articles of incorporation or the bylaws (usually), to receive dividends (if declared), and to receive a distribution of the net assets upon liquidation. The shareholders pay cash for the shares, which gives them only the expectation, but not the guarantee, of receiving cash in the future (dividends) (Berle & Means, 1991).

Capacity/parties

An enforceable contract requires that each party have the legal capacity to enter into a contract (Am Jur 2d, Contracts, §27). Since the parties to a contract must have legal capacity they may not be minors except in very limited circumstances not relevant here. They must have the mental capacity to understand the terms of the contract. Corporations are empowered by state corporation statutes to enter into contracts thus they are considered by law to have capacity to enter into enforceable contracts.

Purpose

An enforceable contract must be for a legal purpose. If a contract is not made for legal purposes, it is not enforceable. On the other hand, a contract may be made for a legal purpose (e.g., buying a house) but may not be enforceable if it does not comply with certain statutory requirements such the statute of frauds which required the sale of real property to be in writing.[68]

The Uniform Commercial Code

The codification of some common law principles of contract law have been codified into the Uniform Commercial Code (UCC). The UCC governs Sales of Goods, Leases, Negotiable Instruments, Bank Deposits and Collections, Funds Transfers, Letters of Credit, Bulk Sales, Documents of Title, Secured Transactions, and Investment Securities (Article 8). The relevant part is:

> ARTICLE 8. INVESTMENT SECURITIES. § 8–102 Definitions. (a) In this Article ... (9) 'Financial asset,' except as otherwise provided in Section 8–103, means: (i) a security ... (15) 'Security,' except as otherwise provided in Section 8–103, means an obligation of an issuer or a share ... .[69]

The UCC also provides rules for determining if an obligation of an issuer is a security: "§ 8–103 Rules for determining whether certain obligations and interests are securities or financial assets. (a) A share ... is a security."

The UCC's classification of shares of stock as Investment Securities and financial assets is important because classifying a share of stock as an investment security removes the purchase of stock from being classified as a trust and places it squarely within contract law. Shareholders purchase an interest in the shares, not in the corporation. Shareholders invest in shares, not in the corporation.

Complete and incomplete contracts

The theory of the firm has evolved from a simple, albeit erroneous, agency theory to a more complex theory of nexus of contracts and more recently incomplete contracts. The nexus of contracts theory of the firm and the incomplete contracts theory of the firm are discussed in chapter 7. At this point it is necessary to consider incomplete contracts in order to understand the monumental error of the theory of incomplete contracts.

When considering incomplete contracts it must be remembered that if any element of contract law is missing as articulated above, there is no contract. A purported contract that has no consideration, for example, is not a contract. A contract must be complete in all its necessary elements, as articulated above, in order to be a contract or else it is not a contract.

> To be enforceable, an agreement must be definite and certain as to its terms and requirements, or contain provisions which are capable in themselves of being reduced to certainty even if there are some formal imperfections in the contract. To have a valid contract, all terms should

be definitely agreed upon, and *the failure to agree to even one essential term means there is no agreement to be enforced …. No enforceable contract comes into being when parties leave a material term for future negotiations, creating a mere agreement to agree* [emphasis added].[70]

Mutual expressions of agreement may fail to consummate a contract for the reason that they are not complete, some essential term or terms not being agreed upon … . However, the absence of agreement on non-essential terms does not render the agreement unenforceable [emphasis added].[71]

Corporations and property law

The Delaware General Corporation Law sets forth the relationship of a corporation to corporate property. To review:

Every corporation created under this chapter shall have power to … [p]urchase, receive, take by grant, gift, devise, bequest or otherwise, lease, or otherwise acquire, own, hold, improve, employ, use and otherwise deal in and with real or personal property, or any interest therein, wherever situated, and to sell, convey, lease, exchange, transfer or otherwise dispose of, or mortgage or pledge, all or any of its property and assets, or any interest therein, wherever situated [emphasis added].[72]

Similarly, the New York Business Corporation Law states:

(a) Each corporation … shall have power in furtherance of its corporate purposes … (4) To purchase, receive, take by grant, gift, devise, bequest or otherwise, lease, or otherwise acquire, own, hold, improve, employ, use and otherwise deal in and with, real or personal property, or any interest therein, wherever situated; (5) To sell, convey, lease, exchange, transfer or otherwise dispose of, or mortgage or pledge, or create a security interest in, all or any of its property, or any interest therein, wherever situated; (6) To purchase, take, receive, subscribe for, or otherwise acquire, own, hold, vote, employ, sell, lend, lease, exchange, transfer, or otherwise dispose of, mortgage, pledge, use and otherwise deal in and with, bonds and other obligations, shares, or other securities or interests issued by others, whether engaged in similar or different business, governmental, or other activities; (7) To make contracts, give guarantees and incur liabilities, borrow money at such rates of interest as the corporation may determine, issue its notes, bonds and other obligations, and secure any of its obligations by mortgage or pledge of all or any of its property or any interest therein, wherever situated; (8) To lend money, invest and reinvest its funds, and take and hold real and personal property as security for the payment of funds so loaned or invested [emphasis added].[73]

The property of the corporation constitutes the resources of the corporation reflected on the balance sheet as the total assets of the corporation which consists of, among other things, the financial capital it received when it issued securities to the public.

Shareholders as owners of corporate property

It is beyond question that corporations, not shareholders, are the owners of corporate property, both total and net. The corporation alone decides, through the directors which resources of production to acquire with its financial capital and how the assets are allocated to production.

So if corporations own corporate property, what do shareholders own? Shareholders own shares. Nothing more. Delaware General Corporation Law declares that shares of stock are personal property while the UCC classifies them as financial assets of the owner of the shares.

The California Supreme Court acknowledged in *Miller v. McColgan* that it is the ownership of shares that is the legally recognized property interest. "The property of the shareholders in their respective *shares* is distinct from the corporate property" (emphasis added),[74] thus negating any ownership interest in the corporation itself. Furthermore, the California Supreme Court continued: "It is fundamental, of course, that the corporation has a personality *distinct from that of its shareholders, and that the latter neither own the corporate property nor the corporate earnings*" (emphasis added).

Shareholders as owners of the corporation

The arguments presented in the previous section are equally applicable to shareholders as owners of the corporation. However, in addition, we turn to the Delaware General Corporation Law.

The Delaware General Corporation Law classifies shares as personal property. "The *shares of stock* in every corporation shall be deemed *personal property* and transferable as provided in Article 8 of subtitle I of Title 6 (emphasis added)."[75] The Uniform Commercial Code defines a security as a financial asset[76] of the owner of the shares, which includes "a share or similar equity interest issued by a corporation." "Investment security" explicitly excludes an interest in a partnership, which is an "economic interest."

Thus, it is the shares that are the property of the shareholder and which the shareholder owns. Shareholders do not own the corporation.

The corporation owns its property; i.e., its assets. The corporation also owes its liabilities. If the corporation owns the total assets and owes its liabilities, then the corporation obviously owns the net assets, i.e., the value of the assets after all liabilities are paid. But the net assets is the equity of the corporation: assets – liabilities equals net assets. If the corporation owns the net assets, then it obviously owns the equity. Thus it is the *corporation's* equity, not the shareholders' equity.

How is the *corporation's* equity magically transformed into *shareholders'* equity? Transforming the net assets which are owned by the corporation, into net assets owned by shareholders is worthy of anything coming out of Wizarding World!

Shareholders as beneficial owners of the corporation

Shareholders as have been categorized as beneficial owners with directors as trustees of shareholders' property by judges, legal scholars, and economists alike. But in order to be a beneficial owner a trust relationship must exist between the shareholders and the directors. In order for a trust relationship to exist, trust law must be applied. If trust law cannot be applied, there can be no trust relationship, no beneficial owners, and no trustees.

In order for trust law to apply, shareholders would have to transfer their property (cash) to the directors. But shareholders do not transfer their cash to directors. They transfer their cash to the corporation in an IPO. Thus, trust law cannot apply, therefore there is no trust relationship and therefore directors are not trustees and shareholders are not beneficial owners.

Shareholders as residual owners/residual claimants of the corporation

In *Applebaum v. Avaya, Inc.*, the Delaware Supreme Court held that "Shares of stock are issued to provide a verifiable property interest for the *residual claimants* of the corporation" (emphasis added).[77]

Thus, it is said that shareholders are residual claimants because it is assumed they have a "residual claim" on the equity (net assets) of the corporation, meaning they have a claim on the equity after corporate debts are paid. Alces (2009) states unequivocally that "the distinction between creditors and shareholders is well reasoned. Shareholders are the residual claimants, the 'owners' of the corporation." But when we examine the law, and logic, of the assumptions we find that shareholders are not owners or claimants, residual or otherwise.

Roberts (1955) describes the balance sheet equation (asset – liabilities = equity) as demonstrating that the corporation is owned by the stockholders and that their claims are residual in nature. But this is incorrect on at least two counts. First, the balance sheet does not show who owns the corporation. It does not even show who owns the equity (net assets). It only shows the value of net assets of the corporation, i.e., the equity, with no regard to ownership.

Second, it does not show shareholders are residual claimants, or any other type of claimant. That shareholders are residual claimants is an assumption not supported by law. In order to be a claimant, a person must have a legally valid, enforceable right.

Shareholders have no enforceable rights against either the corporation, the corporation's assets (whether total or net), or its directors. The rights of shareholders are limited to rights to vote on certain matters and rights to liquidation proceeds. None of those rights encompasses a valid, enforceable claim against either the corporation, the income of the corporation, or the property of the corporation. Without a valid, enforceable claim against either the corporation, the income of the corporation, or the property of the corporation shareholders are not claimants, let alone residual claimants.

Shareholders have no greater claim on the net assets than they do on the total assets. The corporation owns the assets and shareholders have no claim against the total assets. The corporation owns the equity thus the shareholders have no claim against the equity.

Roberts (1955) does correctly note that the dividends are a distribution of the corporation's profits which are residual in nature, i.e., distributed out of net income or retained earnings after all expenses have been paid, whereas the interest paid to the creditors represents a direct claim against the corporation. If the corporation does not pay the interest due to creditors, the creditors may enforce their claims in a court of law.

However, the fact that dividends are residual in nature does not translate into a residual claim by shareholders against the corporation or its net income since shareholders have no claim to dividends. As Berle and Means (1991) note, shareholders traded their property rights with respect to the resources of production for a mere expectation of dividends, which Roberts does acknowledge ("The corporation has an obligation to pay the interest due bondholders but there is no obligation on the corporate enterprise to pay dividends"). But Roberts misses the connection between the corporation having no obligation to pay dividends and shareholders having no claim for dividends. There can be no claim by one person (a shareholder) against another person (the corporation) if the second person (the corporation) has no obligation (duty) to the first person (a shareholder).

Creditors have a claim against the corporation for both interest and principal if neither is paid. Shareholders have no claim against the corporation for dividends or "principal," which Roberts also acknowledges ("the bondholders have a claim for a specific amount to be paid within a certain time period whereas the stockholders have no such claim"). But Roberts, as all the others, nevertheless continues to assert that stockholders are residual claimants which, as a matter of property law and contract law, they cannot be.

Roberts also errs in stating, "The stockholder owns the capital stock which represents a residual interest in the assets of the corporation. The stockholder is the last recipient of distributed corporate assets." Stockholders have no legal interest in the total assets of the corporation. If they have no interest in the total assets of the corporation, they have no legal interest in the net assets of the corporation. Indeed, Roberts states, "The bondholder can demand payment when the debt is due but the stockholder cannot demand payment." Therefore, if stockholders cannot demand payment, they are not claimants.

To see this point in perspective, consider the following cases from Delaware. In *Production Resources v. NCT Group*[78] the court ruled:

By definition, the fact of insolvency places the creditors in the shoes normally occupied by the shareholders—that of residual risk-bearers ... creditors become the residual claimants of a corporation when the equity of the corporation has no value ... when a firm is insolvent, creditors do not become residual claimants with interests entirely identical to stockholders, they simply become the class of constituents with the key claim to the firm's remaining assets.

And in *In re Trados Incorporated Shareholder Litigation*[79] the court stated: "Even when a corporation is insolvent, creditors lack standing to assert a direct claim for breach of fiduciary duty; they merely gain standing to sue derivatively because they have joined the ranks of the residual claimants."

Obviously, as a matter of contract creditors must first be paid in the event of insolvency. But that is not the point. The point is that in a bankruptcy proceeding, all creditors and all shareholders become residual claimants, so to categorize shareholders as residual claimants since they are paid after creditors are paid in a bankruptcy proceeding creates a false impression, particularly since creditors must actually file claims in the bankruptcy court in order to be paid, and shareholders do not.

In *Applebaum v. Avaya, Inc.*,[80] the court stated: "Shares of stock are issued to provide a *verifiable property interest for the residual claimants* of the corporation" (emphasis added). Two points must be made here. One, the court is equating owners of shares with residual claimants, but as discussed above, shareholders are not claimants of any type.

Two, when the court states that shares of stock provide a verifiable property interest the court is not saying that shares of stock provide a verifiable ownership interest in the corporation. Delaware General Corporation Law makes a share of stock an item of personal property and therefore it cannot be a property interest in the corporation. However, corporations are not actually required to issue certificated shares. Owning shares may be uncertificated. The certificated share of stock merely verifies the property interest in the shares.

To see that a share is a verifiable property interest in the shares and not a property interest in the corporation, compare a share of stock to a deed or title to an automobile. A deed to real property is not a financial asset and is obviously not the real property itself. It is the verifiable property interest in the real property; namely, that of owner. The title to an automobile is not a financial asset and is obviously not the personal property that is the automobile. "*Corporate securities* are a species of *property right* that represent not only a firm's fundamental source for raising capital, but also now a publicly traded commodity" (emphasis added).[81] A share of stock is a financial asset as defined by the Uniform Commercial Code, and a publicly traded commodity. Furthermore, shares are personal property according to the Delaware General Corporation Law.

Since the Delaware General Corporation Law, as well as the corporation laws of every other jurisdiction, grants to corporations the right to acquire and own assets but explicitly makes shares of stock personal property as an investment security, shareholders are prohibited by statute from owning the either the corporation or the assets of the corporation and therefore have no claim against the corporation or its assets.

Furthermore, by making shares of stock personal property transferable only in accordance with the Uniform Commercial Code's provision for "Investment Securities," shareholders cannot both own the shares as investment securities, and own the corporation itself.

At first glance, the UCC's definition of a security as "a share or similar equity interest issued by a corporation" suggests an ownership interest in the corporation, but that is not the case. First, the definition does not state that a share *is* an equity interest, only that a share may be *similar* to an equity interest. But that distinction is not controlling.

The Delaware General Corporation Law "shall not be construed as repealing, modifying or restricting the applicable provisions of law relating to incorporations [or] sales of securities ... except insofar as such laws conflict with this chapter."[82] To the extent that the UCC's definition of a security conflicts with the Delaware General Corporation Law, the Delaware General Corporation Law prevails. Thus, while the Delaware General Corporation Law provides that shares of stock shall be sold in accordance with the UCC, the UCC cannot make a share of stock an equity interest in the corporation.

The equity of a corporation is the net assets of the corporation (assts – liabilities = equity), which arises in the first instance when the corporation issues shares in an IPO and subsequently by retained earnings. But the equity is not owned by the shareholder. It is owned by corporation. The shareholder only has a right to receive net assets when the corporation is liquidated and the net assets are required by law to be distributed to the shareholders.

Shareholders have no right as a matter of law to share in the profits and losses of a corporation. They have no right to receive distributions other than in a liquidation. If they have no right, they are not claimants, residual or otherwise.

The Delaware General Corporation Law provides that "The directors of every corporation, subject to any restrictions contained in its certificate of incorporation, *may* declare and pay dividends upon the shares of its capital stock ... ."[83] Thus, not only do directors have no duty to declare dividends, shareholders have no right to receive a dividend until it is declared by the directors. Thus receiving a dividend is no more than a mere expectation, a hope really, as acknowledged by Berle and Means (1991).

Shareholders as investors in the corporation

Shareholders as owners of the corporation is directly related to the question of shareholders as investors in the corporation. It is a commonly held belief that shareholders are investors in corporations.

An investment is something you expect to receive a return from. But to be an investor requires an ownership interest in that which you invest in. An investor can only invest in property to which property rights are attached:

> An investment is an asset or item acquired with the goal of generating income or appreciation … an investment is a monetary asset purchased with the idea that the asset will provide income in the future or will later be sold at a higher price for a profit.[84]

Corporate statutory law is emphatic that corporations own the assets (property). It was also shown above that shareholders do not own the corporation. Therefore. they do not earn a return from investing in the corporation.

The California Supreme Court acknowledged in *Miller v. McColgan* that it is the ownership of shares that is the legally recognized property interest. "The property of the shareholders in their respective *shares* is distinct from the corporate property" (emphasis added),[85] thus negating any proprietary interest in the corporation itself. Furthermore, the California Supreme Court continued:

> It is fundamental, of course, that the corporation has a personality distinct from that of its *shareholders, and that the latter neither own the corporate property nor the corporate earnings.* The shareholder simply has an expectancy in each, and he becomes the owner of a portion of each only when the corporation is liquidated by action of the directors or when a portion of the corporation's earnings is segregated and set aside for dividend payments on action of the directors in declaring a dividend. This well-settled proposition was amplified in Rhode Island Hospital Trust Co. v. Doughton, 270 U.S. 69, 81 [46 S. Ct. 256, 70 L. Ed. 475], wherein appears the following cogent language: 'The owner of the shares of stock in a company is not the owner of the corporation's property. He has a right to his share in the earnings of the corporation, as they may be declared in dividends arising from the use of all its property. In the dissolution of the corporation he may take his proportionate share in what is left, after all the debts of the corporation have been paid and the assets are divided in accordance with the law of its creation. But he does not own the corporate property' [emphasis added].

The California Supreme Court in 1941 in *Miller v. McColgan* relied on the United States Supreme Court ruling in *Rhode Island Hospital Trust Co. v. Doughton*[86]:

> The owner of the shares of stock in a company is not the owner of the corporation's property. He has a right to his share in the earnings of the corporation, as they may be declared in dividends arising from the use of all *its* property. In the dissolution of the corporation he may take his

proportionate share in what is left, after all the debts of the corporation have been paid and the assets are divided in accordance with the law of its creation. But he does not own the corporate property ... . The interest of the shareholder entitles him to participate in the net profits earned by the bank in the employment of *its* capital, during the existence of its charter, in proportion to the number of his shares; and, upon its dissolution or termination, to his proportion of the property that may remain of the corporation after the payment of its debts. This is a distinct independent interest or property, held by the shareholder like any other property that may belong to him [emphasis added].

Miller must be compared to the Model Business Corporation Act, which states:

A *shareholder of the corporation does not have a vested property right* resulting from any provision in the articles of incorporation, including provisions relating to management, control, capital structure, dividend entitlement, or purpose or duration of the corporation [emphasis added].[87]

Thus, since owners of share are not owners of the corporation, owners of shares are not investors in the corporation. Shareholders own shares and invest in the shares. They do not own the corporation and therefore do not invest in the corporation.

Corporations and agency law

Directors have been declared to be agents of shareholders. If directors are agents of shareholders, then agency laws must be applied. If agency law does not apply, then directors cannot be agents of shareholders.

According to agency law, a principal is liable for the acts of her agent either by signing a contract or by causing injury to a person or property. Here we are only concerned with contracts since corporations have been described as *nexuses*[88] of contracts in the theory of the firm.

Oddly enough, while the theory of the firm is concerned with directors as agents and agency costs, it pays no heed to actual agency law to confirm, or negate, the bases on which the theory of the firm are built.

If directors are agents of shareholders, then shareholders are liable for the acts of the directors. If shareholders are not liable for the acts of the directors, then shareholders are not principals. If shareholders are not principals, then directors are not agents of shareholders. Corporations are liable for the acts of the directors, therefore corporations are the principals and directors are the agents of the corporation, not of the shareholders.

The parties required in order to create an agency relationship are the principal and the agent. In order to create the agency relationship, it is the principal who must appoint the agent to act on his or her behalf. An agent cannot appoint a principal to be her principal.

Corporate directors exist before shareholders exist. If directors are agents of shareholders, they are agents of non-existent principals, which is not allowed under agency law. Second, only directors can issue shares. When a corporation is formed, there are no shareholders, only directors. Directors then issue the shares creating shareholders. Thus, agents are creating the principals. This is contrary to agency law and nullifies the theory that directors are agents of shareholders, which undermines the economic theory of the firm.

Purchasing shares in an IPO is a contract, but not a contract of principal and agent relationship. As Easterbrook and Fischel (1989) state, it is a contract of adhesion. The articles of incorporation set forth the terms of shareholders' and directors' respective rights and duties that bind both shareholders and directors and that shareholders explicitly agree to by purchasing the shares in a take-it or leave-it transaction. There is no negotiation.

When you purchase shares in an IPO the corporation offers to sell you shares and the rights accompanying the shares for consideration as determined by the articles of incorporation and the class of stock. You accept the offer by delivering the consideration (cash) to the corporation and surrendering your rights to decide what to do with the cash to the corporation. Such a transaction simply does not fulfill the requirements for a trust relationship.

The mistake is to assume the money paid for shares in an IPO is the shareholders' money after they purchase the shares. It is not. The corporation gave consideration to shareholders during the IPO process in the form of a promise that is legal consideration. The corporation promised to potential shareholders that in exchange for cash the corporation would give them the right to vote for directors and that the shareholders might receive a share of the corporate profits in the form of a dividend (an expectation). The shareholders relinquish all title to ownership to the money just as when a person buys a car he relinquishes title to ownership of the money. The title to the car is not the car; the title to the shares is not the corporation.

Statutory corporate law does not impose on directors a fiduciary duty to shareholders as agents of shareholders, which even Berle and Means acknowledged ("The directors of the corporation ... are not agents of the stockholders," p. xxi)[89] but which is almost universally ignored. Indeed, the entire theory of the firm is built on the theory that directors are agents of shareholders. Robé (2011) explains (although without evidence):

> In fulfilling their duties, the directors are required to act under the high standards imposed on fiduciaries. The directors of the corporation have to make their decisions in the best interests of the corporation, with a duty of loyalty and a duty of care ... the duty of care requires that ...

directors act in the honest belief that the action taken was in the best interest of the company (not the shareholders) ... .

(p. 34, emphasis added)

Berle and Means go on to explain, "In place of actual physical properties over which the owner could exercise direction and for which he was responsible, the owner now holds a piece of paper representing a set of rights and expectations with respect to an enterprise" (p. 64). They continue, "It follows from all the foregoing that the shareholder in the modern corporate situation has surrendered a set of definite rights for certain indefinite expectations" (p. 244).

Corporations and trust law

Directors have been declared to be trustees of shareholders. If directors are trustees of shareholders, trust law must be applied.

A trust is a relationship involving three persons wherein one person, the grantor (also referred to as a donor, settlor, or trustor), transfers legal title to property (the trust res, or trust corpus) to a second person, the trustee, for the benefit of a third person, the beneficiary (or beneficial owner), according to the terms of a trust agreement.

The trustee has an obligation to manage the property for the benefit of the beneficiary according to the trust agreement. The trustee has a fiduciary duty to the beneficiary.

The trustee has discretion as to how to manage the trust property for the benefit of the beneficiary. An agent has no such discretion. Importantly, neither the trustor nor the beneficiary exercises any control over the trustee as a principal exercises control over the agent. The trustee takes legal title to the property. The agent does not. A beneficial owner has no rights to choose, name, appoint, or vote for a trustee, which is an important point to keep in mind when considering whether shareholders can be beneficial owners since they vote for directors.

To see how judges and legal scholars confound corporate law, consider that many legal scholars disparage corporate governance for separating ownership and control, arguing for greater shareholder rights. This criticism is echoed by judges. Courts have ruled that shareholder owners are beneficial owners and directors are trustees. But a beneficial owner of a trust does not control the trust; the trustee does. So if, according to popular theory, shareholders are beneficial owners and directors are their trustees, shareholders cannot by definition have rights of control so they have no justifiable right to complain about non-control.

In yet another way that judges and legal scholars confuse corporate law and trust law is that trustees have legal title to the trust property. The trustor transfers the trust property to the trustee for the benefit of the beneficiary. Yet in a shareholder-corporation-director relationship, shareholders do not transfer legal title to trustee-directors. Trustee-directors do not have legal title to any property; the corporation does.

Chapter summary

This chapter reviewed the creation of corporations; governance and operation of corporations; ownership and control of corporations; corporations and contract law, property law, agency law, and trust law; and shareholders and contract law, property law, agency law, and trust law.

As proven in *Corporate Law and the Theory of the Firm: Reconstructing Corporations, Shareholders, Directors, Owners, and Investors* and presented here in condensed form, shareholders do not own corporations (whether direct, beneficial, or residual), shareholders are not investors in corporations, and directors are not agents of shareholders thus obliterating any validity for the agency theory of the firm and incomplete contracts.

Furthermore, corporations whose shares are traded in the market and corporate law, property law, and agency law have a direct relationship to economics, finance, investment and accounting, as well as capital and ownership of capital, capitalists, and capitalism.

Notes

1 Summarized and adapted from *Corporate Law and the Theory of the Firm: Reconstructing Corporations, Shareholders, Directors, Owners, and Investors,* © 2020 Wm. Dennis Huber, with permission.
2 Delaware General Corporation Law § 101.
3 New York Business Corporation Law Sec. 401.
4 Delaware General Corporation Law § 106.
5 New York Business Corporation Law Sec. 403.
6 Delaware General Corporation Law § 106. "Commencement of corporate existence. Upon the filing with the Secretary of State of the certificate of incorporation, executed and acknowledged in accordance with § 103 of this title, the incorporator or incorporators who signed the certificate, and such incorporators or incorporators' successors and assigns, shall, from the date of such filing, be and constitute a body corporate, by the name set forth in the certificate, subject to § 103(d) of this title and subject to dissolution or other termination of its existence as provided in this chapter."
7 Delaware General Corporation Law § 141(a).
8 New York Business Corporation Law Sec. 701.
9 Delaware General Corporation Law § 216.
10 New York Business Corporation Law Sec. 404(a).
11 Delaware General Corporation Law § 108, "Organization meeting of incorporators or directors named in certificate of incorporation. (a) After the filing of the certificate of incorporation an organization meeting of the incorporator or incorporators, or of the board of directors if the initial directors were named in the certificate of incorporation, shall be held, either within or without this State, at the call of a majority of the incorporators or directors, as the case may be, for the purposes of adopting bylaws, electing directors (if the meeting is of the incorporators) to serve or hold office until the first annual meeting of stockholders or until their successors are elected and qualify, electing officers if the meeting is of the directors, doing any other or further acts to perfect the organization of the corporation, and transacting such other business as may come before the meeting."
12 New York Business Corporation Law Sec. 404(a). "After the corporate existence has begun, an organization meeting of the incorporator or incorporators shall be held…for the purpose of adopting by-laws, electing directors to hold office until the first annual meeting of shareholders."

13 Delaware General Corporation Law § 107.
14 Delaware General Corporation Law § 152. Shares issued in an IPO are issued for cash.
15 Delaware General Corporation Law § 158. Stock certificates; uncertificated shares. "The shares of a corporation shall be represented by certificates, provided that the board of directors of the corporation may provide by resolution or resolutions that some or all of any or all classes or series of its stock shall be uncertificated shares."
16 Delaware General Corporation Law § 151.
17 Delaware General Corporation Law § 152.
18 New York Business Corporation Law Sec. 504(a).
19 Delaware General Corporation Law § 122(i)(2).
20 New York Business Corporation Law Sec. 202(a)(2).
21 Delaware General Corporation Law § 121(a).
22 Delaware General Corporation Law § 121(b).
23 New York Business Corporation Law Sec. 202(a()16).
24 Delaware General Corporation Law § 122(4).
25 New York Business Corporation Law Sec. 202.
26 Delaware General Corporation Law § 121(b).
27 The New York Court of Appeals is the highest court in New York, the equivalent of the "supreme court."
28 Mason v. Curtis, 223 N. Y. 313 (NY, 1918).
29 The court went on to state, "The relation of the directors to the stockholders is essentially that of trustee and *cestui que trust*," and stockholders "are the complete owners of the corporation," which, although not supported by law, is not unusual for either that time period or this.
30 Shareholders do not invest in corporations. They invest in the shares of the corporation.
31 Federal securities laws impose fiduciary duties on publicly traded corporations. See chapter 8.
32 Delaware General Corporation Law § 102(b)(7).
33 Loft v. Guth, 2 A.2d 225 (Del. Ch. 1938).
34 "The Delaware Court of Chancery is widely recognized as the nation's preeminent forum for the determination of disputes involving the internal affairs of Delaware corporations." https://courts.delaware.gov/chancery/.
35 Lofland et al. v. Cahall, Rec'r., 13 Del. Ch. 384 (Del. 1922).
36 Recognizing that there is no fiduciary relation existing between directors and stockholders does not imply that the final judgment in the case would have been different; only that the reason for the final judgment may have been different.
37 Malone v. Brincat, 722 A.2d 5, 8 (Del. 1998).
38 North American Catholic Educational Programming Foundation, Inc v. Rob Gheewalla, Gerry Cardinale and Jack Daly, 930 A.2d 92 (2007).
39 New York Business Corporation Law Sec. 717.
40 Am Jur 2d, Agency, § 192.
41 Am Jur 2d, Agency, § 192.
42 Cede & Co., v. Technicolor, Inc., 634 A.2d at 361 (DE, 1994).
43 Pepper v. Zions First Nat'l Bank, N.A., 801 P.2d 144, 151, 1990 (UT, 1990).
44 Delaware General Corporation Law § 102(b)(7).
45 Delaware General Corporation Law § 212.
46 New York Business Corporation Law Sec. 501.
47 Delaware General Corporation Law § 102(a).
48 Delaware General Corporation Law § 151(a).
49 New York Business Corporation Law Sec. 402(c).
50 New York Business Corporation Law Sec. 612(a).
51 New York Business Corporation Law Sec. 703(a).
52 Delaware General Corporation Law § 282.

53 New York Business Corporation Law Sec. 628,630.
54 Delaware General Corporation Law § 170(a).
55 New York Business Corporation Law Sec. 510.
56 Delaware General Corporation Law § 281(b).
57 New York Business Corporation Law Sec. 1005(d).
58 California General Corporation Law § 300(a).
59 Delaware General Corporation Law § 203(c)(4).
60 It is rare for an individual to own 20% of the voting stock of a publicly traded corporation. A publicly traded corporation can own 20% or more of another publicly traded corporation in which case it would be reported as a subsidiary according to Generally Accepted Accounting Principles. There can be several tiers of subsidiary corporations but eventually the shares of the parent of all subsidiary tiers would be owned by individuals.
61 American Jurisprudence, 2nd, 17A Contracts, § 1.
62 American Jurisprudence, 2nd, 17A Contracts, § 10.
63 American Jurisprudence, 2nd, 17A Contracts § 1.
64 Contract. Legal Information Institute. www.law.cornell.edu/wex/contract.
65 American Jurisprudence, 2nd, 17A Contracts, § 3.
66 Am Jur 2d, Contracts, § 101.
67 American Jurisprudence, 2nd, 17A Contracts, § 71.
68 Am Jur 2d, Contracts, § 6.
69 Uniform Commercial Code, § 8–102.
70 AmJur 2nd, § § 180. Requisites of definiteness and certainty, generally.
71 AmJur 2nd, § 183. Invalidation for uncertainty due to absence of express provision as to essential terms.
72 Delaware General Corporation Law § 122(4).
73 New York Business Corporation Law Sec. 202.
74 Miller v. McColgan, 17 Cal.2d 432, 436 (CA, 1941).
75 Model Business Corporation Act § 159.
76 Delaware General Corporation Law §§ 8–102(a)(9)(i).
77 Applebaum v. Avaya, Inc., 812 A.2d 880 (2002).
78 Production Resources v. NCT Group, 863 A.2d 772 (DE, 2004).
79 In re Trados Incorporated Shareholder Litigation, 73 A.3d 17 (DE, 2013).
80 Applebaum v. Avaya, Inc., 812 A.2d 880 (2002).
81 Kalageorgi v. Victor Kamkin, Inc., 750 A.2d 531, 538 (DE, 1999).
82 Delaware General Corporation Law § 619.
83 Delaware General Corporation Law § 170.
84 Investment. *Investopedia*, www.investopedia.com/terms/i/investment.as.
85 Miller v. McColgan, 17 Cal.2d 432, 436 (CA, 1941).
86 Rhode Island Hospital Trust Co. v. Doughton, 270 U.S. 69, 81, 46 S.Ct. 256 70, L. Ed. 475 (1926).
87 Model Business Corporation Act § § 10.01(b).
88 From Latin *nectere* "to bind." The plural of *nexus* is either *nexus* or *nexuses.*
89 It must be noted that even Berle and Means acknowledged that directors are not agents of the stockholders. Yet, agency theory, which dominates the theory of the firm, is built on the concept that directors are agents of stockholders.

Bibliography

Cases

Applebaum v. Avaya, Inc., 812 A.2d 880 (2002).
Cede & Co. v. Technicolor, Inc., 634 A.2d at 361 (DE, 1993).
In re Trados Incorporated Shareholder Litigation, 73 A.3d 17 (DE, 2013).

Kalageorgi v. Victor Kamkin, Inc., 750 A.2d 531, 538 (DE, 1999).
Lofland et al. v. Cahall, Rec'r., 13 Del.Ch. 384, 118 A. 1 (DE, 1922).
Loft v. Guth, 2 A.2d 225 (DE, 1938).
Malone v. Brincat, 722 A.2d 5 (DE, 1998).
Mason v. Curtis, 223 N. Y. 313 (NY, 1918).
Miller v. McColgan, 17 Cal.2d 432 (CA, 1941).
North American Catholic Educational Programming Foundation, Inc v. Rob Gheewalla, Gerry Cardinale and Jack Daly, 930 A.2d 92 (DE, 2007).
Production Resources v. NCT Group, 863 A.2d 772 (DE, 2004).
Rhode Island Hospital Trust Co. v. Doughton, 270 U.S. 69, 81, 46 S.Ct. 256 70, L.Ed. 475 (1926).

Authors, publications, and statutes

Alces, K.A. (2009). Debunking the corporate fiduciary myth. *Iowa Journal of Corporation Law*, 35 (2), 239–282. Retrieved from https://ssrn.com/abstract=1352595.
Banner, S. (2011). *American property: A history of how, why, and what we own.* Boston: Harvard University Press.
Berle, A.A., & Means, G.C. (1991). *The modern corporation and private property* (2nd ed.). New York: Routledge.
Delaware General Corporation Law. https://delcode.delaware.gov/title8/title8.pdf.
Easterbrook, F., & Fischel, D.R. (1989). The corporate contract. *Columbia Law Review*, 89, 1416–1448. Retrieved from https://chicagounbound.uchicago.edu/cgi/viewcontent.cgi?article=2163&context=journal_articles.
Friedman, M. (1970). The social responsibility of business is to increase its profits. *N.Y. Times Magazine*, Sept. 13, p. 2.
Green, R.M. (1993). Shareholders as stakeholders: Changing metaphors of corporate governance. *Washington and Lee Law Review*, 50 (4), 1409–1421. Retrieved from https://scholarlycommons.law.wlu.edu/wlulr/vol50/iss4/4.
Huber, W.D. (2017). The saga of Huber vs. the American Accounting Association: Forensic accounting and the law. *Journal of Forensic & Investigative Accounting*, 9 (2), 870–879. Retrieved from https://papers.ssrn.com/sol3/papers.cfm?abstract_id=2970636.
Huber, W.D. (2020). *Corporate law and the theory of the firm: Reconstructing shareholders, directors, owners, and investors.* London: Routledge.
Jensen, M.C., & Meckling, W.H. (1976). Theory of the firm: managerial behavior, agency costs and ownership structure. *Journal of Financial Economics*, 3, 305–360. doi:10.1016/0304-405X(76)90026-X.
Levitt, A., Jr. (2008). How to boost shareholder democracy. *Wall Street Journal*, July 1, p. A17.
Masten, S.E. (1993). A legal basis for the firm. In Oliver E. Williamson and Sidney G. Winter (Eds.), *The nature of the firm: Origins, evolution, and development.* London: Oxford University Press.
Model Business Corporation Act. www.americanbar.org/content/dam/aba/administrative/business_law/corplaws/2016_Model_Business_Corporation_Act.authcheckdam.pdf.
New York Business Corporation Law. https://newyork.public.law/laws/n.y._business_corporation_law.
Posner, R.A. (2014). *Economic analysis of law* (9th ed.). New York: Wolters Kluwer.

44 *Review of corporations and corporate law*

Reich-Graefe, R. (2011). Deconstructing corporate governance: Director primacy without principle? *Fordham Journal of Corporate and Financial Law*, 16, 465–506. Retrieved from https://ssrn.com/abstract=1971300.

Robé, J.-P. (2011). The legal structure of the firm. *Accounting, Economics, and Law—A Convivium*, 1 (1), 1–85. doi:10.2202/2152-2820.1001.

Robé, J.-P. (2019). The shareholder value mess (and how to clean it up). *Accounting, Economics, and Law—A Convivium*, 9 (3), 1–27.

Roberts, A.T. (1955). The proprietary theory and the entity theory of corporate enterprise (Doctoral Dissertation). Louisiana State University and Agricultural & Mechanical College, Retrieved from https://digitalcommons.lsu.edu/gradschool_dis stheses/132/.

Shepherd, J.C. (1981). *The law of fiduciaries*. London: The Carswell Company.

Suojanen, W.W. (1954). Accounting theory and the large corporation. *Accounting Review*, 29 (3), 391–398. Retrieved from www.jstor.org/stable/241556?seq=1#metada ta_info_tab_contents.

Stigler, G.J., & Friedland, C. (1983). The literature of economics: The case of Berle and Means. *Journal of Law & Economics*, 26 (2), 237–268. doi:10.1086/467032.

Stout, L. (2012). *The shareholder value myth: How putting shareholders first harms investors, corporations, and the public*. Oakland, CA: Berrett-Koehler Publishers.

Velasco, J. (2010). Shareholder ownership and primacy. *University of Illinois Law Review*, 2010 (*3*), 897–956. doi:0.2139/ssrn.1274244.

Part I

Economic, finance, investment, and accounting considerations

With the review of corporate law completed, including corporations and contract law, property law, agency law, and trust law, we now turn our attention to economic, finance, investment, and accounting considerations. It is necessary to understand the foundation and basic principles of economics, finance, investment, and accounting in order to understand the nature of the firm, the theory of the firm, capital, capitalists capitalism, and Marx's inherent contradictions, when they are placed in context. The review necessarily encompasses federal securities laws, generally accepted accounting principles (GAAP), the Financial Accounting Standards Board, and what is known as capital markets theory.

There are naturally overlaps of economics, finance, investment, and accounting but each must be considered separately before they are placed in context. Reviewing the foundation and basic principles of economics, finance, investment, and accounting will allow a common denominator to be found that links them together and with capital, capitalists, and capitalism.

2 Corporations and economic considerations

Introduction

Having completed a review of corporate law we are now in a better position to understand the relationship between corporations and economics, much of which has been perverted by the theory of the firm because the theory of the firm ignores corporate law.

Economics, as defined by every introductory economics textbook, is the science of the allocation of scarce resources. Property in its various forms constitutes resources to the owner of the property. Property law is the legal structure that determines who owns the property (e.g. government or private persons), which resources are allocated and controlled (labor or capital), and how they are allocated and controlled (market or centrally planned by the government).

In this chapter I review basic principles and assumptions of economics in order to establish the framework for an analysis of the relationship between corporations and economic principles, and resources of production and ownership of those resources, which is necessary in order to fully understand the theory of the firm, capitalism, and the contradictions between and within law and economics. In particular, I review micro- and macroeconomics and how property law determines the relationship of corporations and economic principles to corporate property. The review is basic and assumes the reader has no, or at least insufficient, background in economics, and may therefore be considered as "Economics 101."

Some parts of this chapter are adopted and summarized from *Corporate Law and the Theory of the Firm: Reconstructing Shareholders, Directors, Owners, and Investors* with permission. Some parts of this chapter are adopted and summarized from *The FASB Conceptual Framework: A Case of the Emperor's New Clothes* with permission.

Corporations and microeconomic considerations

Microeconomics deals with such things as demand and supply for resources of production at the firm level—in particular the supply of resources, resources of production,[1] production functions, and costs of production.[2]

Supply

Basic microeconomic theory posits that the quantity of goods supplied by a producer depends not only on price but also on the cost of the resources used in production since producers must earn a profit that is the price minus the cost of producing the goods (Krugman & Wells, 2008). The cost of production depends on the costs of individual resources of production that are the scarce or limited resources used in production.

The resources of production and the costs of the resources of production are traceable to the goods produced,[3] either directly or indirectly.[4] Production includes both the cost of the actual production of the goods and the cost of delivering the goods and administering the enterprise. Although the costs of production and administering the enterprise and delivering the goods are treated differently in financial statements (see chapter 5), since all costs are costs incurred by the enterprise from the very beginning of production to the point where the goods are in the possession of purchasers, either consumers or other businesses, they are considered costs of production.

The supply of resources is naturally a function of the profitability of the resources. The supply of a resource will in general be greater when the profitability of the resource is greater. The supply of labor, for example, will be higher when the wages of labor are higher. Yet the owners of some resources will try to suppress the profitability of owners of other resources. Owners of capital resources of production, for example, will try to suppress the profitability (wages) of labor, one of Marx's central postulates. But the contentious issue that is seen to exist between labor and the owners of capital resources of production is universally clouded by the failure to correctly identify the owners of the capital resources of production.

Scarce resources and resources of production

A scarce resource is only scarce and only a resource if it is a resource of production. A resource of production is simply a scarce resource used in production, which includes both actual production of the goods and the operation of the enterprise. There are three types of scarce, or limited, resources used in production: land, labor, and capital (Krugman & Wells, 2008; Federal Reserve Bank of St. Louis, n.d.).

Land includes not only the land itself but also natural resources in, on, or under the land or produced by the land, including minerals and trees (Worstall, 2016; Krugman & Wells, 2008).[5] Some aspects of land constitute raw materials (e.g., trees) which are transformed into finished goods (e.g., lumber for houses). While land is fixed in location, the supply of land used in production can be expanded by such things as clearing forests or discovering more mineral deposits (Krugman & Wells, 2008). Only land owned by producers of goods is a resource of production. Land owned by consumers is naturally excluded.

Labor is more problematic due to its variability. Labor encompasses all aspects of human activity related to the production and distribution of goods. This includes manual or physical labor used directly or indirectly, as well as managerial and intellectual (mental) labor necessary to produce the goods and operate the enterprise and to distribute the goods. Entrepreneurship (see chapter 8) or managerial labor are occasionally considered as separate resources of production. However, that is a false distinction. If the resource is not land or capital (machines), it is labor. Furthermore, the classification of labor for financial statement purposes (direct or indirect labor as part of cost of goods manufactured) or administrative labor (office personnel as administrative expense) is irrelevant. "Management is a type of labor but with a special role—coordinating the activities of inputs and carrying out the contracts agreed among inputs, all of which can be characterized as 'decision making'" (Fama, 1980, p. 290). All human activities are labor and the distinction or classification does not affect the arguments made herein. Like the supply of land, the supply of labor used in production can be increased such as by an increase in population (Krugman & Wells, 2008). Certain types of labor supply can be increased through education and training.

Physical capital is anything created, manufactured, or produced by human labor that is used as a resource in the production of other goods—tools, machines, computers, computer programs to operate machines or administer the enterprise (Krugman & Wells, 2008).[6] Capital can be increased by, e.g., inventing new machines such as the cotton jenny, computer programs, or robots. Obviously, things such as a computer program are not a physical, i.e., tangible, resource. Yet, intangible resources of production are capital resources of production as much as tools and machines are because they are produced by labor for use in producing other goods. Since "capital" with no adjective is also frequently used to refer to money or financial capital which is not a resource of production, I will use the terms "physical capital," "productive capital," or "capital resource of production" to refer to "capital" and to distinguish it from "financial capital." "Capital" is discussed in detail in chapter 8.

Importantly, omitted from consideration as a resource used in production is cash. Cash, i.e., financial capital, is not a resource of production. Cash is not used in production. Cash is not a scarce resource. (Although, as the author can attest to, cash may be scarce, it is not a resource of production.) Cash cannot be traced to goods, either directly or indirectly. Cash has no production value. While some resources can be substituted for others, e.g., capital for labor, an enterprise cannot substitute cash for labor, cash for capital, or cash for land in order to increase production. While cash can be used to acquire resources of production, cash is not itself a resource of production.

The "capital" that providers of capital provide to corporations who shares are publicly traded is financial capital, i.e., cash which is provided to the corporation when the corporations sells its securities to the public and the shareholders purchase the securities in an IPO: "Business enterprises raise capital for production and marketing activities not only from financial institutions and small groups of individuals but also from the public through issuing equity and debt securities that are widely traded in highly developed securities markets" (FASB, 1978).

The FASB correctly links financial capital to savings:

> Production and marketing of goods and services often involve long, continuous, or intricate processes that *require large amounts of capital*, which in turn require *substantial savings in the economy*. Savings are often invested through a complex set of intermediaries which offer savers diverse types of ownership and creditor claims.
>
> (FASB, 1978, 11, emphasis added)

It is important to keep in mind at all times—in law, economics, finance, and accounting—that it is the corporation that owns all the resources, both financial capital and capital resource of production. When a shareholder purchases shares in an IPO, the equation A = L + E (assets = liabilities + equity) is created. The corporation owns the assets and owes the liabilities. Therefore, A − L = E, or assets minus liabilities equals equity where E = the net assets. In other words, the corporation owns the net assets, or equity, of the corporation, not the shareholders, and it is the corporation that decides how to use and allocate the resources of production that it owns and how to use the financial capital that it owns to acquire resources of production.

As noted, the term "capital" is frequently used to refer to the financial capital, i.e., the cash provided by purchasers of stock in an IPO, such as in the FASB statement quoted in the preceding paragraph. At other times, "capital" is distinguished from "cash." For example, *Statement of Financial Accounting Concepts No. 1, Objectives of Financial Reporting by Business Enterprises* (2008) states, "saving and investing in *productive resources* (capital formation) are generally considered to be prerequisite to increasing the standard of living in an economy" (FASB, 1978, 33, emphasis added).[7]

Production functions and allocation of resources of production

Production functions explain how resources of production are combined and how one resource of production may be substituted for another resource of production while achieving the same level of output or expanding output up to a maximum. A simple Leontief production function, for example, assumes that resources of production are used in fixed proportions with no substitutability between resources. Labor, for example, cannot be substituted for capital or vice versa (Nakamura, 2009). Expanding capital or labor resources does not result in an increase in output without a proportional increase in labor or capital resources. The capital/labor ratio is constant and the production function is linear homogeneous. On the other hand, according to the Cobb-Douglas production function, resources of production can be substituted for each other (Sato & Hoffman, 1968). For example, capital resources can be substituted for labor resources and vice versa. Increasing capital resources can result in an increase in output without a proportional increase in labor resources. The capital/labor ratio is non-linear.

Resources can only be considered as "scarce resources" in relation to production and production functions. Scarce resources will be allocated by the owner of the resources from less efficient production methods to more efficient production methods in order to reduce costs of production. One scarce resource will be substituted by the owner of the resource for another scarce resource in order to produce more quantity or to produce more efficiently or more cheaply. The corporation is the owner of the resources of production and the corporation alone decides how to allocate its resources of production.

It bears repeating and emphasizing that it is the corporation that owns the assets (resources) and it is the corporation alone that decides how to combine its physical capital with the land that it owns and its labor to decide the optimal production function. This fact is almost universally ignored in theories of the firm and debates about capital and capitalism. When one speaks of the ownership of capital as an indication of whether or not a particular regime is capitalist, there is great deal of inconsistency and confusion in how the term is used and what it means.

While there is financial capital, physical capital is only that which is a resource (factor, means, mode) of production, along with land and labor. Marx himself recognized this, as did Weber, although they at times were inconsistent in their discussions of what is meant by "capital." Neither socialism nor communism lies at the end of the spectrum opposite capitalism as is universally believed since production under both socialist and communist regimes must rely on physical capital for production. What lies at the end of the spectrum opposite capitalism is more accurately described as *"laborism."*

As seen in production functions, labor and capital may be substituted for each other given that land is fixed. Land is an endogenous variable, not a variable in a production function.

There is, of course, an entire field of economics dedicated to the labor market, i.e., the supply of and demand for labor as a resource of production, referred to simply as "labor economics." Yet, while capital resources of production are necessary for a production function, there is no field within economics referred to as the "capital market" or "capital economics," i.e., the supply of and demand for capital resources as a resource of production. What is erroneously referred to as the "capital market" is nothing more than the supply of and demand for financial capital[8] that a corporation receives when it issues shares to the public. Financial capital is discussed in greater detail in chapter 8.

Production costs and resources of production

The costs of production are the costs associated with the scarce resources used in production. Land owners receive rent (Krugman & Wells, 2008). Labor receives wages or salaries (Krugman & Wells, 2008). Capital resource owners receive a profit (also called "interest" or "return") on their capital (Krugman & Wells, 2008).

However, in the case of corporate enterprises it is the corporate enterprise that legally owns the capital resources (machines, computers, computer programs) and receives the return (profit) on the capital resources used in production, referred to as "return on assets" or ROA. (See chapter 5). The enterprise initially acquires its capital resources of production by using the cash received from shareholders in an IPO to acquire the capital resources in the resource market. The enterprise does not receive capital resources from purchasers of shares. The profit earned by the enterprise on capital resources is then distributed to the shareholders in the form of dividends (cash) but only if the directors declare a dividend, and thus it is the shareholders who, although it is only an expectation and not a right, ultimately receive the profit (return) on the capital resources or production (Krugman & Wells, 2008).[9]

Total costs associated with scarce recourses of production—rent, wages/salaries, return—might not be internalized by the enterprise, i.e., there may be no "sacrifice of future benefits."[10] Internalized costs are the costs the enterprise reports in its financial reports (see chapter 5), while externalized costs are costs that are not reported because they are exported to others outside the enterprise without a sacrifice by the enterprise (Krugman & Wells, 2008). Thus, enterprise profit will be higher if costs can be externalized. All things equal, the highest return goes to that enterprise that can best externalize costs.[11] Internalized costs are the only costs the enterprise reports on its financial reports (see chapter 5).

Corporations and macroeconomic considerations

Macroeconomics deals with economic issues at the national level. Relevant to the arguments in this book are gross domestic product, and savings and investment.

Gross domestic product and national income

As every standard introductory economics text explains, gross domestic product (GDP) using the expenditure approach is defined as total expenditures for consumption by consumers (C), investment expenditures made by a businesses for acquiring capital resources (I), and expenditures made by the government (G), which gives the well-known equation GDP = C + I + G (Krugman & Wells, 2015).[12] Consumption is the largest part of GDP in free-market economies. Business investment is the most important part of GDP for purposes of this book.

Gross domestic product is measured from the output side, but GDP can also be measured from the income side (Krugman & Wells, 2015). GDP measured from the income side rather than from the output side is called "national income." Gross national income measures the distribution of national income among the resources of production: land, labor, and capital (Krugman & Wells, 2015). National income does not differentiate between types of labor. Capital is the physical capital used in production, not the financial capital used to acquire the physical capital used in production.

Savings and investment

The "I" of C + I+ G refers to the investment by business enterprises to acquire capital resources (Krugman & Wells, 2015).[13] Consumers do not invest. They save. Anything not spent on consumption (i.e., goods or services purchased for personal consumption) is by definition saved (Krugman & Wells, 2015). When consumers invest, they invest in stock or other instruments such as bonds. They may also deposit their funds in a savings account. While consumers may allocate cash not spent on consumption among various types of savings such as savings accounts, if consumers allocate savings to stocks rather than savings accounts they are considered as investors in the stock, but they are nevertheless still saving when they purchase the stock of a corporation, either in an IPO or in the market. They invest in the stock, they do not invest in the corporation. (See chapter 1, and Huber, 2020.)

Shareholders do not allocate or commit scarce resources of production to an enterprise as the *FASB Conceptual Framework* erroneously claims. Shareholders only allocate cash (financial capital) to an enterprise when they purchase shares in an IPO (see Securities Act of 1933, chapter 3). The cash the enterprise receives from purchasers of stock in an IPO comes ultimately from consumer savings and is reported in the statement of cash flows as financing activities. The enterprise uses the cash received from purchasers of stock to invest in capital resources. Thus, we have the equation savings equals investment, or S = I. The "I" is the capital expenditures in C + I + G and is reported on the statement of cash flows as investing activities (Weygandt, Kimmel, & Kieso, 2015; see also chapter 5).

As previously pointed out, the FASB correctly links financial capital to savings:

> Production and marketing of goods and services often involve long, continuous, or intricate processes that *require large amounts of capital*, which in turn require *substantial savings in the economy*. Savings are often invested through a complex set of intermediaries which offer savers diverse types of ownership and creditor claims.
>
> (FASB, 1978, 11, emphasis added)

Chapter summary

This chapter provided a very basic review of relevant microeconomic principles (identification of resources of production, supply of resources of production, and production functions) and macroeconomic principles (gross domestic product, gross national income, and savings and investment) necessary to establish a foundation for understanding how economics and contract law, property law, agency law, and corporate law are contradictory.

Notes

1 The term "resource of production" is more apropos than "factor of production" and will be used in this book.
2 Both micro- and macroeconomics also encompass consumer issues. However, the economics of consumer supply and demand are not relevant to this book.
3 Costs of the resources of production applies to the production of both goods and services, but for simplicity only the production of goods is considered here.
4 Tracing the costs of the resources of production to the goods produced is the domain of cost accounting, which is beyond the scope of this book.
5 There is an ongoing political and economic debate regarding renewable recourses. That debate is not relevant to te issues discussed in this book.
6 Capital is sometimes classified as human capital and physical capital (Krugman & Wells, 2008). That classification confuses the meanings of labor and capital. Human capital is labor.
7 The Securities Exchange Act of 1934 also uses the term "capital" to mean "cash." "CONSIDERATION OF PROMOTION OF EFFICIENCY, COMPETITION, AND CAPITAL FORMATION. Whenever pursuant to this title the Commission is engaged in rulemaking, or in the review of a rule of a self-regulatory organization, and is required to consider or determine whether an action is necessary or appropriate in the public interest, the Commission shall also consider, in addition to the protection of investors, whether the action will promote efficiency, competition, and capital formation" (15 U.S.C. § 78(f)).
8 Capital market research occupies a significant part of accounting and finance research with entire journals devoted to capital market theory and research. For example, the *Journal of Capital Markets Studies* publishes "high-quality research in the areas of economics and finance with a specific focus on capital markets." (www.emeraldgrouppublishing.com/services/publishing/jcms/index.htm). Capital market research is discussed in chapter 5.
9 The *FASB Conceptual Framework* recognizes that investors contribute cash to an enterprise in expectation of receiving more cash in the future.
10 Cost is the sacrifice incurred in economic activities in order to produce (FASB, 1978, CON1, Footnote 11).
11 Costs such as mitigating environmental degradation, which an enterprise may try to externalize, are an integral and necessary part of resource s of production and production costs, but are beyond the scope of this paper.
12 GDP also includes net exports, which is not relevant here.
13 The Securities Act of 1933 also uses the term "capital expenditures" to refer to investing in capital resources. 15 U.S.C. § 77z–2i(1)(A).

Bibliography

Fama, E.F. (1980). Agency problems and the theory of the firm. *Journal of Political Economy*, 88 (2), 288–307. Retrieved from www.jstor.org/stable/1837292.
Financial Accounting Standards Board (FASB) (1978). *Statement of Financial Accounting Concepts No. 1, Objectives of Financial Reporting by Business Enterprises.* Norwalk, CT. Retrieved from www.fasb.org/resources/ccurl/816/894/aop_CON1.pdf.
Federal Reserve Bank of St. Louis (n.d.) Retrieved from www.stlouisfed.org/education/economic-lowdown-podcast-series/episode-2-factors-of-production.
Huber, W.D. (2020). *Corporate law and the theory of the firm: Reconstructing shareholders, directors, owners, and investors.* London: Routledge.

Huber, W.D. (2020). The FASB Conceptual Framework: A case of the emperor's new clothes. *Journal of Accounting, Ethics & Public Policy*, 21 (1), 77–114. Retrieved from https://papers.ssrn.com/sol3/papers.cfm?abstract_id=3400769.

Krugman, P., & Wells, R. (2008). *Microeconomics* (2nd ed.). New York: Worth Publishers.

Krugman, P., & Wells, R. (2015). *Macroeconomics* (4th ed.). New York: Worth Publishers.

Nakamura, H. (2009). Micro-foundation for a constant elasticity of substitution production function through mechanization. *Journal of Macroeconomics*, 31 (3), 464–472. doi:10.1016/j.jmacro.2008.09.006.

Sato, R., & Hoffman, R. (1968). Production functions with variable elasticity of factor substitution: Some analysis and testing. *Review of Economics and Statistics*, 50(4), 453–460. doi:10.2307/1926813.

Weygandt, J.J., Kimmel, P.D., & Kieso, D.E. (2015). *Financial accounting* (10th ed.). Hoboken, NJ: Wiley.

Worstall, T. (2016). Economics is scarce resources allocation: What resource constraint does urban farming solve? *Forbes*, Aug. 15.

3 Corporations and finance considerations

Introduction

Unlike sole proprietors and partnerships, which are created by acts of investing cash in their proprietor or partnership, corporations whose shares are traded in the market are not created by acts of investing cash in the corporation. When a sole proprietor or partnership is created, it is usually accompanied by the simultaneous transfer of cash (or other property) by the proprietor or partners to the sole proprietor or partnership.

A corporation has no cash (or any other property) when it is created. A corporation can only be created by an act of filing appropriate papers with the state and receiving approval from the state, as explained in chapter 1. Subsequently, the only way a corporation can finance the acquisition of their capital assets is to issue first stock and then bonds. Since this chapter is concerned only with corporations whose shares are traded in the market, the ownership and control of corporations whose shares are traded in the market, and the relationship between corporations whose shares are traded in the market and economics, only stock is relevant to this chapter.

Furthermore, since we are concerned only with corporations and the stock (and bonds) issued by corporations whose shares are traded in the market we must take into account federal securities laws that govern the issuance of stock and bonds to the public.

Finance considerations: corporations

The balance sheet reveals that corporate assets are financed either by stock or debt—assets equals liabilities plus corporate equity which consists of stock that is initially required before the corporation assumes operating (see chapter 1), plus liabilities (debt) and retained earnings if the corporation has any. The statement of cash shows also shows that the cash used to acquire capital resources of production (investing activities) comes from issuing stock or bonds to the public (financing activities).

The cash corporations receive when they issue shares (and bonds) to the public provides their financial capital which they subsequently use to acquire capital resources of production.[1] The financial capital corporations receive is owned by the corporation. It is not owned by the shareholders. The capital resources of production are owned by the corporations. They are not owned by the shareholders. Thus, it is the corporation that allocates the resources.

Note that we are not here concerned with the value of the firm since that is a matter of evaluation by the owners of, and investors in, the shares of the corporation.

Corporations, financial capital, securities laws, and the securities market

There are two federal securities laws relevant to the financing of corporations whose shares are traded in the market: the Securities Act of 1933 ("'33 Act"), which applies to initial issues of securities (initial public offering or IPO), and the Securities Exchange Act of 1934 ("'34 Act"), which applies to securities traded on exchanges subsequent to an initial issue. In an initial issue of securities to the public the seller (the firm, the corporation, the enterprise) is the issuer. In a transaction traded on an exchange, the seller is someone different than the issuer (Fox 1997).[2]

It is important to recognize at this point that neither act was intended by Congress to facilitate the allocation of resources, scarce or otherwise. Neither act even mentions the allocation of resources.[3] The securities laws are intended only to protect and facilitate the efficient operation of the securities markets (Huber, 2016).

Corporations and the Securities Act of 1933

The purpose of the Securities Act of 1933 ("'33 Act") is to "provide full and fair disclosure of the character of securities sold in interstate and foreign commerce and through the mails, and to prevent frauds in the sale thereof, and for other purposes."[4]

The '33 Act applies to securities issued by an enterprise for the first time in an initial public offering. The securities issued in an IPO are not traded in the market or on an exchange but issued by the corporation and purchased directly from the issuer through an underwriter (Reilly & Brown, 2009). Recent examples include Uber[5] and Lyft.[6] It is only after the shares are issued by the corporation that they are traded on an exchange.

An infusion of cash to a corporation by purchasers of securities via an IPO, what the statement of cash flows classifies as a financing activity (see chapter 5), enables the corporation to expand its resources of production—acquire or expand capital resources, for example, or hire additional labor resources— thus expanding its output and production function. An infusion of cash to a corporation by purchasers of securities is not an allocation of a scarce resource to a corporation since cash, although it may be as scarce to the reader as it is to the author, is not a scarce resource. Furthermore, the forum and mechanism for distributing shares in an initial issue does not allow shares to be issued in exchange for resources other than cash since securities prices in an IPO are set in cash.

Issuing securities to the public for the first time requires a corporation to have a registration statement in effect with the Securities Exchange Commission (SEC): "Unless a registration statement is in effect as to a security, it shall be unlawful for any person, directly or indirectly—to sell such security through the use or medium of any prospectus or otherwise ..." (15 U.S.C. § 77e(a)). The registration statement must disclose what the enterprise plans to do with the cash it receives from the offering.[7]

Only after the registration statement is in effect is the corporation allowed to issue securities to the public via a prospectus. The registration statement is effective weeks in advance of the actual issuance of the securities which are offered to the public through an underwriter who issues the securities to purchasers on behalf of the corporation. Purchasers of the securities purchase the securities from the corporation via the underwriter by subscribing to the security in advance of the actual issuance after receiving a prospectus.

It is important to be aware first that the prices of securities issued in an IPO are not market determined. (For example, see the recent IPOs of Uber[8] and Lyft.[9]) "The pricing of initial public offerings is performed not by a market mechanism but by the underwriters involved with the transaction ... courts hold that the pricing by the underwriters is essentially subjective and is not dependent on the market price ..." (Lockwood, 1989).

Second, the issuance of shares in an IPO does not allow the shares to be issued in exchange for property or other "resources." Securities prices in an IPO are set in cash. The '33 Act specifically acknowledges that securities issued to the public for the first time are not traded on an exchange.[10]

Decisions on how to allocate actual scarce resources are made by the corporation issuing the securities in an IPO. Purchasers of securities do not make decisions on how to allocate scarce resources because they do not own the scarce resources. It is only at the time of an initial public offering that purchasers of securities decide to commit cash, not other resources, to the corporation by purchasing stock directly from the corporation.[11]

The corporation's scarce resources are the land, labor, and capital that the corporation uses in production. Land, labor, and capital cannot be committed to a corporation in an initial public offering. Purchasers of securities cannot and do not allocate other resources to a corporation in an IPO because prices of securities are set in cash and determined by the issuer and underwriter, not as a function of supply and demand in the market.

Corporations and the Securities Exchange Act of 1934

Trading securities on an exchange subsequent to the initial issue contributes nothing to a corporation's financial capital. However, while the '33 Act applies directly to initial issues, the '34 Act also contains provisions relevant to initial issues.

The purpose of the Securities Exchange Act of 1934 ("'34 Act") is, "AN ACT To provide for the regulation of securities exchanges and of over-the-counter markets operating in interstate and foreign commerce and through the mails, to prevent inequitable and unfair practices on such exchanges and markets, and for other purposes."[12] The Congressional finding as declared in the '34 Act was that "transactions in securities as commonly conducted upon securities exchanges and over-the-counter markets are affected with a national public interest ... ." (See Huber, 2016).[13]

> For the reasons hereinafter enumerated, transactions in securities as commonly conducted upon securities exchanges and over-the-counter markets are affected with a national public interest which makes it necessary to provide for regulation and control of such transactions and of practices and matters related thereto, including transactions by officers, directors, and principal security holders, to remove impediments to and perfect the mechanisms of a national market system for securities ... in order to protect interstate commerce, the national credit, the Federal taxing power ... and to insure the maintenance of fair and honest markets in such transactions.
>
> (15 U.S.C. § 78b)

Therefore, the '34 Act requires

> every issuer of a security registered pursuant to section 12 of this title file with the [Securities Exchange] Commission ... for the proper protection of investors and to insure fair dealing in the security—such information and documents...as the Commission shall require ... *annual reports* ... certified ... by independent public accountants.
>
> (15 U.S.C. § 78m(a), emphasis added)

The annual reports issued by a corporation include the balance sheet, income statement, and statement of cash flows. The opinion of the independent public accountant (Certified Public Accountant, CPA) states whether, in the auditor's opinion, the financial statements are in conformity with generally accepted accounting principles (GAAP) which are determined by the Financial Accounting Standards Board, subject to oversight by the SEC.

Section 12 of the '34 Act sets forth the registration requirements for securities[14] as determined by the '33 Act:

> Unless a registration statement is in effect as to a security, it shall be unlawful for any person, directly or indirectly (1) to make use of any means or instruments of transportation or communication in interstate commerce or of the mails to sell such security through the use or medium of any prospectus or otherwise.[15]

Corporations, financial capital, securities markets, and scarce resources

To better understand corporations and the relationship of financial capital, securities markets, and scarce resources we must consider not only what are scarce resources of production, but also the purposes of federal securities laws and the Financial Accounting Standards Board (FASB) created in 1973 as discussed in chapter 5.

Securities laws are not concerned with the allocation of resources, scarce or otherwise. Securities laws are only concerned with "capital formation" and what is called the "capital market." "Capital formation" refers to the ability of corporations to acquire financial capital in the securities market. (See chapter 8 for a more in-depth discussion of the meaning of "capital formation" and a discussion of why "capital market" is an incorrect label.)

Financial capital is the cash a corporation receives when it issues shares to the public (described as financing activities in the statement of cash flows) that is then available for the corporation to acquire capital resources of production, the long-term assets on the balance sheet (described as investing activities in the statement of cash flows).

The *FASB Conceptual Framework* incorrectly assumes that markets allocate resources: "Well-developed *securities markets* tend to allocate *scarce resources* to enterprises that use them efficiently and away from inefficient enterprises" (FASB, 1978, 13). However, securities markets are not resource markets and are not used to allocate scarce resources, whether these are land, labor, or capital. Securities markets are merely the fora investors use to exchange securities (hence the Securities and *Exchange* Commission) amongst themselves for cash.

Furthermore, securities markets do not allocate scarce resources. Markets do not own resources. It is the participants in the resource markets—the buyer of a resource and the seller of a resource—that own and allocate resources such as labor (labor market) or raw materials (commodities market).[16] Resource markets are simply the fora in which the allocation of resources take place. "Factors of production are bought and sold in factor markets, and the prices in factor markets are known as factor prices" (Krugman & Wells, 2008).

According to the *FASB Conceptual Framework*, general purpose financial reporting "is intended to provide information … for making reasoned choices among *alternative uses of scarce resources* …" (FASB, 1978, CON1), and "Business enterprises are producers and distributors of *scarce resources* …" (FASB, 1978, 19, emphasis added). Therefore, we must ask, who makes reasoned choices among alternative uses of scarce resources? To answer that question we must first acknowledge what scarce resources are.

Scarce resources are land, labor, and capital, keeping in mind that cash is not a scarce resource. Who then decides how to use land, labor, and capital? Purchasers of securities do not and cannot make reasoned choices among alternative uses of scarce resources because they do not own the scarce resources. Only the enterprise can decide where and how to allocate scarce resources because it is the enterprise that owns the resources of land and capital. Purchasers of securities only allocate cash (monetary capital, financial capital). It is the enterprise, or more specifically, the managers and directors of the enterprise, which then decides how to use the financial capital it receives to allocate or reallocate the land, labor, and capital.[17]

When purchasers of securities allocate or commit cash to an enterprise when they purchase shares in an IPO, the cash allocated to the enterprise is from their savings. Even if the cash from savings comes from selling stock in another enterprise, it is not taking the cash from that enterprise to allocate to another enterprise since no cash from the sale of stock on an exchange is transferred to or from any corporation.

Finance considerations: owners of shares and investors in shares

Ultimately, only individuals can provide financial capital to corporations. Even if one corporation forms another corporation and owns 100% of its shares, the financial capital of the first corporation that is transferred to the second corporation came from shareholders. But what we must carefully distinguish is that the owners of the shares are not the owners of the corporation and the investors in the shares are not investors in the corporation.

Owners of shares and investors in shares: financial capital and securities markets

Individuals provide financial capital to corporations when they take cash from their savings to purchase shares in an IPO. When a corporation issues shares in an initial public offering, it is referred to as the "primary market" although it is not the actual securities market per se because the shares are not purchased and sold in the securities market or on a securities exchange. They are sold by the corporation directly to the purchaser through an underwriter. It is only a market in the sense that there is a purchase and sale.

The price of the shares issued by a corporation is not set by market supply and demand. There is no market price because the shares have not been traded. The price is determined by the corporation's directors. When the shares are issued, the purchasers become the owners of the shares, not owners of the corporation. They become investors in the shares, not investors in the corporation. The cash the corporation receives is now the financial capital of the corporation, not the financial capital of the shareholders.

Owners of shares and investors in shares: scarce resources

Although the *FASB Conceptual Framework* states that "Well-developed *securities markets* tend to allocate *scarce resources* to enterprises that use them efficiently and away from inefficient enterprises" (FASB, 1978, 13), this is incorrect. Owners of shares do not provide scarce resources (land, labor, capital) to the corporation in which they own shares. Owners of shares only provide financial capital (which is not a scarce resource) to the corporation when they purchase the shares in an IPO. After purchasing the shares, they no longer own the financial capital they used to purchase the shares. The corporation owns it. What the shareholders own are the shares of stock which are financial assets, not capital assets. The financial assets of course form a part of individual savings.

Chapter summary

This chapter reviewed finance considerations pertaining to corporations, owners of shares, and investors in shares. Federal securities laws govern how corporations whose shares are traded in the market obtain their financial capital that is used to acquire scarce resources—land and capital resources of production—and to pay labor until enough cash is generated through operations.

The review of finance considerations included a review of federal securities laws, and the *FASB Conceptual Framework*'s misconception of the relationship of shareholders and scarce resources.

The review concluded that federal securities laws do not address the allocation of scarce resources, and that owners of, and investors in, shares do not provide scarce resources to the corporation; they only provide financial capital.

Notes

1 Corporations also receive cash from operations which is added to their financial capital via retained earnings that are not paid out in dividends.
2 Organizations other than corporations may issue securities other than shares of stock, such as limited partnerships or local governments.
3 A word search reveals that "allocation" is not even mentioned.
4 Securities Act of 1933, 15 U.S.C. § 77.
5 Uber IPO: 5 things you need to know about the biggest IPO in years. www.market watch.com/story/uber-ipo-5-things-you-need-to-know-about-potentially-the-biggest -ipo-in-years-2019-04-12.
6 Lyft to Price Shares Above Targeted Range of $62 to $68 in IPO. www.wsj.com/a rticles/lyft-to-price-shares-above-targeted-range-of-62-to-68-in-ipo-11553614735.
7 For example, see Uber's registration statement at www.sec.gov/Archives/edgar/da ta/1543151/000119312519144716/d647752d424b4.htm.
8 Uber IPO: 5 things you need to know about the biggest IPO in years. www.market watch.com/story/uber-ipo-5-things-you-need-to-know-about-potentially-the-biggest -ipo-in-years-2019-04-12.
9 Lyft to Price Shares Above Targeted Range of $62 to $68 in IPO. www.wsj.com/a rticles/lyft-to-price-shares-above-targeted-range-of-62-to-68-in-ipo-11553614735.
10 The SEC sets registration fees for IPOs based on "a baseline estimate of the aggregate maximum offering prices for any fiscal year" (15 U.S.C. § 77e(a)(6)(B)).
11 Universally overlooked is the fact that only the initial purchasers of securities commit cash directly to the enterprise in an IPO. Purchasers of securities on an

exchange do not commit cash to the enterprise. (An exception is when treasury shares are re-issued in the market.) However, because the use of the term "investor" to mean anyone who owns securities regardless whether they purchased them in an IPO or on an exchange is so entrenched in the literature it will similarly be used here.

12 15 U.S.C. § 78.
13 15 U.S.C. § 78b.
14 14 U.S.C. § 78l.
15 15 U.S.C. § 77e(5).
16 Technically, resources markets are not used to allocate resources. Resource markets are used to buy and sell resources. Buying and selling resources is not an allocation of a resource.
17 "Directors and professional managers commonly control enterprise resources and decide how those resources are allocated in enterprise operations" (FASB, 1978, 12).

Bibliography

Financial Accounting Standards Board (FASB) (1978). *Statement of Financial Accounting Concepts No. 1, Objectives of Financial Reporting by Business Enterprises.* Norwalk, CT: Financial Accounting Standards Board.

Fox, M.B. (1997). Securities disclosure in a globalizing market: Who should regulate whom? *Michigan Law Review*, 95 (8), 2048–2632. Retrieved from https://repository.law.umich.edu/mlr/vol95/iss8/5.

Huber, W.D. (2016). The myth of protecting the public interest: The case of the missing mandate in federal securities laws. *Journal of Business & Securities Law*, 16 (2), 402–423. Retrieved from https://papers.ssrn.com/sol3/papers.cfm?abstract_id=2605301.

Krugman, P., & Wells, R. (2008). *Microeconomics* (2nd ed.). New York: Worth Publishers.

Lockwood, L.B (1989). The fraud-on-the-market theory: A contrarian view. *Emory Law Journal*, 38, 1269–1318. Retrieved from https://heinonline.org/HOL/LandingPage?handle=hein.journals/emlj38&div=45&id=&page=.

Reilly, F.K., & Brown, K.C. (2009). *Investment analysis and portfolio management* (9th ed.). New York: South-Western College.

4 Corporations and investment considerations

Corporations, owners of shares and investors in shares

Introduction

Besides "capital," "investment" and "investor" are two of the most misused terms in corporate law, accounting, finance, and economics. The misuse of investment and investor has contributed significantly to the confusion and contradictions between economics, finance, accounting, and corporate law.

It is universally accepted that owners of shares of a corporation are investors in the corporation that issued the shares. Myriads of judicial rulings and publications by economists and legal scholars shamelessly refer to shareholders as investors in the corporation, and the ownership of shares as investment in the corporations. That is incorrect.

Investment from the perspective of a corporation is not the same as investment from the perspective of individuals. Their purposes are different, as are the results. What they invest in is different. Nevertheless, there is a common element in that they are two sides of the same coin, so to speak.

Investment from the perspective of a corporation encompasses not only financial statement items but also what is erroneously referred to as the "weighted average cost of capital." Investment from the perspective of individuals also involves financial statement items but also what is erroneously referred to as the "Capital Asset Pricing Model" (CAPM).

In this chapter I examine investment considerations from the perspective of both corporations and individuals in order to demonstrate that while they are not the same, they do share certain common elements, and to understand how investment considerations from the perspective of a both corporations and individuals are related to the allocation of resources.

Investment considerations: corporations

Investment considerations by corporations have three distinct elements—what corporations invest in, how they invest, and how investment is reported. To see these three elements I review first corporate investment and economics and then corporate investment and financial statements.

Corporate investment and economics

As explained in chapter 2, in the GDP equation C + I + G, "I" refers to business investment; i.e., corporations' purchases capital assets (capital resources of production, long-term assets on the balance sheet). Consumers do not invest. Consumers save ("S"), which provides the financial capital that corporations need to acquire capital assets of production when shares are issued in an IPO. Thus S = I, or consumer savings equals business investment. Owning shares is a type of saving since by definition whatever consumers do not spend, they save.

One way the term "invest" or "investment" has been misused is with reference, e.g., to "invest" in human capital. For example, "Since human capital is based on the investment of employee skills and knowledge through education, these investments in human capital can be easily calculated."[1] Certainly expenditures are made in acquiring and training labor (the factor of production) with diverse skill sets, e.g., manual labor or skilled labor. Yet such expenditure are still wages as the expenditures are paid to or on behalf of labor regardless of the label that is applied to those expenditures.

Another example of how "invest" or "investment" is misused is with reference to "working capital investment." For example, "Working capital investments are required to pay for unexpected and planned expenses ... . Working capital investment is the amount of money you require to expand your business, meet short-term business responsibilities and cover business expenses."[2]

Both examples share a common misuse of the term, which is that, as used in these contexts, it is unrelated to either legal, economic, finance, or accounting principles. The term "human capital" is not labor as a scarce resource of production. Labor is paid wages. Human capital, on the other hand, refers to

> an intangible asset or quality not listed on a company's balance sheet. It can be classified as the economic value of a worker's experience and skills. This includes assets like education, training, intelligence, skills, health, and other things employers value such as loyalty and punctuality.[3]

Investment from a corporate perspective properly and accurately refers to one thing only—the purchase of capital assets of production since that is the only thing that is common to law, economics, finance, and accounting. To impose on "investment" from a corporate perspective any meaning other than the purchase of capital assets of production isolates the concept from any relationship to law, economics, finance, or accounting and renders it meaningless.

Corporate investment and financial statements

Corporations acquire capital resources of production using the financial capital received when purchasers of securities purchase shares in an IPO issued in accordance with securities laws and subsequently from the cash retained from their earnings. They acquire physical capital in the factor market—machines, equipment, tools, etc.—the "I" in GDP. Corporate investment is reported in the corporation's financial statements as long-term assets (usually labelled "property, plant, and equipment") on the balance sheet and as investing activities in the statement of cash flows. The corporation makes investments using its financial capital.

Wages paid to labor as a resource of production appears on the income statement as either direct labor (cost of goods manufactured) or indirect labor (general expenses), and ultimately on the balance sheet as inventory in a manufacturing firm. Working capital is simply current assets that appear on the balance sheet (sometimes referred to as net working capital after current liabilities are subtracted) simply as cash and other current assets (see chapter 5). There is no category for investment in human capital or investment in working capital. Those terms are misleading and serve only to detract from the actual meaning of capital (see chapter 8).

Weighted average cost of financing

What is called the "weighted average cost of capital" is intricately related to what is erroneously called the Capital Asset Pricing Model, discussed in the next section, and is equally erroneous. It is also inseparable from the misuse of "capital," meaning the right side of the balance sheet.

What is called the "weighted average cost of capital" is the weighted average of the cost of debt plus the cost of equity, conveniently arranged in (very simplified) equation form as $k_a = (\%debt * k_d) + (\%equity * k_e)$ where k_d is the cost of debt and k_e is the cost of equity. On the statement of cash flows, issuing debt and stock constitute financing activities, not capital activities. The financing activities are used to finance investment activities; i.e., the acquisition of physical capital resources of production.

Since the right side of the balance sheet (debt plus equity) is not capital, to call the weighted average of the cost of debt plus the cost of equity the weighted average cost of capital is fallacious. What is called the "cost of capital" is, in reality, the cost of financing—the weighted average of the cost of financing with debt plus the cost of financing with equity (noting that it is the corporation's equity, not the shareholders'). Yet, the "cost of financing" has been, for the most part, relegated to the cost of using debt to finance the acquisition of long-term assets or services by both consumers and businesses. The "cost of financing" has been written into federal and state consumer "Truth in Lending" laws, and even into the California Commercial Financing Disclosures law[4], while the fallacious term "cost of capital" has been enshrined in the math and equations taught in every introductory corporate financing course.

Investment considerations: owners of shares and investors in shares

Owners of shares and investors in shares

As noted in chapter 2, individuals do not invest; they save. Anything consumers do not spend on consumption goods is saved by various methods. One method of saving is by a savings account in a bank. Another is by purchasing shares in a corporation.

Purchasing and owning shares in a corporation is not tantamount to owning the corporation. Nor does it constitute investing in the corporation. Individuals invest in stock the same way they invest in bond. Investing in shares is not the equivalent of investing in the corporation any more than investing in bonds constitutes investing in the corporation.

Unlike sole proprietors who invest their money in their businesses, shareholders do not invest in the corporation in which they own shares. Unlike partners who invest their money in their partnership, shareholders do not invest in the corporations in which they own shares. Investment requires an ownership interest. If there is no ownership, there is no investment.

Shareholders do not own the corporation. They own the shares. Consider the fact that many corporations issue bonds to the public.[5] When you purchase a bond, whether from the corporation or in the market, you do not own the corporation. You own the bond.

Financial Asset Pricing Model

Capital market research, which encompasses a large percentage of accounting and finance research, focuses on the relationship of risk and return of securities and the price of securities in the securities market.

Michie (2014) observes that

> In corporate capitalism [see chapter 9], the company was center stage with everything directed towards furthering its success. In financial capitalism [see chapter 9] it was the investment that was center stage, with everything directed towards maximizing the returns obtained.
>
> (p. 236)

This reality is reflected in the emphasis on "capital market" research and modern portfolio theory. In fact, the concept of financial capital is so well known that it earned Harry M. Markowitz, Merton H. Miller, and William F. Sharpe the 1990 Nobel prize in economics for their work in portfolio and capital markets theory.[6] Particularly noteworthy here is Sharpe's (1964) Capital Asset Pricing Model.

The Capital Asset Pricing Model (CAPM) is a rather simple equation that is used to estimate the price of what he calls a capital asset, i.e., a security, in the market (not in an IPO):

$$E_r = R_f + \beta(R_m - R_f)$$

where E_r is the expected return on a security, R_f is the risk-free rate of return (U.S. Treasury Bills), β (simply referred to as "beta") is the risk of the security as measured by its correlation with the market risk premium, R_m is the market rate of return, and $R_m - R_f$ is the market risk premium which is based solely on the risk of changes in the market prices of the securities. The risk is a function of shareholders' investment in the securities, not their investment in the corporation. Since the return is on the financial asset, not the capital asset, the correct term of the model is the Financial Asset Pricing Model (FAPM).

The model presents several issues. First, it only applies to securities traded in the market, not to securities issued in an IPO. The model is used to evaluate the equilibrium prices of securities and how securities' prices relate to each other and to the market factoring in risk. Thus, it has no relationship to corporations and therefore has no direct relationship to corporations issuing securities to raise financial capital.

Recall that financial capital is money. It is not stock. Financial capital is acquired when shares are issued in an IPO and used to acquire physical capital (capital assets). Capital assets are physical assets used in production. If, as the model alleges, the securities traded in the market are capital assets, what is it that purchasers of the securities own? If the purchaser is an individual, the securities form part of her portfolio and are a part of her total assets along with bonds, real property, art, or jewelry. Securities are, by legal definition, personal property and financial assets. Capital assets are assets used in production (see chapter 8). Individuals do not invest in or own capital assets because they don't produce anything. Individuals consume and save.

Securities traded on an exchange cannot be capital assets because no capital is involved since no financial capital is transferred to the corporation and the corporation is not acquiring physical capital. Capital can only be either financial capital raised by a corporation from the savings of individuals when the corporation issues securities in an IPO or physical capital acquired by a corporation as a resource of production using the financial capital received from the purchasers of the securities issued in an IPO. The securities traded on an exchange are neither financial capital nor physical capital because no cash is received by the corporation and corporations do not acquire physical capital with cash traded for securities in the market.

The first important point to understand here is that financial capital, money, is not a resource of production that both the FASB and SEC acknowledge. Labor cannot use financial capital (money) to produce anything. Financial capital (money) cannot be substituted for labor or physical capital in a production function. Nor can financial capital (money) be substituted for land. Money may, of course, be used to acquire capital resources of production, referred to as capital expenditures and "Investment Activities" on the statement of cash flows, but money is not itself a resource of production (see chapter 2). The cash owned by the corporation is used to pay the owners of the resources (factors) of production – land, labor, and capital. The corporation does not, and cannot, use cash to pay the owner of cash–itself–and therefore is not a resource of production.

The second important point is that shares of stock, whether issued in an IPO or traded in the market as Sharpe's model suggests, are not capital assets and neither the securities laws nor the UCC refer to them as such. While "capital" may be ambiguous and exhibit chameleon-like characteristics when used inconsistently, there are only two types of capital assets—money (financial) and physical (resource of production)—relevant to corporations and purchasers of shares. Purchasers of shares do not own resources of production. They own cash (their savings) until they purchase the corporation's shares, at which time they are still saving but now the corporation owns the cash as its financial capital. The corporation, once purchasers purchase the shares in an IPO, uses the financial capital to acquire capital assets (the capital resource of production). A Nobel prize was basically awarded for something that does not exist—namely, capital assets. While the model is arithmetically sound since it is merely an equation (although it is not empirically validated, but that is beyond the scope of this book), the name of the model is completely specious. Stocks are *financial* assets not *capital* assets, whether from the corporation's or shareholder's position, thus again, the correct term of the model is the Financial Asset Pricing Model (FAPM).

Chapter summary

This chapter highlighted the fact that there is one thing that investment from a corporate perspective and investment from a shareowner perspective have in common—they both own what they invest in. There is no investment if there is no ownership. Corporations own the long-term assets (capital assets of production). Investors own the shares they purchase. Shareowners do not own the corporation. They own the shares. Therefore, shareowners do not invest in the corporation. They invest in the shares.

The Capital Asset Pricing Model is not the Capital Asset Pricing Model. It is the Financial Asset Pricing Model (FAPM). The weighted average cost of capital is not the weighted average cost of capital. It is the weighted average cost of financing.

Notes

1 Human Capital. www.investopedia.com/terms/h/humancapital.asp.
2 Working Capital Investment. www.capital-investment.co.uk/working-capital-investment/.

3 Human Capital. www.investopedia.com/terms/h/humancapital.asp.
4 CALIFORNIA FINANCING LAW: COMMERCIAL FINANCING DIS-
   CLOSURES.   https://dbo.ca.gov/california-financing-law-commercial-financing-di
   sclosures/.
5 Issuing bonds also requires compliance with securities laws.
6 The Nobel Prize. www.nobelprize.org/prizes/economic-sciences/1990/press-release/.

Bibliography

Michie, R. (2014). The rise of capitalism from ancient origins to 1948. In L. Neal
   & J.G. Williamson (Eds.), *The Cambridge history of capitalism*, Vol. 2, pp. 239–263.
   Cambridge: Cambridge University Press.
Sharpe, W. (1964). Capital asset prices: A theory of market equilibrium under condi-
   tions of risk. *Journal of Finance*, 19 (3), 425–442. doi:10.1111/j.1540-6261.1964.
   tb02865.x.

5 Corporations and accounting considerations

Corporations, owners of shares, and investors in shares

Introduction

> I suggested that the accounts could be a valuable source of data on firm beha-
> viour, and, if I am right, it follows that their use could greatly assist in the
> development of a theory of the firm. Then I argued that a theory of the
> accounting system is part of the theory of the firm.
>
> (Coase, 1990)

Thirty years later, Coase's suggestion and argument have yet to be acted upon
and, given the disparity between generally accepted accounting principles and
the theory of the firm, it is not likely to happen in the foreseeable future.

Corporations are required by securities laws to issue financial statements on
an annual basis prepared in accordance with GAAP and audited by an independent public accountant (in the U.S, Certified Public Accountant or CPA)
who must issue an opinion stating whether or not the corporation's financial
statements are prepared in conformity to GAAP. Failure to conform to
GAAP may result in civil damages, fines, and even imprisonment. Yet, as I
show in this chapter, the financial statements required to be issued by corporations pursuant to securities laws are inherently misleading, not with
respect to the numbers (although they may be), but by the very nature of the
financial statements themselves and the classification of items on the financial
statements.

Accounting considerations are broad and encompass securities laws,
judicial opinions, the Financial Accounting Standards Board or FASB (the
U.S. accounting standard-setting body), and accounting textbooks (at the
introductory, intermediate, and advanced levels), as well as property law and
corporate law.

This chapter is concerned with financial reporting (accounting) as it relates
to corporations, owners of shares, and investors in shares. It may appro-
priately be titled "Accounting 101" because it reviews basic corporate financial statements as required by generally accepted accounting principles
(GAAP) and federal securities laws. Readers who have a fear of accounting
may rest assured that there are no debits and credits in this chapter. While
accountants (practicing or academics) will find the discussion of accounting

in this chapter familiar and be tempted so skip it, I encourage them to read it in order to have it fresh in their minds when they read the chapters that follow.

I begin by considering corporate financial reporting as required by GAAP, and then proceed to consider financial reporting from the perspectives of owners of shares and investors in shares. Owners of shares are investors in shares but I treat them differently to emphasize the fact that owners of shares are not investors in the corporation.

Accounting considerations: corporations and financial reporting

Corporations are required by securities laws to issue financial statements (what the FASB refers to as "general purpose financial statements") on an annual basis[1] prepared in accordance with GAAP as determined by the Financial Accounting Standards Board. Corporations must also submit audited financial statements to the SEC in order to receive authorization to issues shares to the public.[2] The statements must be audited by an independent public accountant who must issue an opinion stating whether or not the corporation's financial statements are prepared in conformity to GAAP.[3]

The SEC was given exclusive authority by Congress to make, amend, and rescind rules and regulations defining accounting, including

> the items or details to be shown in the balance sheet and earning statement, and the methods to be followed in the preparation of accounts, in the appraisal or valuation of assets and liabilities, in the determination of depreciation and depletion, in the differentiation of recurring and non-recurring income, in the differentiation of investment and operating income ... .[4]

In 2002 Congress authorized the SEC to explicitly recognize accounting standards established by a private standard-setting body provided the private standard-setting body met certain criteria.[5] The SEC subsequently recognized the FASB in 2002 as the sole private standard-setting body. (See Huber (2016) for an argument that the SEC's recognition of the FASB as a standard-setting body was an *ultra vires* act.)

Interestingly, law determines the economic and financial dynamics of the corporation in a way that is contrary to the "ajuridical approaches of most theories of the firm" (Biondi, Canziani, & Kirat, 2007, p. 7). Generally accepted accounting principles require the valuation of assets and liabilities as specified in the firm's contracts, thus "Accounting provides a better understanding of the economic and financial dynamics of the firm, driving to the very comprehension of such matters as assets, liabilities, revenues, prices, transactions, as well as to the appropriate representation of them" (Biondi, Canziani, & Kirat, 2007, p. 7).

But as I show in this section, those financial statements are inherently misleading because of the nature of the financial statements themselves and the classification of items on the financial statements.

Corporations, corporate financial statements, and the capital account

There are three financial statements relevant to the purposes of this book. Each is discussed separately, but they are interconnected.

The balance sheet

The structure of the balance sheet, also known as the statement of financial position, per U.S. GAAP[6] is assets (the left side of the balance sheet, or sometimes the top) equals liabilities plus equity (the right side of the balance sheet or sometimes the bottom) or what is known as the basic accounting equation: $A = L + E$. What constitutes assets and liabilities (debt) and how they are measured or valued is defined by the FASB.[7] Simple arithmetic then shows that assets minus liabilities equals equity, or $A - L = E$, where again, equity is the net assets. (In other countries, the balance sheet is shown as $A - L = E$.)

The asset section of the balance sheet is divided between current assets and long-term assets.[8] The current assets include cash (and what is called "cash equivalents" such as Treasury bills) and other items that will be converted into cash very quickly. Long-term assets are the resources of production—land and the capital assets of production (machines, equipment, etc.).

Prior to the beginning of operations the cash received from shareholders in an IPO constitutes the financial capital of the corporation. At that time, total assets equals net assets because there is no debt. The cash the corporation owns equals the equity the corporation owns. Immediately after receiving cash in an IPO the corporation uses part of its financial capital to acquire capital resources of production. The balance sheet still balances. The assets are still owned by the corporation, not the shareholders. The equity is still owned by the corporation, not the shareholders. But the financial capital no longer equals equity. (See chapter 8 for a more in-depth explanation.)

The liabilities, or debt, are self-explanatory.

Property law and corporate statutory law mandate that it is the corporation that owns the assets, not the shareholders,[9] and it is the corporation that is responsible for the liabilities; i.e., shareholders have no legal liability for payment of corporate debts.[10] (See chapter 1.)

The equity section is divided into stock and retained earnings. Stock is divided into common stock and preferred stock. But common stock is frequently referred to as "capital stock."[11] Furthermore, not only is common stock frequently referred to as capital stock, the entire right side of the balance sheet is referred to as "capital." (See chapter 8 for an explanation of why this is incorrect.)

While that is the structure of the balance sheet, the labels are misleading. Every introductory, intermediate, and advanced accounting textbook; every scholarly paper in accounting, finance, economics, and law; and every judicial opinion refers to the equity as "stockholders' equity." To refer to equity as stockholders' equity is a perversion of both property law and corporate law. As I explained in chapter 1 and *Corporate Law and the Theory of the Firm: Reconstructing Corporations, Shareholders, Directors, Owners, and Investors*, to transform corporate ownership of total assets into shareholder ownership of net assets, and therefore equity, is worthy of anything coming out of Wizarding World! It is the corporation that owns the equity, not the stockholders.

The income statement

The structure of the income statement, also known as the profit and loss statement, is revenue minus expenses equals net income or net earnings. What constitutes revenue and expenses and how they are measured is defined by the FASB. The net income is then added to retained earnings to become part of the corporation's equity. Dividends may be paid to owners of, and investors in, shares, which reduces the corporation's retained earnings that are part of its equity. Retained earnings is not cash.

Statement of cash flows

The structure of the statement of cash flows reports the cash flows in and out of the corporation according to operating activities, investing activities, and financing activities. Operating activities show the increase of decrease in cash from daily operations. The financing activities report cash received (or paid) from issuing stock or bonds. The investing activities report the corporation's investment in resources of production: long-term assets (capital) and land.

Corporations and the "capital account"

According to historians, economists, and sociologists like Werner Sombart, Basil Yamey, and others, the capital account was the greatest invention since the proverbial sliced bread, paving the way for the introduction of capitalism. (See chapters 8 and 9.) The introduction of double-entry bookkeeping[12] in the thirteenth century (or possibly before) introduced along with it the "capital account" that allowed individuals to separate their personal assets from their business assets.

The capital account and double-entry bookkeeping began with individual firms or partnerships (mostly merchants) to record how much financial capital they invested in their firms and how much was added through operations. On the importance of double-entry bookkeeping, Levy (2014) states:

double-entry bookkeeping made possible the separation of the profit and loss statement from the capital account, or the transformation of wealth into profit-seeking capital ... . Accounts have audiences. Double-entry bookkeeping, for instance, emerged from the complex forms of partnership and debt that constituted merchant capital in late medieval Italian city-states—which created the need for new forms of accountability. The issue of audience well illustrates capital's struggle to assert its own temporality.

(pp. 177–178)

Winjum (1971) concurs:

Double-entry bookkeeping permits a separation of ownership and management and thereby promotes the growth of the large joint stock company. By permitting a distinction between business and personal assets it makes possible the autonomous existence of the enterprise. Its standardized techniques make it a means of communication readily understood by many rather than by just the owner-manager and his bookkeeper.

(pp. 335–36)

From the capital account the term "capital stock" was born. But the capital account is not an account of either financial capital or physical capital. It does not record anything actually related to capital. "Capital stock" is a remnant of a time before there were corporations whose shares were traded in the market:[13]

Some respondents to the Exposure Draft [of the *Conceptual Framework*] said that the reporting entity is not separate from its equity investors or a subset of those equity investors. This view has its roots in the days when most businesses were sole proprietorships and partnerships that were managed by their owners who had unlimited liability for the debts incurred in the course of the business. Over time, the separation between businesses and their owners has grown. The vast majority of today's businesses have legal substance separate from their owners by virtue of their legal form of organization, numerous investors with limited legal liability, and professional managers separate from the owners. Consequently, the [Financial Accounting Standards] Board concluded that financial reports should reflect that separation by accounting for the entity (and its economic resources and claims) rather than its primary users and their interests in the reporting entity.

(FASB, 2010, BC1.8)

The capital account was injected into corporations almost by reflex; a label subsequently applied to corporations with no thought of what it meant or how, or even if, the capital account can apply to corporations. Eight hundred years later, there has been no improvement in the capital account. That is, there is still no correspondence between the "capital account" and either financial capital (money, cash) or physical capital as a means of production. Nor is there any relationship between "capital stock" or financial capital or physical capital. The "capital account" shows equity, not capital. (The balance sheet and the capital account are discussed in greater depth in chapter 8.)

Accounting considerations: owners of shares and investors in shares[14]

Owners of shares, investors in shares, and corporate financial statements

The FASB's *Statement of Financial Accounting Concepts (Concepts Statement)* is part of the Financial Accounting Standards Board's *Conceptual Framework*. The FASB issued its first *Conceptual Framework* in 1978 and has gone through several revisions since then. For convenience, all versions are referred to simply as the *Conceptual Framework*, with appropriate dates.

From the corporate perspective, "Concepts Statements are intended to set forth objectives and fundamental concepts that will be the basis for development of financial accounting and reporting guidance. The objectives identify the goals and purposes of financial reporting" (FASB, 2010, 5).

However, while the objectives of the *Conceptual Framework* are to identify the goals and purposes of financial reporting and therefore the *Conceptual Framework* applies to corporations, the *Conceptual Framework* actually has much to say about whom it refers to as "users" of corporate financial reports and their decisions. According to the *Conceptual Framework*, the objectives of general purpose financial reporting "focus on a particular kind of economic decision—committing (or continuing to commit) cash or other resources to a business enterprise" (FASB, 1980, 26).

General purpose financial reporting, as determined by the FASB, is intended for investors[15] to make resource allocation decisions (FASB, 2018, D32d). Thus, according to the *Conceptual Framework*, investors make economic decisions, specifically decisions about committing (or continuing to commit) cash or other resources to an enterprise, based on general purpose financial reporting. But this is, for the most part, false.

In the latest iteration, the FASB announced that the *Conceptual Framework* was

> intended to provid[e] structure and direction to financial accounting and reporting to facilitate the provision of unbiased financial and related information. *That information helps capital and other markets to function efficiently in allocating scarce resources in the economy and society.*
>
> (FASB, 2018, emphasis added)

The *Conceptual Framework's* proposition that investors decide to commit or continue to commit cash or other resources to an enterprise based on general purpose financial reporting is misleading. If an enterprise does not and cannot receive cash (or other resources) from purchases of securities based on general purpose financial reports issued annually,[16] then purchasers of securities do not and cannot commit cash (or other resources) to an enterprise based on general purpose financial reporting. It is only during an IPO that purchasers of securities commit cash to an enterprise. Furthermore, purchases of securities cannot commit "other resources" to an enterprise. Purchasers of securities can only commit cash to an enterprise during an IPO.

The *Conceptual Framework*'s declaration that "the objective of general purpose financial reporting is to provide financial information about the reporting entity that is useful … in making decisions about *providing resources to the entity*" (FASB, 2018, emphasis added) is incorrect. The only thing that investors in shares can "commit" to an enterprise is cash. Cash is not a scarce resource and not a resource of production.

The *Conceptual Framework* assumes that markets allocate resources. "Well-developed *securities markets tend to allocate scarce resources to enterprises* that use them efficiently and away from inefficient enterprises" (FASB, 1978, 13, emphasis added). However, securities markets are not resource markets and are not used to allocate scarce resources. Enterprises do not receive or acquire resources from purchasers of securities.

The *Conceptual Framework* correctly states that "Numerous, perhaps most, transactions in those markets are transfers from one investor or creditor to another with no part of the exchange price going to the issuing enterprise" (FASB, 1978, 13). That is, the exchange price in the market is the cash exchanged among buyers and sellers in the market for the security, with no cash going to the enterprise.

General purpose financial reports are issued annually. If purchasers of securities used general purpose financial reporting to decide to commit cash to an enterprise, it necessarily follows that purchasers of securities decide to commit cash to an enterprise annually. But that is not possible. They only decide to commit cash to an enterprise in an initial public offering.

We must first ask, who makes reasoned choices among alternative uses of scarce resources? To answer that question we must first acknowledge what scarce resources are. Scarce resources are land, labor, and capital, keeping in mind that cash is not a scarce resource. Who then decides how to use land, labor, and capital? Purchasers of securities do not and cannot allocate scarce resources to an enterprise or decide where to allocate the resources. They can only allocate cash to the firm. It is the enterprise, or more specifically, the managers and directors of the firm, that decides how to (re)allocate the land, labor, and capital (FASB, 1978, 12).

Owners of shares and investors in shares: the "capital account" revisited

Assuming for the sake of argument that the equity account is the capital account, as it has been since the thirteenth century, it is the capital account of the individual or partnership owners of the firm. The capital account, as it was conceived in the thirteenth century, reports the financial capital invested in the firm by the owner(s). Shareholders do not own the corporation. Thus, the capital account does not represent, and cannot report, the capital of shareholders. Nor does it represent, or report, the capital of the corporation, which is the left side of the balance sheet, i.e., the financial capital and productive capital. What is referred to as the corporation's capital (the capital account) is nothing more than the corporation's equity.

Chapter summary

This chapter examined accounting and its relationship to corporations, owners of shares, and investors in shares. It examined the relevant federal securities laws and relevant generally accepted accounting principles as determined by the Securities and Exchange Commission and the Financial Accounting Standards Board.

We saw that, apart from whether or not the numbers on the financial statements are misleading. The balance sheet, e.g., is misleading because it portrays corporate equity as shareholders' equity. We saw that the right side of the balance sheet—liabilities and equity—is considered the corporation's capital, rather than the left side that actually reports the corporation's financial capital and productive capital resources.

We saw the that the "capital account" was invented for use by individuals and partnership to record their initial investment of financial capital in their firms which allowed owners of the firm to separate their business assets from their personal assets. We further saw the subsequent misuse and misinterpretation of the capital account by transposing it into corporations.

Notes

1 15 U.S.C. § 78m(a).
2 15 U.S.C. § 77g.
3 It is worth noting that auditors' opinions are addressed "To the board of directors and *shareholders* of the corporation," not to the "owners."
4 15 U.S.C. § 77s(a)).
5 Sarbanes-Oxley Act of 2002.
6 Other countries use different generally accept accounting principles, but they are substantially similar.
7 Financial Accounting Standards Board. Codification. https://asc.fasb.org/.
8 There are also other types of assets such as intangible assets which is beyond the scope of this book.
9 Delaware General Corporation Law § 122(4).
10 Delaware General Corporation Law § 282.
11 See, e.g., www.sec.gov/Archives/edgar/data/1652044/000119312515336577/d82837d ex991.htm.
12 Luca Pacioli is credited with the introduction of double-entry bookkeeping in 1494 although he did not invent it. He merely wrote about common practices of the time.

13 While there are different classes of common stock and accounts for each class, for convenience the accounts for all classes of common stock will be referred to simply as the "capital account."
14 Adapted and summarized from Huber (2020) with permission.
15 The *FASB Conceptual Framework* adopts the term "users," which encompasses more than investors in shares. It includes creditors, employees, and suppliers. However, the term "investors" will frequently be used since it focuses only on those who invest in shares. Investors only invest in shares, not the corporation.
16 It should be noted here that audit reports are addressed to the shareholders, not the owners.

Bibliography

Biondi, Y., Canziani, A., & Kirat, T. (2007). Coming back to the enterprise entity. In Y. Biondi, A. Canziani, & T. Kirat (Eds.), *The firm as an entity* (pp. 3–8). London: Routledge.

Coase, R.H. (1990). Accounting and the theory of the firm. *Journal of Accounting and Economics*, 12, 3–13. doi:10.1016/0165-4101(90)90038-6.

Financial Accounting Standards Board (FASB) (1978). *Statement of Financial Accounting Concepts No. 1, Objectives of Financial Reporting by Business Enterprises.* Norwalk, CT: FASB.

Financial Accounting Standards Board (FASB) (1980). *Statement of Financial Accounting Concepts No. 2, Qualitative Characteristics of Accounting Information.* Norwalk, CT: FASB.

Financial Accounting Standards Board (FASB) (2010). *Statement of Financial Accounting Concepts No. 8, Conceptual Framework for Financial Reporting.* Norwalk, CT: FASB.

Financial Accounting Standards Board (FASB) (2018). *Statement of Financial Accounting Concepts No. 8, Conceptual Framework for Financial Reporting.* Norwalk, CT: FASB.

Huber, W.D. (2016). The SEC's ultra vires recognition of the FASB as a standard-setting body. *Richmond Journal of Law & the Public Interest*, 19 (2), 120–152. Retrieved from https://papers.ssrn.com/sol3/papers.cfm?abstract_id=2662634.

Huber, W.D. (2020). The FASB Conceptual Framework: A case of the emperor's new clothes. *Journal of Accounting, Ethics & Public Policy*, 21 (1), 77–114. Retrieved from https://papers.ssrn.com/sol3/papers.cfm?abstract_id=3400769.

Levy, J. (2014). Accounting for profit and the history of capital. *Critical Historical Studies*, 1 (2), 171–214. Retrieved from www.jstor.org/stable/10.1086/677977.

Winjum, J.O. (1971). Accounting and the rise of capitalism: An accountant's view. *Journal of Accounting Research*, 9 (2), 333–350. Retrieved from www.jstor.org/stable/2489937.

Part II

The nature and theory of the firm

The nature of the firm and theory of the firm are naturally highly related but not identical. The theory of the firm—or more precisely the economic theories of the firm, since there are more than one—are augmentations of the nature of the firm. The nature and theories of the firm all share the assumptions that shareholders are owners of the firm and directors are their agents. From these assumptions emerge agency cost, transaction cost, property rights, nexus of contracts, and incomplete contracts theories.

In this section I first review the nature of the firm as attributed to Ronald Coase, who in 1937 explained that the reason corporations are formed is in order to reduce agency and transaction costs. I then review the theory of the firm, beginning with Jensen and Meckling, who in 1976 suggested the relationship of shareholders and directors of corporations is one of pure agency. This in turn is followed by Hart and Moore, who in 1990 identified a corporation by the assets it possesses. The nexus of contracts theory is also traced to Jensen and Meckling but was enlarged upon by Fama and others beginning in 1980. The incomplete contracts theory stems from Grossman and Hart in 1986 and Hart and Moore in 1990 and explains corporations as consisting of a series of incomplete contracts.

There is of course a great deal of overlap between the theories, and the dates are not hard and fast. Nevertheless, the various theories are clearly identifiable as are the assumptions, all of which are contradicted by contract law, property law, agency law, and corporate law.

6   The nature of the firm

Introduction

> A physicist, an engineer, and an economist are stranded in the desert. They are hungry. Suddenly, they find a can of corn. They want to open it, but how?
>
> The physicist says, "Let's start a fire and place the can inside the flames. It will explode, and then we will all be able to eat."
>
> "Are you crazy?" says the engineer. "All the corn will burn and scatter, and we'll have nothing. We should use a metal wire, attach it to a base, push it, and crack the can open."
>
> "Both of you are wrong!" states the economist. "Where the hell do we find a metal wire in the desert? The solution is simple: Let us assume we have a can opener."
>
> (Source unknown)[1]

Ronald Coase, recipient of the 1991 Nobel prize in economics, is lauded as introducing the nature of the firm (corporations) as an explanation for why firms exist. Since, according to Coase, there is a trend in economic theory towards beginning an analysis of individual firms he believes it is necessary that a clear definition of the word "firm" be given. In deriving a definition of a firm, Coase first considers the economic system as it is considered by economists. At the same time, Coase readily admits that "economic theory has suffered in the past from a failure to state clearly its assumptions. Economists in building up a theory have often omitted to examine the foundations on which it was erected." This chapter examines the foundations on which the nature of the firm was erected.

Since in economic theory the allocation of resources of production among different uses is determined and coordinated by the price mechanism, Coase asks, "Why is such organisation necessary?" If production is in fact regulated by the price mechanism, production should be able to be accomplished without an organization. Coase finds the price mechanism does not apply in many areas of the real world. For example, if a workman moves from one department to another it is because he is told to do so, not because of a change in relative prices. Coase then uses the concept of transaction costs to explain the nature and limits of firms, concluding that the reason firms exist is in order to reduce transaction costs.

Coase uses the term "entrepreneur" to refer to the "person or persons who, in a competitive system, take the place of the price mechanism in the direction of resources." As will be seen in chapters 8 and 9, Coase's use of the term "entrepreneur," as well as his concept of the nature of the firm and his assumptions, are in conflict with corporate law, property law, agency law, capital, and capitalism.

This chapter is not an exhaustive, or even comprehensive, review of the subject. The works discussed in this chapter are merely representative of various views of the nature of the firm.

Multiple natures of the firm

Many researchers who write about the nature of the firm or the theory of the firm do not define what they mean by the firm. Some researchers do define a firm, but as with so many other things, how a firm is defined depends on whom you ask. Many researchers define a firm contrary to law. They define what is the nature of the firm or the theory of the firm economically without actually understanding what a firm is legally, something encountered much too frequently in the literature.

I begin with what is considered to be the origination of "the nature of the firm." In 1937 Ronald Coase published *The Nature of the Firm*, which he followed up in a series of lectures in 1988. Coase (1937) asks, what is a firm and why does a firm exist? He begins by defining a firm as "consist[ing] of the system of relationships which comes into existence when the direction of resources is dependent on an entrepreneur" (p. 393)—which includes individual proprietorships and partnerships but necessarily excludes corporations, which he fails to acknowledge.

Coase does acknowledge that

> it is not possible to draw a hard and fast line which determines whether there is a firm or not. There may be more or less direction. It is similar to the legal question of whether there is the relationship of master and servant or principal and agent.
>
> (p. 392)

But that is, of course, the point. The existence of a firm *is* a legal question, as I explained in chapter 1 and *Corporate Law and the Theory of the Firm: Reconstructing Corporations, Shareholders, Directors, Owners, and Investors*, but the legal question is never asked, let alone answered, with respect to corporations. Strangely, however, Coase begins his analysis by "considering the legal relationship normally called that of 'master and servant' or 'employer and employee'" and even ventures into contracts.

Coase understands the essentials of the legal concept of the employer and employee is not identical to the economic concept of a firm because the firm may "imply control over another person's property as well as over their labour" (p. 404). This is, as I'm sure the reader is well aware, incorrect. Coase in fact correctly contends that the firm (enterprise, corporation) has no control over another person's property whether it be the property of the shareholder or the employees. Nevertheless, Coase perceives the identity of employer-employee and the economic concept of the firm to be "*sufficiently close for an examination of the legal concept*" to be of value in appraising the worth of the economic concept" (p. 403, emphasis added). But it is *not* "sufficiently close," which undermines his entire thesis.

Coase correctly argues that the essentials of the employer-employee relationship require that the servant owe a duty of "rendering personal services to the master or to others on behalf of the master, otherwise the contract is a contract for sale of goods or the like" and that he master has the right to control the servant's work, either personally or through an agent (pp. 403–404). However, Coase's thesis of the nature of the firm suffers from a failure to differentiate the legal parameters of the firm, which are the legal relationships between shareholders and the corporation and between shareholders and directors. Coase, as many others, erroneously equates a corporation to an entrepreneur, which I will further explain in chapter 9.

Coase suggests that the distinguishing mark of the firm is the suppression of the price mechanism. In other words, the price mechanism only works interfirm and not intrafirm. The difference between the allocation of resources within a firm and their allocation between firms is seen in Adam Smith's description of the capitalist:

'It began to be seen that there was something more important than the relations inside each factory or unit captained by an undertaker [one who undertakes a project, not one who runs a funeral home]; there were the relations of the undertaker with the rest of the economic world outside his immediate sphere ... the undertaker busies himself with the division of labour inside each firm and he plans and organises consciously,' but 'he is related to the much larger economic specialisation, of which he himself is merely one specialised unit. Here, he plays his part as a single cell in a larger organism, mainly unconscious of the wider role he fills.'

(p. 389)

We will return to this distinction when we examine capitalism and Marx in chapters 9 and 10. For now we will examine Coase's purpose to

bridge what appears to be a gap in economic theory between the assumption (made for some purposes) that resources are allocated by means of the price mechanism and the assumption (made for other purposes) that this allocation is dependent on the entrepreneur-co-ordinator.

(p. 389)

Coase concludes that "The main reason why it is profitable to establish a firm would seem to be that there is a cost of using the price mechanism" (p. 390), costs which include negotiating contracts but which are greatly reduced within the firm. He explains:

> A factor of production (or the owner thereof) does not have to make a series of contracts with the factors with whom he is co-operating within the firm, as would be necessary, of course, if this co-operation were as a direct result of the working of the price mechanism [outside the firm] ... . The contract is one whereby the factor [owned or controlled by the firm], for a certain remuneration (which may be fixed or fluctuating), agrees to obey the directions of an *entrepreneur* within certain limits.
>
> (p. 391, emphasis added)

He continues to explain his concept of master-servant and its relation to firms: "The master must have the right to control the servant's work, either personally or by another servant or agent. It is this right of control or interference ... which is the dominant characteristic in this relation ..." (p. 404).[2] This is true of course in a master-servant relationship, except that the firm is not an entrepreneur, as I explain in chapter 9. Coase, like all before and after, uses "firm" (i.e., corporation) interchangeably with entrepreneur, which has no logical, legal, or economic validity and contributes to the vast confusion that exists within the theory of the firm (see chapter 7) and the notion of capitalism (see chapter 9).

Presaging the theory of incomplete contracts, part of the theory of the firm discussed in greater detail in chapter 7, Coase posits that a party to a contract may not know which of several courses he will want to take. Therefore, the service being provided in the contract is expressed in general terms, with the exact details left to fill in at a later date. However, if the essential requirements of a contract are absent, there is no contract, therefore it is not incomplete, it is unenforceable and cannot be completed by a court.

Coase sums up his argument by saying,

> the operation of a market costs something and by forming an organisation and allowing some authority (*an 'entrepreneur'*) to direct the resources, certain marketing costs are saved. The *entrepreneur* has to carry out his function at less cost, taking into account the fact that he may get factors of production at a lower price than the market transactions which he supersedes, because it is always possible to revert to the open market if he fails to do this.
>
> (p. 392, emphases added)

Coase unwaveringly maintained his argument through at least 1990:

Resources are not employed in those uses where they make the most valuable contribution ... because of the existence of what has come to be called transaction costs ... firms emerge because they are able to achieve some of those more productive arrangements of factors of production.

(Coase, 1990, p. 10)

and later emphatically states that "transaction cost considerations undoubtedly explain why firms come into existence" (p. 11).

But this makes no sense. Corporations do not "emerge" or "come into existence." They do not self-create. They do not appear out of nowhere. Although corporations are created *ex nihilo*,[3] they are created by people and the reason people create firms is not to reduce costs. People create corporations first to allow a large number of individuals to amass their financial capital by transferring it to a corporation by purchasing shares in the corporation in order to acquire a large amount of physical capital in order to produce and sell a greater amount of commodities thereby making a greater profit. (In the case of non-manufacturing firms such as financial institutions, the principle is the same.) Reducing costs, including transaction costs, is a result, not the purpose, of creating firms.

Second, people create corporations to avail themselves of limited risk.[4] People simply do not get together and say, "Let's create a corporation to reduce costs." That is simply not their motive. Corporations need large amounts of capital (Milhaupt, 1998). Therefore people say, "Let's create a corporation in order to pool our financial capital and to limit our risk of loss in order to increase production and sales (and profit)."

Corporations are often created by capitalist-entrepreneurs who are individuals or partnerships who own all the assets (the financial capital and the means of production) of the corporation, which is merely an extension or alter ego of the individuals who own the shares of the corporation. However, once the corporation sells shares to the public, the capitalist-entrepreneur ceases to exist since she no longer owns the means of production.

Like Coase over a half century earlier, Hart and Moore (1990) ask, what is a firm, and how do transactions within a firm differ from those between firms? They propose a mathematical/ statistical model to answer those questions.

Hart and Moore "identify a firm with the assets it possesses and take the position that ownership confers residual rights of control over the firm's assets" (p. 1120). They emphasize that the approach they take makes a distinction between ownership in the sense of possession and ownership in the sense of entitlement to an asset's profit stream. They argue there is crucial difference between a party owning a firm, which they refer to as integration, and contracting with another party who owns a different firm, or non-integration. However, they continually vacillate between discussion of an owner of a firm, which necessarily means an individual, and a corporation, which is not owned by the owners of the shares. While stating they make a distinction between ownership in the sense of possession and ownership in the sense of entitlement to an asset's profit stream, they fail to actually do so given the way they use the terms "owner" and "ownership."[5]

Their identification of a firm based on the assets its owners control presents a problem right from the start. The only way a firm could have *owners* is if the firm were a partnership, not an individual. A corporation, (the firm) has no owners to control its assets. It is the corporation that controls its assets.

The problem becomes more severe since they

> take the position that ownership confers residual rights of control over the firm's assets: the right to decide how these assets are to be used except to the extent that particular usages have been specified in an initial contract.
>
> (p. 1120)

Calling on property law, they correctly

> suppose that the sole right possessed by the owner of an asset is his ability to exclude others from the use of that asset. That is, the owner of a machine can decide who can and who cannot work on that machine ... .
>
> (p. 1121)

This, in turn, leads them to conclude that the owner of the machine allows the owner to indirectly control labor. If the firm is a collection of physical assets (i.e., capital resources of production; see chapters 2 and 8) they conclude that "a *person* will have more 'control' over an asset's workers if he employs them ... than if he has an arm's-length contract with another employer of the workers" (p. 1121, emphasis added).

This is a misleading and inaccurate use of terms. While it is obvious that the owner of a machine controls the worker who uses the machine, the owner of the machine is not a person when the subject of their analysis is the firm (corporation) that consists of a collection of capital resources of production. The owner of the machine is the firm (corporation), while the person who has control over the worker is the supervisor, manager, foreperson, etc., who has no ownership rights in the machine.

Additional careless and incorrect use of terms is reflected in their use of "agent," which they use with no regard for what "agent" means or the relationship of agents to corporations, as seen in the following statement:

> the existence of asset specificity means that an agent's marketability or bargaining position will depend on which assets he has access to ... an agent's actions will depend not only on whether he owns a particular asset ... an *agent* is more likely to own an asset if his action is sensitive to whether he has access to the asset ... a key right provided by ownership [of assets] is the ability to exclude people from the use of assets authority

over assets translates into authority over people: an *employee* will tend to act in the interest of his boss.

(pp. 1150–1151, emphasis added)

Hart and Moore are here referring to the employees of a corporation; otherwise the entire discussion concerning firms makes no sense. But even so, agents are not employees and employees are not agents regardless of the type of firm.

Putterman (1993) looks at the ownership of firms from both a theoretical and a comparative standpoint. He discusses capitalization requirements, agency costs of separating ownership of the firm from work and public ownership. Thus, immediately we know that he is referring to corporations, which he considers to be "capitalist economic institutions." We also know immediately that he is making the almost universal error of assuming owners of shares of a corporation own the corporation.

According to Putterman, economists in recent years have been devoting more attention to capitalist economic institutions in terms of property rights, the nature of contracts, and organizational form. Without explaining what is capitalism, what is a capitalist, or what private ownership means with respect to shareholders, corporations, and corporate property, Putterman states:

> In a capitalist setting, the existence of an owner or owners who hold the right of control [over assets], the right to net revenue, and the right to alienate is an aspect of business organization that is usually taken for granted [and] private ownership can be presumed ... .

(p. 244)

The conflict between a corporation's "demands for the aggregation of funds" and financiers' demands for portfolio diversification is resolved in different ways depending on the amount and type of "required capital," the degree of difficulty in monitoring decision making, and the retention of control rights by the holders of residual claims. The holders of residual claims are considered, incorrectly, to be the shareholders, as I explained in chapter 1 and *Corporate Law and the Theory of the Firm: Reconstructing Corporations, Shareholders, Directors, Owners, and Investors*. The "demand for funds" is, of course, financial capital (the cash provided by purchasers of shares or bonds in an IPO), while "type of capital" refers to debt vs. stock. (See chapter 8 for a discussion of types of capital.)

But Putterman commits a serious error. "The resulting separation of ownership and work," he states, "is the basic cause of the familiar agency problem between employer and employee" (p. 24). The familiar agency problem is as wrong as it is familiar. The separation of ownership and work does not cause an agency problem between employer and employee because employers are not principals and employees are not agents. The separation of ownership and work is an issue all too familiar to economists—capitalists and labor (discussed in chapter 9).

But his error does not stop there. It is true that "In most business firms, decision-making rights are held by persons who are also financial risk-bearers and suppliers of funds. The holders of these rights are known as the owners of the firm" (p. 245). But that refers to sole proprietorships and partnerships. which in terms of numbers are greater than corporations whose shares are traded in the market and therefore are "most business firms." However, it is not true of corporations whose shares are traded in the market.

Putterman compounds the confusion:

> Ownership refers to a bundle of rights that an economic agent is entitled to exercise over an asset ... . The firm as an ownable asset is an entity that acts as a legal agent in the market place, entering into contractual agreements with other agents in order to produce and sell goods.
>
> (p. 245)

First, ownership is not a bundle of rights that an economic agent is entitled to exercise over an asset. An agent has no ownership rights. Ownership rights belong to the principal. Second, unless the firm is a sole proprietorship or partnership, the firm (corporation) is not an ownable asset. Third, the corporation is not a "legal agent" that enters into contracts with other agents to produce and sell goods. The firm itself is the principal on whose behalf its agents, the directors and officers, enter into contracts.

"With respect to a firm," he states, "the right of utilization means the right to determine what contracts the firm enters into" and to complete incomplete contracts "with some agents, e.g., employees" (p. 245), again incorrectly equating agents and employees.

Putterman takes the existence of the ownership of firms by shareholders as given and the rights of ownership of firms are characteristics of a social order under capitalism. Firms in modern market economies are entities empowered to act as legal agents in the market and contract with other such entities and economic agents. The rights to direct firms' activities, according to Putterman, constitute ownership of the firm.

Firms are not entities empowered to act as legal agents in the market because they are not agents. If firms are agents, their principals must be identifiable, which they are not. The right to direct firms' activities does not constitute ownership of the firm. The right to direct firms' activities is under the board of directors, not the shareholders.

The joining of control rights with revenue and alienation rights will, under ideal assumptions, cause firms to direct the resources they control into their most socially valued uses, without reference to the time preferences or horizons of the immediate decision makers.

Chapter summary

This chapter reviewed the nature of the firm. The "nature of the firm" is nothing more than the can opener in the desert; that is, assumptions contrary to facts, which in this case means contrary to law, compounded by an incorrect use of terms. Those assumption and incorrect use of terms include assuming owners of shares are owners of the corporation and the confusing and incorrect use of employer-employee (master-servant), owner-employer, owner-manager, firm-entrepreneur, and employee-agent.

The nature of the firm has been defined by the assets it possesses, which is then ignored by attributing the ownership of assets to the shareholders, and the relationships which come into existence when the direction of resources is dependent on an entrepreneur, which is erroneously considered to be the firm.

The nature of the firm ignores the psychological motivation of incorporators. The nature of the firm proclaims that incorporators create corporations in order to reduce costs. However, that is not the reason why corporations are created. People are motivated to create corporations in order to pool their financial capital in order to increase production and to reduce risk. Reducing costs is a result, not the purpose, of creating a firm (corporation).

The nature of the firm serves as an introduction to a more in-depth examination of the theory of the firm in the next chapter.

Notes

1 There are several variations to the joke, but the intent of all versions is clear—assumptions contrary to facts.
2 Master and servant is an archaic term for employer-employee relationships.
3 *Ex nihilo* is Latin for "out of nothing," usually used in a theological sense. Unlike sole proprietorships and partnerships, corporations have no antecedent existence.
4 As I explained in *Corporate Law and the Theory of the Firm: Reconstructing Corporations, Shareholders, Directors, Owners, and Investors* and in chapter 1, "limited risk" is mistakenly referred to as "limited liability." However, according to corporate law shareholders have no liability whatsoever. They have limited risk of loss, the maximum amount of which is the amount they paid for their shares. Furthermore, in the event of liquidation, the corporation loses its equity, but the equity is the corporation's, it is not the shareholders' equity. The maximum amount shareholders lose in liquidation is the amount they paid for their shares when the market price drops to zero.
5 If they are referring to an individual who owns a firm and not to a corporation their entire argument is pointless.

Bibliography

Coase, R.H. (1937). The nature of the firm. *Economica*, 4 (16), 386–405. doi:10.1111/j.1468-0335.1937.tb00002.x.

Coase, R.H. (1990). Accounting and the theory of the firm. *Journal of Accounting and Economics*, 12 (1–3), 3–13. doi:10.1016/0165-4101(90)90038-6.

Hart, J.A. & Moore, J. (1990). Property rights and the nature of the firm. *Journal of Political Economy*, 98 (6), 1119–1158. doi:10.1086/261729.

Huber, W.D. (2020). *Corporate law and the theory of the firm: Reconstructing corporations, shareholders, directors, owners, and investors.* London: Routledge.

Milhaupt, C.J. (1998). Property rights in firms. *Virginia Law Review*, 84 (6), 1145–1194. doi:10.2307/1073696.

Putterman, L. (1993). Ownership and the nature of the firm. *Journal of Comparative Economics*, 17, 243–263. Retrieved from https://EconPapers.repec.org/RePEc:eee:jcecon:v:17:y:1993:i:2:p:243-263.

7   The theory of the firm

Introduction

The nature of the firm introduced by Coase in 1937 (see chapter 6) morphed into what later became known as the theory of the firm, originally based entirely in economics. There are now many theories of the firm other than economic—behavioral, organizational, and management (Walker, 2016), to name a few—plus variations within each theory, and at least 21 different concepts of the firm (Orts, 2013). However, the theories of the firm that are the subject of this chapter are economic-based theories, considered together here simply as "the theory of the firm." "Firm" as used in this chapter, indeed the entire book, is synonymous with "corporation" or "enterprise" unless otherwise stated.

Economic-based theories of the firm each has its own label—agency theory, property rights, nexus of contracts, and incomplete contracts—but they all share two common errors; errors of such magnitude that they void all economic-based theories of the firm. They are all based on the error that (1) shareholders own corporations; and (2) directors (and managers) are agents of shareholders. It is legally impossible for shareholders to own the corporation and for directors to be agents of shareholders. This chapter examines each economic-based theory of the firm and demonstrates how the erroneous assumptions that shareholders own the corporation and that directors (and managers) are agents of shareholders invalidate the economic-based theories of the firm.

This chapter is not an exhaustive, or even comprehensive, review of the subject. The works discussed in this chapter are merely representative of various views of the theory of the firm in order to demonstrate the confusion and contradictions embedded in the theories. To those who will charge that I omitted certain works or authors, I again plead guilty as charged.

The theory of the firm

The heart of the theory of the firm according to Coase (1990) is that

> Resources are not employed in those uses where they make the most valuable contribution ... because of the existence of what has come to

be called transaction costs ... firms emerge because they are able to achieve some of those more productive arrangements of factors of production.

(p. 10)

Coase continues to advance his thesis emphatically stating, "transaction cost considerations undoubtedly explain why firms come into existence" (p. 11).

In reviewing the theory of the firm over ten years prior to 1942, Boulding (1942) notes that the while the theory of the firm is almost universally attributed to Coase and to Jensen and Meckling, there was an explicit recognition of the theory of the firm as an integral division of economic analysis at least as early as 1932. However, the early reference to the theory of the firm bears little resemblance to the modern theory of the firm.

Demsetz (1983) explicitly links the theory of the firm to the separation of ownership and control. He considers that the separation of ownership and control in corporations as proclaimed by Berle and Means in 1932 continues to maintain a key position in the economic theory of the firm. He interprets the separation of ownership and control as shareholders experience a "loss of control" over their resources because ownership of the corporation is so broadly dispersed that they cannot exercise real power to oversee management of the corporation. "The issue of the alleged separation between ownership and control is based on an *empirical presumption* that ownership of the modern corporation is so diluted among the multitude of shareholders that their interests are essentially unrepresented" (p. 387, emphasis added).[1] However, shareholders do not lose control. They sell control to the corporation in exchange for shares of stock.

The difficulty with Demsetz and others' interpretation of the separation of ownership and control, however, is that shareholders' "loss of control" has nothing to do with the "ownership of the corporation [being] so broadly dispersed." Ignoring the fact that shareholders do not own the corporation, in corporate statutory law shareholders are prohibited from exercising *any* power to oversee managerial performance of the corporation, regardless of how many shareholders there are or how widely dispersed they may be.[2] To blame "the separation of ownership and control" on the dispersion of shareholders is a red herring.[3]

Oddly, Demsetz states,

> For all these commentators on the modern corporation, the cutting edge is the separation between ownership and control. A closer look at the problem of ownership structure is warranted, if for no other reason than that these commentators fail to examine either the theoretical problem or the empirical premise carefully.
>
> (p. 376)

Yet, Demsetz himself fails to examine the theoretical problem.

Hart (1989) attempts to provide lawyers with highlights of several ideas of how economists think about firms, which include neoclassical theory, principal-agent theory, transaction cost economics, nexus of contracts, and property rights.

Neoclassical economics theory views the firm as a set of feasible production plans but does not explain how conflicts of interest between the corporation's owners, managers, and workers are resolved. Principal-agent theory also views the corporation as a production set but with a professional manager making investment or allocation decisions that the firm's owners do not observe. Transaction cost economics was introduced in 1937 by Coase, who argued that the main cost of transactions is the cost of negotiating the terms of trade, but which can be reduced by delegating authority to one person to negotiate the terms of trade within limits. The delegation of authority is what defines a firm but introduces other costs. The firm as a nexus of contracts emphasizes that the firm's contractual relations with employees, suppliers, customers, creditors, and others are an essential aspect of the firm.

Hart describes the property rights approach to the theory of the firm as differing from the transaction cost theory by focusing on the physical assets in a contractual relationship. The property rights approach "relies on the idea that ... the firm's *owner* has the right to decide who uses the firm's assets" (p. 1771, emphasis added). But, Hart then says, "one of the weaknesses of the property rights approach ... is that it does not take account of the separation of ownership and control present in *large, publicly held corporations*" (p. 1773, emphasis added). Note the use of the singular "owner." Hart explains that "Although *owners* (shareholders) typically retain some control rights ... in practice *they* delegate many others to *management*, at least on a day-to-day basis" (p. 1773, emphases added). But changing the analysis from the single owner of a corporation to a corporation whose shares are publicly traded on an exchange alters the legal parameters of the corporation and the owner, thereby changing the relationships and the economic dynamics which Hart neglects to take into account. "The world of law shapes the reality of economic and financial dynamics in an essential way [that is] contrary to the ajuridical approaches of most theories of the firm" (Biondi, Canziani, & Kirat, 2007, p. 7).

Hart switches between a singular owner who has the right to decide the use of her firm's assets and plural owners (shareholders) without exhibiting any awareness that corporations have no owners and that shareholders do not delegate control to management. Control of a corporation is limited by corporate statutory law solely to the board of directors. Shareholders' voting for directors does not delegate control to the directors. Control by the board of directors is mandated by corporate statutory law. If a corporation has a million shares outstanding and one shareholder who owned only one share who was the only shareholder to vote for directors, directors would, again by corporate statutory law, still control the corporation although elected by only one shareholder.

Three things should be kept in mind while reading this chapter. First, due to space limitations, the review of economic-based theories of the firm is not exhaustive, or even comprehensive. It is representative. Second, the economic-based theories of the firm reviewed here are related to each other and are all based to some degree on the errors that owners of shares own the corporation and directors are their agents.

Third, the authors of the works that are reviewed here are frequently not precise in their use of terms. They often use some terms incorrectly, thereby causing a great deal of confusion and misunderstanding. For example, they often use "managers" when they mean "directors." This is particularly important when considering that directors are not managers, and both are sometimes referred to, incorrectly, as agents of shareholders. "Agent" has a precise legal meaning. (See chapter 1, and *Corporate Law and the Theory of the Firm: Reconstructing Corporations, Shareholders, Directors, Owners, and Investors*). Furthermore, directors are elected by shareholders; managers are not. Managers are hired by directors. Managers are not accountable to shareholders and shareholders cannot remove them, while directors are accountable to shareholders since shareholders can remove them. This confusion of terms is one source of their erroneous assumptions and conclusions.

The theory of the firm is an umbrella theory under which are found certain branches or sub-theories. Accordingly, I first discuss agency theory, agency costs, and transaction costs theory of the firm. Next, the theory of the firm and property rights will be examined. Third, the theory of the firm and the nexus of contracts will be considered. This will be followed by an examination of the theory of incomplete contracts. I explain why each of these theories has no basis in law and therefore can have no basis in economics.

Agency theory, agency costs, and transaction costs

I begin with what is considered to be the origination of the theory of the firm. In 1976 Michael Jensen and William Meckling published *The Theory of the Firm: Managerial Behavior, Agency Costs, and Ownership Structure*. Although the term "theory of the firm" is much older, Jensen and Meckling's work subsequently initiated a wave of modern economic-based theories of the firm. It was not widely received at first, but slowly generated a groundswell of economics research that eventually infiltrated legal scholarship.

Jensen and Meckling attempted to "integrat[e] elements from the theory of agency, the theory of property rights and the theory of finance to develop a theory of the ownership structure of the firm." It was both a huge success, at least in terms of generating an entire field of research on the theory of the firm, and a dismal failure.

A Google Scholar search of the title "Theory of the Firm: Managerial Behavior, Agency Costs and Ownership Structure" returned 38,600 hits, while the Social Science Research Network reports 132,895 downloads and 7,421 citations as of March 2020, although it was not posted on SSRN until 1998,

22 years after publication, a success by any measure or definition. Of course, not all the citations would necessarily have been favorable, but the sheer number of citations is indicative of its widespread influence.

But, its outward show of success is overshadowed by its colossal inward failure, heretofore essentially ignored in both legal and economic scholarship: it fails to actually integrate elements from the theory of agency, the theory of property rights, and the theory of finance to develop a theory of the ownership structure of the firm. Granted that they do develop *a* theory of the ownership structure of the firm, the ownership structure of the firm they construct is, like all others, contrary to, and contradicted by, the very theories of contract law, agency law, and property law that they profess to rely on to construct their theory of the ownership structure of the firm. Furthermore, let the reader keep in mind that their entire theory is backwards. That is, economic relationships do not determine the legal structure of the firm. The legal structure of the firm determines economic relationships.

Although the errors are many, the most egregious error, and the error from which all other errors spring, is their construction and use of "agency." They first define, correctly, an agency relationship as "a contract under which one or more persons (the principal(s)) engage another person (the agent) to perform some service on their behalf which involves delegating some decision making authority to the agent" (p. 308). This is consistent with the legal definition of agency as discussed in chapter 1 and *Corporate Law and the Theory of the Firm: Reconstructing Corporations, Shareholders, Directors, Owners, and Investors*. Unfortunately, they subsequently do not correctly apply the legal definition of agency to the relationship between stockholders and directors (whom they incorrectly identify as managers)[4]:

> Since *the relationship between the stockholders and manager* [sic] *of a corporation fit* [sic] *the definition of a pure agency relationship* it should be no surprise to discover that the issues associated with the 'separation of ownership and control' in the modern diffuse ownership corporation are intimately associated with the general problem of agency. We show below that an explanation of why and how the agency costs generated by the corporate form are born leads to a theory of the ownership (or capital) structure of the firm.
>
> (p. 309, emphasis added)

The fundamental error is, of course, that neither directors nor managers are agents of shareholders. There is no agency relationship, pure or otherwise, between the stockholders and directors (or managers) of a corporation. Their imprecise, and at times contrary to corporate law, use of the term "manager" to refer to directors confuses the entire theory.

Jensen and Meckling go on to define agency costs (based on their misunderstanding of agency law) and show how agency costs are related to the "separation [of ownership] and control issue." They then investigate the nature of agency costs generated by debt and equity, and determine who bears the agency costs. Finally, they provide a definition of the firm:

> The private corporation or firm is simply one form of legal fiction which serves as a nexus for contracting relationships and which is also characterized by the existence of divisible residual claims on the assets and cash flows of the organization which can generally be sold without permission of the other contracting individuals.
>
> (p. 311)

By private corporation Jensen and Meckling are referring to non-government corporations whose shares are traded in the market (sometimes referred to as public corporations, or publicly traded corporations), not corporations whose shares are not publicly traded, as evidenced by the fact that what they refer to as "residual claims" can be sold without permission.

At least two other errors are revealed in their quoting, with implicit agreement, Adam Smith:

> The directors of such [joint-stock] companies however, being the managers rather of other people's money than of their own, it cannot well be expected, that they should watch over it with the same anxious vigilance with which the partners in a private copartnery frequently watch over their own. Like the stewards of a rich man, they are apt to consider attention to small matters as not for their master's honour, and very easily give themselves a dispensation from having it. Negligence and profusion, therefore, must always prevail, more or less, in the management of the affairs of such a company. (Adam Smith, The Wealth of Nations, 1776, Cannan Edition (Modern Library, New York, 1937) p. 700).
>
> (p. 305)

The first error repeats their previous error. That is, neither directors, nor managers, manage other people's money. Once the shares are purchased in an IPO, the money received by the corporation from the purchaser is no longer the money of the owners of the shares. When shares are purchased in the market the money never goes to the corporation.

The second error, which is actually Smith's error, but which was uncritically adopted by Jensen and Meckling, is that directors are not managers. That is, directors are not involved in the actual managing of the day-to-day activities of the corporation.[5] Directors hire managers—officers, CEOs, etc.—to manage the day-to-day activities of the corporation. Directors can fire managers. And, while shareholders elect directors, directors have no duty to shareholders, as explained in chapter 1 and *Corporate Law and the Theory of the Firm: Reconstructing Corporations, Shareholders, Directors, Owners, and Investors.* Shareholders cannot fire directors. Managers, on the other hand, have a duty to obey the directives of the directors or risk being fired.

Jensen and Meckling early on constructed the firm as a "nexus of contracts" discussed in this chapter, although they did not use that exact term:

It is important to recognize that most organizations are simply legal fictions which serve as a *nexus for a set of contracting relationships among individuals.* This includes firms, non-profit institutions such as universities, hospitals and foundations, mutual organizations such as mutual savings banks and insurance companies and co-operatives, some private clubs, and even governmental bodies such as cities, states and the Federal government, government enterprises such as TVA, the Post Office, transit systems, etc.

(p. 310, emphasis added)

The firm as a "nexus for contracting relationships" would later be adopted as a separate theory of the firm. By limiting the *"nexus for a set of contracting relationships among individuals"* they fail to include or consider that it is the corporation itself that enters into contracting relationships, not individuals.

It is also more than just interesting that they recognize that there is a contract between the corporation and "residual claims." Residual claims are generally considered to be held by shareholders (see chapter 1), but they unfortunately fail to develop, or even to recognize the importance of that contract. The contract between shareholders and the corporation is one in which shareholders sell their rights to control resources to the corporation.

They define a legal fiction as an "artificial construct under the law which allows certain organizations to be treated as individuals" (p. 310). This, of course, presents other problems. First, if most organizations are simply legal fictions which serve as a nexus for a set of contracting relationships among individuals, there is no longer anything unique about publicly traded corporations so why study them as opposed to, say, the Post Office or private clubs which have no shareholders or owners?

In addition, the contracts are not always contracting relationships among individuals. Jensen and Meckling in fact state outright that "The firm is not an individual" (p. 311). Corporations, which are not individuals, form contracts with other corporations, which are also not individuals even when considered as a fictitious person. The importance of this is made clear when the theory of incomplete contracts is reviewed.

Second, they omit partnerships, in particular large partnerships such as Big Law or the Big 4 accounting firms, which are as much nexuses of contracts as corporations.

Third, and more important, Jensen and Meckling omit the most important set of contractual relationships of all—the contract between the corporation and owners of shares formed during an IPO.

Contractual relations are, according to Jensen and Meckling, the essence of the firm, not only with employees but with suppliers, customers, creditors, etc. (which are often other firms, not individuals). But as noted by Jensen and

Meckling, firms include non-profit institutions such as universities, hospitals, and foundations, mutual organizations such as mutual savings banks and insurance companies and co-operatives, some private clubs, and even governmental bodies such as cities, states, and the Federal government, government enterprises such as TVA, the Post Office, transit systems, etc. They claim, with absolutely no analysis of agency law, all those contractual relations with all those firms present problem of agency. But none of the firms they include in their list of firms are purported to be owned by anyone as corporations are said to be owned by shareholders.

While Jensen and Meckling omit from their list of contractual relationships the contractual relationship that is formed in an IPO by the corporation and owners of shares, they do allude to such a relationship, albeit in a somewhat cryptic manner which is puzzling. The legal fiction of a publicly traded corporation, which serves as a nexus for contracting relationships, is characterized by the existence of divisible residual claims on the assets and cash flows of the organization. But claims, whether or not residual, are matters of contract law and property law. Elsewhere they say,

> We have assumed throughout our analysis that we are dealing only with a single investment-financing decision by the *entrepreneur* and have ignored the issues associated with the incentives affecting future financing-investment decisions which might arise after *the initial set of contracts are consumated* [sic] *between the entrepreneur-manager, outside stockholders* and bondholders.
>
> (p. 351, emphases added)

Jensen and Meckling's definition of a firm is not simple. The private corporation or firm is one form of legal fiction which serves as a nexus for contracting relationships and which is also characterized by the existence of divisible residual claims on the assets and cash flows of the organization that can generally be sold without permission of the other contracting individuals (p. 311). (Note that they are here equating a firm to a private corporation, i.e., one whose shares are publicly traded, although their list of firms includes non-publicly traded corporations and organizations.)

Residual claims, as used by Jensen and Meckling, can refer to no one other than owners of shares since (a) they are defining a firm as a private corporation and (b) no other party is said to have any claim on organizational assets or cash flows.[6] Owners of shares are traditionally considered as "residual claimants" (although owners of shares also have no legal claim on corporate assets, whether total or net, revenues, or cash flows as I explained in *Corporate Law and the Theory of the Firm: Reconstructing Corporations, Shareholders, Directors, Owners, and Investors*).

Jensen and Meckling recognize that their definition of the firm has little substantive content, but in another glaring omission they maintain that their definition presents a firm as "a multitude of complex relationships (i.e., contracts) between the legal fiction (the firm) and the *owners of labor, material and capital inputs and the consumers of output*" (p. 311, emphasis added). The omission is, of course, the contractual relationship formed between the corporation and owners of shares formed in an IPO.

In another unmistakable display of confusion, Jensen and Meckling posit the existence of an agency conflict between the owner-manager of a firm and outside shareholders deriving from the manager's tendency to appropriate the firm's resources for his own consumption. But who is the owner-manager and who are the outside shareholders? If shareholders own the firm such that directors are their agents, there is no owner-manager who appropriates resources to himself. Even if he does so as a manager, he is not the owner of those resources.

Since their "permanent assumption" is that outside shareholders are non-voting, they're equating outside shareholders with preferred shareholders. If outside shareholders are non-voting, there can be no separation of ownership and control any more than there is a separation of ownership and control of preferred shareholders.

But if outside equity has voting rights then the manager will be concerned about the effects on his long-run welfare of reducing his ownership below the point where "he loses control of the corporation" (here they use "corporation" rather than "firm") and the outside equity holders can fire him. But outside shareholders cannot fire either the directors or the managers. Indeed, they state, "A complete analysis of this issue will require a careful specification of the contractual rights involved on both sides, the role of the *board of directors*, and the coordination (agency) costs borne by the stockholders in implementing policy changes" (p. 352, emphasis added).

Jensen and Meckling mistakenly believe that it is the entrepreneur that issues shares to outside equity holders. But it is the corporation, not the entrepreneur, that issues the shares and forms the contract with outside equity holders, an important oversight by Jensen and Meckling when discussing nexus of contracts.

Jensen and Meckling of course pay homage to Coase and at the same time introduce property rights:

> An independent stream of research with important implications for the theory of the firm has been stimulated by the pioneering work of Coase ... . While the focus of this research has been '*property rights*', the subject matter encompassed is far broader than that term suggests. What is important for the problems addressed here is that specification of individual rights determines how costs and rewards will be allocated ... .
> (p. 306–307, emphasis added)

Jensen and Meckling are extremely careless in their use of the terms "manager" and "directors/board of directors;" so careless that it reduces the value of their theory to mere speculation.

Jensen and Meckling correctly believe that property rights are human rights:

> Property rights are of course human rights, i.e., rights which are possessed by human beings. The introduction of the wholly false distinction between property rights and human rights in many policy discussions is surely one of the all time great semantic flimflams.
>
> (p. 307)

While not relevant to the theory of the firm, it is also not completely accurate. Property rights are indeed human rights, but property rights are not limited to human beings.[7] By state statutes, corporations have property rights and corporate property rights are protected by the U.S. Constitution. The introduction of the "distinction between property rights and human rights is not one of the all time great semantic flimflams" since corporations do not have the rights accorded to humans.[8] Thus, property rights and human rights are not coterminous. Thus, Jensen and Meckling's limiting property rights to human beings unnecessarily constricts the scope of their analysis, thereby leading to faulty conclusions. At the same time, since state corporate statutes confer upon corporations the right to own property, then the property rights of corporations are equal to the rights of humans to own property and it is the corporation that owns the financial capital and capital resource of production, not the shareholders.

Masten (1993) sees a contradiction in the logic of Jensen and Meckling. Masten thinks "it makes little or no sense" that according to Jensen and Meckling,

> to try to distinguish those things which are 'inside' the firm ... from those things that are 'outside' of it. There is in a very real sense only a multitude of complex relationships (i.e., contracts) between the legal fiction (the firm) and the owners of labor, material and capital inputs and the consumers of output.
>
> (p. 311)

At the same time they say,

> This view of the firm [as a nexus of contracts] points up the important role which the legal system and the law play in social organizations, especially, the organization of economic activity. Statutory laws sets [sic] bounds on the kinds of contracts into which individuals and organizations may enter without risking criminal prosecution. The police powers of the state arc available and used to enforce performance of contracts or to enforce the collection of damages for non-performance. The courts adjudicate conflicts between contracting parties.
>
> (p. 311)

Masten sees this as a contradiction because while they urge it makes no sense to "distinguish things which are 'inside' the firm ... from those things that are 'outside' of it," at the same time they say their view of the firm points to the important role which the legal system and the law play in social organizations. The law does in fact "distinguish things which are 'inside' the firm ... from those things that are 'outside' of it."

Meurer (2004) makes a distinction between agency theory and the theory of the firm: "Economists merely use agency theory to study the firm and the problems presented when a principal delegates authority to an agent. The theory of the firm uses agency theory to study why firms exist." His distinction admits to two problems. To study the firm and the problems presented when a principal delegates authority to an agent is to impose upon the firm a problem that cannot legally exist since directors are not agents of shareholders.

However, it is more than just a contradiction. It is a total failure to acknowledge that property law prohibits shareholders from owning corporations and agency law prohibits directors from being agents of shareholders, as I explain in chapter 1 and *Corporate Law and the Theory of the Firm: Reconstructing Corporations, Shareholders, Directors, Owners, and Investors.*

Cooper (1951) proposes extending the theory of the firm, but in doing so he "muddies the waters." "As a terminological convenience all intermediaries who participate in the management process will be referred to as agents—as distinct from factors" (p. 90). But his "terminological convenience" uses terms contrary to their meaning, not unlike Humpty Dumpty. Not all intermediaries who participate in the management process are, or can be, agents. Many are employees.

He also makes unrealistic, misleading, and contradictory assumptions. He first says, "the entrepreneur is regarded as operating directly on (more or less) 'will-less' factors of production ... . The 'factors' are assumed to know immediately what is expected of them ..." (p. 90). If factors are will-less they would not know what is immediately, or ever, expected of them. Land and capital certainly do not know "what is expected of them" since they are inanimate Labor may not know unless it is told what to do by the entrepreneur.

Cooper goes on to say,

> the entrepreneur is assumed to know instantly what is being done ... the characteristic entrepreneur-factor relation assumed in economic theory may be viewed as a type of organization ... . The firm, or entrepreneur, is viewed as operating with respect to a more or less uncertain world.
>
> (p. 90)

Cooper is undeniably here equating entrepreneurs to individuals. But he then changes to mean entrepreneurs are firms. With no argument to support it, he is magically transforming firms into entrepreneurs.

There simply is no agency problem, or agency costs, because there are no agents. Agency theory has no basis in law, and therefor can have no basis in the economic theory of the firm.

Property rights

"Property rights are where the whole debate began" in 1932 with the publication of Berle and Means' *The Modern Corporation and Private Property* (Milhaupt, 1998, p. 1145). Because corporations need vast amounts of financial capital they issue shares to a large number of shareholders which allows the control of corporations to be concentrated in the hands of managers. "Corporate governance ... focuses on aligning the interests of shareholder 'owners' who provide the capital and corporate managers who run the firm" (Milhaupt, 1998, p. 1145).

Hart and Moore (1990), as so many others do, build on Coase (1937). But, although the title of their paper is *Property Rights and the Nature of the Firm*, they frame their analysis of property rights in the context of contracts and not according to the law of property.[9] Furthermore, they do not actually discuss "the nature of the firm." Rather, the major part of their analysis focuses on how employees' incentives change as integration occurs and asset ownership becomes more or less concentrated.

Hart and Moore identify a firm according to the assets it possesses and take the position that ownership of assets confers residual rights of control over the assets, which means the right to decide how the assets will be used. This is partly right and partly wrong. It is partly right because according to the law of property firms own the assets. Although they do not place the ownership of assets within the law of property, they are essentially just restating the law of property using economic concepts and mathematical models. It is partly wrong because the concept of residual rights applies only to shareholders (although shareholders have no residual rights—see chapter 1 and *Corporate Law and the Theory of the Firm: Reconstructing Corporations, Shareholders, Directors, Owners, and Investors*) who, by law, are not permitted to say how corporate assets will be used.

Their approach is to distinguish the difference between the ownership of assets in the sense of possession of residual control rights and ownership of assets in the sense of entitlement to the assets' profit stream. But neither one fulfills any legal, or even economic, concept of rights or ownership. The ownership of assets in the sense of possession of residual control rights can only be attributable (although erroneously) to shareholders who do not have any ownership rights of assets, while ownership of assets in the sense of entitlement to the assets' profit stream applies only to corporations who own the assets and therefore the profit generated by the profit stream. Shareholders are not entitled to the corporation's cash flow or profit stream.

According to the property rights approach, the possession of control rights over an asset is crucial for a firm's decisions on whether to acquire part of another firm's profit stream, which it can do by contract, or to acquire control over an asset by integration. Their explanation of integration (one party owns the firm), and non-integration (two firms contract with each other) is somewhat convoluted and much more complex than presented here. As Hart and Moore explain it, the issue is whether (1) a particular asset should be owned by firm 1 and another asset owned by firm 2, which they call non-integration; (2) both assets should be owned by firm 1, which they consider to be an integrated firm, and firm 1 controls the integrated firm; or (3) both assets should be owned by firm 2, which they consider to be an integrated firm, and firm 2 controls the integrated firm. In non-integrated firms (alternative 1), since each firm owns and controls its own assets the two firms contract with each other to buy or sell goods or services. They develop elaborate mathematical models in order to decide which alternative is optimal.

However, as with agency theory, agency costs, and transaction costs, a close examination of their analysis reveals several flaws. First, they identify a corporation "with the assets it possesses." However, as seen in chapter 1, a corporation exists prior to its owning any assets. Therefore, a corporation cannot be identified with the assets it possesses. It must be identified by its legal existence, which is defined by corporate statutory law

Second, they fail to clearly and explicitly distinguish the difference between corporations as the owners of the resources of production (i.e., its land and physical capital) and the owners of the shares of the corporation. For example, they argue

> that the crucial difference for party 1 between owning a firm (integration) and contracting for a service from another party 2 who owns this firm (nonintegration) is that, under integration, party 1 can selectively fire the workers of the firm (including party 2) if he dislikes their performance, whereas under nonintegration he can 'fire' (i.e., stop dealing with) only the entire firm... .
>
> (p. 1119)

If they are dealing with one-person corporations this makes perfect sense. But they are not. They are dealing with corporations whose shares are publicly traded and which have no owner. Thus, they confuse the relationships between firms with each other and the relationship of firms with their shareholders.

Property rights theory of the firm is basically the property rights of owners of shares considered as owners of the corporation, rather than the rights of corporations as the owners of financial capital and capital resources of production. But corporate law and property law do not permit shareholders to be owners of the corporation. Thus, the property rights theory of the firm has no basis in law, and therefore can have no basis in economics.

In a series of internally contradictory and inconsistent statements, Alchian and Demsetz (1972) say,

It is this entire bundle of rights: 1) to be a residual claimant; 2) to observe input behavior; 3) to be the central party common to all contracts with inputs ... and 5) to sell these rights, that defines the ownership (or the employer) of the classical (capitalist, free-enterprise) firm.

(p. 783)

To be a residual claimant and to sell the rights is to be a shareholder but to observe input behavior and be a party common to all contracts means to be the corporation, so together these rights do not define the ownership or employer unless the corporation is a small, close corporation whose shares are not publicly traded, in which case there is no point in talking about economic organization.

But they are not finished. The simultaneous occurrence of all these rights is known as

classical capitalist firms with (a) joint input production, (b) several input owners, (c) one party who is common to all the contracts of the joint inputs, (d) who has rights to renegotiate any input's contract independently of contracts with other input owners, (e) who holds the residual claim, and (f) who has the right to sell his contractual residual status."

(Alchian & Demsetz, 1972, p. 783, 794)

They again exhibit a confusion of shareholders who are considered to have residual claims and can sell those claims (but see chapter 1 and *Corporate Law and the Theory of the Firm: Reconstructing Corporations, Shareholders, Directors, Owners, and Investors*) and the corporation who is a party to all contracts.

Alchian and Demsetz state that in their explanation of the capitalist firm, "the residual claimant must have power to revise the contract terms and incentives of individual members without having to terminate or alter every other input's contract" (p. 782), and "If we look within a firm to see who monitors—hires, fires, changes, promotes, and renegotiates—we should find him being a residual claimant." (p. 786).

Again, residual claimants are considered to be shareholders who have no rights to monitor or revise contracts. They even say, "The residual claim on earnings enjoyed by shareholders does not serve the function of enhancing their efficiency as monitors in the general situation" (p. 789).

How do they resolve these inconsistencies? By assuming a can opener in the desert. "The entrepreneur-organizer, who let us assume is the chief operating officer [COO] and sole repository of control of the corporation, does not find his authority residing in common stockholders ..." (p. 789). Of course, authority does not reside in common stockholders, and the COO is not an entrepreneur and certainly not the sole repository of control of the corporation. That function, by law, resides with the board of directors.

Finally, Weinstein (2007) compounds the confusion concerning who owns property and who enters into contracts concerning the property:

> Property rights theory concerns the possession of assets *by individuals*, not by the firm ... one of the essential characteristics of the modern firm is the fact that the firm itself owns most of the productive assets ... it is the firm – not the directors or managers – which enters into contractual relationships ... .

(p. 29, emphasis in original)

Nexus of contracts

How important is the nexus of contracts theory? Although it is an economic theory of the firm, "The nexus of contracts theory has been extremely influential in shaping corporate law theory over the past three decades" (Hayden & Bodie, 2011, p. 1130). Both critics and advocates agree nexus of contracts theory has "in the last decade swept the legal theory of the corporation" (Kornhauser, 1989, p. 1449). The nexus-of-contracts theory along with the principal-agent theory of the firm "have had profound implications for some of the most important issues of corporation law" (Ulen, 1993, p. 303).

The view which dominates the current economic analysis of the firm is that "the firm is a *'nexus of contracts* between *individuals'*" (Weinstein, 2007, p. 24, emphasis in original). What is called the nexus of contracts theory is basically an outgrowth of the property rights theory (Foss, 2000).

The corporation as a nexus of contracts was alluded to by Jensen and Meckling (1976), although they did not use that exact term and did not fully develop it. To review, a corporation as a nexus of contracts means that most organizations serve as "a nexus for a set of contracting relationships among individuals."

Fama (1980) is to be commended for his choice of words—owners of the securities of the corporation (firm) rather than owners of the corporation: "This paper attempts to explain how the separation of *security ownership* and control, typical of large corporations, can be an efficient form of economic organization" (p. 288) and "The main thesis of this paper is that separation of security ownership and control can be explained as an efficient form of economic organization within the 'set of contracts perspective'" (p. 289). Unfortunately, he then proceeds to ignore the meaning of *security ownership* and continues to adhere to agency theory.

Fama thinks that "the striking insight of Alchian and Demsetz (1972) and Jensen and Meckling (1976) is in viewing the firm as a set of contracts among factors of production," with each factor motivated by its self-interest (p. 289). That "insight," however, is inconsistent with Jensen and Meckling's theory, which is that the firm is "a nexus for a set of contracting relationships among *individuals*." It is impossible for factors of production—land and capital—to make contracts. Only the owners of the factors of production can make contracts. In addition, the firm (in most instances) owns the capital resource of production and the land, only making contracts with labor. (Of course, firms also make contracts with other firms for raw materials, etc., and with shareholders when the firm issues securities in an IPO.)

If a corporation is a nexus of contracts, the question naturally arises, why do corporate governance, separation of ownership and control matter, or agency relationships and duties matter? The more emphasis placed on corporations as nexusus of contracts, the less emphasis can be placed on corporate governance, separation of ownership and control, or agency relationships and duties. Indeed, Fama even discusses "The irrelevance of the concept of ownership of the firm" (p. 290) and correctly notes, but then ignores, "ownership of capital should not be confused with ownership of the firm" (p. 290).[10]

Fama should again be applauded for insisting that because

> in this 'nexus of contracts' perspective, ownership of the firm is an irrelevant concept ... dispelling the tenacious notion that a firm is owned by its security holders is important because it is a first step toward understanding that control over a firm's decisions is not necessarily the province of security holders. The second step is setting aside the equally tenacious role in the firm usually attributed to the entrepreneur.
>
> (p. 290)

I will have more to say about entrepreneurs and corporations in chapter 9. For now, the reader need be aware that Fama again ignores his own observation that the owners of securities are not the owners of the corporation.

A corporation as a nexus of contracts does not require shareholders. It does not even require a corporation, whether publicly traded or a small, close corporation. Everything is a nexus of contracts. A sole proprietorship, a partnership, even a household are all nexuses of contracts. Even Jensen and Meckling admit that "it is important to recognize that *most organizations are simply legal fictions which serve as a nexus for a set of contracting relationships* among individuals" (p. 311). A corporation as a nexus of contracts contributes little if anything to understanding the corporation, whether it is considered a corporation, a firm, or an enterprise.

If one firm is a nexus of contracts, and another firm is a nexus of contracts, and a third firm is a nexus of contracts, etc., etc., and they all enter into contracts with each other, you no longer have the firm as a nexus of contracts. You have a market and a price system, the analysis of which is precisely what the theory of the firm was trying to avoid.

Williamson (1987) "first examin[es] the relation between the firm and each of its constituencies—labor, capital, suppliers, customers, the community, and management—in contractual terms" (p. 298). He thus lends support to the nexus of contracts theory of the firm. In the context, by juxtaposing capital with labor it appears he means capital as a resource of production. But capital as a resource of production is an inanimate object. All of the other "constituents" are either persons (labor, suppliers, customers, the community, and management) or other firms (suppliers, customers), none of which are items on a balance sheet. Furthermore, he does not include "shareholders" as a constituent of the firm, the most important "constituent" since shareholders provide the firm's initial financial capital. But if by "capital" he means the right side of the balance sheet, an all too common error, it is strange he does not specify "creditors" in the list of constituents.

Williamson argues that the board of directors is "a governance structure safeguard between the firm and owners of equity capital" (p. 298). He accepts the common belief that "'owner' is usually reserved for stockholders [and] a well-developed market in shares permits individual stockholders to terminate ownership easily" (p. 304). But here he does at least implicitly acknowledge that there is a contract between the corporation and shareholders: "Labor, suppliers in the intermediate product market, debt-holders, and consumers all have opportunities to renegotiate terms when contracts are renewed. Stockholders, by contrast, invest for the life of the firm ..." (pp. 305–305). However, shareholders do not invest in the firm, only in the shares. Furthermore, his argument that the board of directors is a governance structure safeguard between the firm and owners of equity capital has two weakness. First, there is no such thing as "equity capital." There is capital (financial and productive) and there is equity. Second, assuming he means equity, the owner of equity capital is the corporation, not the shareholders.

Incomplete contracts

Perhaps the most contorted version of the theory of the firm is that of incomplete contracts.

The theory of incomplete contracts is attributable to Grossman and Hart's (1986) *The costs and benefits of ownership: A theory of vertical and lateral integration*, expanded by Hart and Moore (1990) in *Property Rights and the Nature of the Firm*, and Hart (1995) *Firms, Contracts, and Financial Structure*.

Much of the theory of incomplete contracts employs sophisticated, complex mathematical models (complex enough for Hart to earn a Nobel prize) for solving optimization, negotiation, and incentive issues associated with what is referred to as "incomplete contracts." Mathematical models will not be used here, nor will they be evaluated or critiqued. Mathematical models are not relevant to the purpose of this book. We are not concerned with negotiations and incentives.

I begin with Grossman and Hart (1986), who ask "What is a firm" and, "What are the determinants of how vertically or laterally integrated the activities of the firm are?" They base their theory on Coase (1937) and his examination of transaction costs and contracts. Coase suggested that a firm's transactions will be organized inside the firm when the cost is lower than the cost of using the market. Grossman and Hart's focus is on an insurance retailing firm using employees vs. independent agents, and they offer elaborate mathematical proofs to support their thesis (which is not relevant here).

Interestingly, they narrowly define a firm as "consist[ing] of those assets that it owns or over which it has control." Even more interesting, they do not distinguish between ownership and control and "virtually define ownership as the power to exercise control. In a corporation the shareholders as a group have control and delegate this control to the board of directors (i.e., management)" (p. 694). Immediately their error is revealed since by law shareholders do not delegate control to the board of directors and the board of directors is not management.

Notably, Grossman and Hart's failure to distinguish between ownership and control, and their emphasis that shareholders control the corporation (i.e., the firm) who then delegate control to the board of directors, is contrary to Berle and Means' theory of the separation of ownership and control. But in their failure to distinguish between ownership and control they also continue to sustain the legal impossibility that shareholders own the corporation.

Grossman and Hart begin by reviewing transactions cost-based arguments for how vertically or horizontally integrated the activities of the firm are by building on Coase (1937). Coase, they note, suggested that transactions will be organized within the firm when the cost of organizing activities within the firm is lower than the cost of using the market. The allocation of factors of production is determined outside the firm by the price mechanism. But inside the firm the allocation of factors of production is accomplished without reliance on the price mechanism as is evident in vertical integration (Coase, 1937):

> A factor of production (or the owner thereof) does not have to make a series of contracts with the factors with whom he is co-operating within the firm, as would be necessary, of course, if this co-operation were as a direct result of the working of the price mechanism [in the market] ... .
> The contract is one whereby the factor, for a certain remuneration (which may be fixed or fluctuating), agrees to obey the directions of an entrepreneur within certain limits.
>
> (p. 391)

This statement presents serious problems. First, what Grossman and Hart neglect to consider is who owns the factors of production. It is obvious that capital resources of production do not make contracts with the corporation. The owner of capital resources of production does not make contracts with the corporation or agree to obey the directions of an "entrepreneur" (which must be interpreted as the corporation) because the corporation is the owner of the capital resources of production. The corporation, as owner of the capital factor of production, does not contract with itself.

It is the owner of a factor of production that makes the contract, and it is the corporation that owns the capital factor of production. Labor is not owned by anyone. Labor contracts to sell their labor to the corporation, which is implicit in Coase's statement that "[a] contract is one whereby the factor, for a certain remuneration (which may be fixed or fluctuating), agrees to obey the directions of an entrepreneur within certain limits." The only factor that agrees to obey the "entrepreneur" for a certain remuneration is labor. But the corporation is not an entrepreneur. (It is assumed that the corporation also owns the land.)

Hart was a co-recipient of the 2016 Nobel Prize in Economics for his work on developing the theory of incomplete contracts. It therefore deserves special attention.

As Hart (1995) describes it, an incomplete contract is one which, due to the cost of writing a complete contract, intentionally contains gaps, missing provisions, and ambiguities. The problem is, the theory is actually contradicted by contract law.

Recall from chapter 1 that certain elements must exist in order to create a contract and the absence of any one of them nullifies the existence of a contract, i.e., makes it unenforceable. In particular, the terms must be definite, identifiable, and complete—parties, consideration, promises, etc.:

> There is not a complete or valid contract if any material thing remains to be done to establish contractual relations. Except for quasi-contracts, *the law does not make a contract* if the parties intend none, nor does it treat an arrangement as completed *if the parties see it as incomplete. A contract is not complete*, binding, or enforceable *until there is a meeting of the minds as to all essential terms.* If any essential matters are left open for further negotiation or consideration, the contract is not complete. However, not every detail of a contract need be specifically spelled out. Also, the court will enforce a contract if the parties have completed negotiating the essential elements, even when the parties have expressly left other elements for future negotiation and agreement.
>
> (17A Am Jur 2d Contracts § 35, emphases added)

If a contract contains gaps, missing provisions, or ambiguities that are essential, it is not a contract. In order for a contract to be considered incomplete it must first actually be a valid, enforceable contract. The gaps, missing provisions, or ambiguities must be for non-essential terms. If one party to the contract fails to adhere to the essential terms of a contract such that court intervention is necessary, it is considered a breach of contract, not an incomplete contract. While a contract may be incomplete with respect to non-essential elements, if it incomplete with respect to essential elements it is non-existent, essentially void *ab initio*. If the gaps, missing provisions, or ambiguities are non-essential such that a contract may be considered incomplete but enforceable, then the theory of incomplete contracts loses all significance since the missing items are, by definition, not significant. As Weber (1978) puts it,

"It is essential to include the criterion of power of control and disposal in the sociological concept of economic action, if for no other reason than that at least a modern market economy essentially consists in *a complete network of exchange contracts.*"

(p. 67, emphasis added)

Economic action requires valid, enforceable contracts, not incomplete contracts.

Hart states, "The basic idea is that firms arise in situations where people cannot write good contracts [complete contracts] and where the allocation of power and control is therefore important" (p. 1). That is false for at least two reasons.

One, corporations are created (1) as a means of sharing and reducing risks; (2) to undertake projects that one person alone lacks sufficient financial capital to undertake; and (3) to acquire what has come to be known as "limited liability."[11] The second reason it is false is revealed in the very nature of the theory itself—it is backwards. The theory of incomplete contracts is not that people create corporations based on their inability to write good contracts. The theory of incomplete contracts is that firms write incomplete contracts *after* the corporation is created. Corporations cannot write contracts until they are created according to corporate statutory law.

"Economists have written a great deal about why property rights are important ... . However, they have been less successful in explaining why it matters who owns a piece of private property" (Hart, 1995, p. 5, emphasis in original). Unfortunately, Hart not only fails to explain the importance of the fact that it is the corporation that owns the assets, both total and net, he makes assumptions to the contrary:

"I have assumed that an owner [i.e., the shareholder] will exercise residual control rights over the assets; e.g. an equity holder [owner of shares] will use her votes to replace a bad manager [by manager Hart means director, since owners of shares do not use votes to replace managers] ... ."

(p. 9)

This is confirmed by his later statement, which echoes Berle and Means:

"those who own the company [by which they mean the corporation], the shareholders, are too small and numerous, to exercise control on a day-to-day basis. Given this, they delegate day-to-day (residual rights of) control to a board of directors who in turn delegate it to management."

(p. 127)

Hart also argues that the principal-agent theory leads to a more realistic portrayal of firms, but in so arguing he fails to understand that owners of shares do not own the corporation and directors are not the agents of the owners of shares.

Hart develops complex mathematical equations (a prerequisite for a Nobel prize in economics!) incorporating the Nash equilibrium. But he does not relate the rights of property owners, i.e., the corporation as owner of the corporate assets (capital factors of production) to the theory of the firm. His analysis of property rights leads him to conclude that the best choice of the ownership structure of assets is determined by computing and comparing total surplus. But the ownership structure of assets is not based on merely computing and comparing total surplus, but by contract. Property rights are determined by law, not surplus calculations.

Scott (2006) examines one of the main insights of the theory of incomplete contracts, which is that legal enforcement alone cannot ensure the complete realization of cooperative ventures. The law and economic theory of incomplete contracts has developed analytic tools relying on advances in the economics of information for understanding how the contracting conundrum can best be resolved. It is a field that is less than thirty years old but that has produced three Nobel laureates (p. 281).

But incomplete contracts theory of the firm is contrary to legal and accounting requirements (Biondi, 2007). Incomplete contracts theory of property rights is contrary to the legal principles that judges apply in the context of corporations (Biondi, 2007). Incomplete contracts theory of assets, liabilities, costs, and revenues is inconsistent with the generally accepted accounting principles valuation of assets and liabilities as specified in the firm's contracts (Biondi, 2007; Biondi, Canziani, & Kirat, 2007, p. 7). Incomplete contracts cannot be audited.

Thus, Hart's Nobel prize-winning theory of incomplete contracts is the can opener in the desert, based, as are all theories of the firm, on assumptions contrary to contract law, property law, agency law, and corporate law. The theory of incomplete contracts basically has no meaning in spite of the theory winning a Nobel prize. To say that a contract is incomplete is an oxymoron when used in the context of the theory of the firm.[12] The theory of incomplete contracts plus $3.00 will get you a cup of coffee at your local coffee shop. Or a Nobel prize.

Chapter summary

This chapter highlighted some of the more relevant arguments concerning the economic theory of the firm and the major sub-theories—agency theory and agency costs (transactions costs); property rights; nexus of contracts; and incomplete contracts.

To paraphrase Coase (1990), who in turn quoted from an article published in 1939 in *The Accountant*, ideas that are nonsense are made dangerous by the fog of words in which assumptions are disguised as truths. The nonsense in the theory of the firm is that all economic theories of the firm ignore property law, agency law, and corporate law. The fog of words in which assumptions are disguised as truths and the danger that those assumptions pose is that owners of shares own the firm and directors are their agents. The assumptions are blindly accepted in a Matrix-like trance, insulated from reality.

The theory of the firm attempts to accomplish two things: explain why firms arise (e.g., Coase); and who owns, controls, and governs the firm (e.g., Berle and Means; Jensen and Meckling). But the theory of the firm fails to achieve either. The explanation for why firms exist disregards the motivations for creating corporations, alleging that the reason is to reduce transaction costs rather than to pool financial capital and reduce risk of loss.

Explaining who owns, controls, and governs the firm relies on assumptions contrary to law. Economic theory of the firm simply cannot be used to develop ownership structure of the firm. The legal ownership structure of the firm determines the economic theory of the firm. While economic theory is useful for analyzing such things as the behavior of the firm and the relationships of firms to each other, any legitimate economic theory of the firm must be bound by the parameters of contract law, property law, agency law, and corporate law. Where a law exists, the law must determine economics and economic behavior.

In spite of all the propositions, assumptions, lemmas, formulas, equations, models, and mathematical proofs, the economic theory of the firm—all of them—is still nothing more than assuming a can opener in the desert because, like the nature of the firm, the assumptions are contrary to facts which means contrary to law.

Considering the issues related to the nature of the firm and the theory of the firm together, the appropriate label for the field of study would be "the theory of the nature of the firm." But any theory of the firm must be grounded in actual law, not assumptions contrary to law. Regardless of the theory of choice, there is no escaping from the legally incorrect, and therefore economically incorrect, doctrine that shareholders own corporations and directors are agents of shareholders. The theory of the firm twists and distorts the meaning of agency law, property law, and contract law.

Notes

1 One must question his use of "empirical presumption." If there is empirical evidence to support the issue of separation of ownership and control, it cannot be a presumption. If it is a presumption, the presumption must have some valid legal basis. In addition, it would not be empirically based.
2 Delaware General Corporation Law provides "The business and affairs of every corporation organized under this chapter shall be managed by or under the direction of a board of directors." Delaware General Corporation Law, § 141(a).
3 "A red herring is something that misleads or distracts from a relevant or important question." Red herring, https://en.wikipedia.org/wiki/Red_herring.
4 Delaware General Corporation Law, § 141(a).
5 Delaware General Corporation Law, § 141(a).
6 Creditors of course have claims against the corporation for interest and principal payments.

7 Article 7 of the United States Bill of Rights states, "No person shall ... be deprived of life, liberty, or property, without due process of law... ." www.archives.gov/founding-docs/bill-of-rights-transcript.
8 For example, corporations have property rights under the U.S. Constitution but not rights against self-incrimination.
9 "Property rights" is only referred to once other than in the title of their paper and the title of a reference that is an earlier draft of their own work.
10 This begs the question, if ownership is irrelevant, why has so much emphasis been placed on the separation of ownership and control for the last ninety years?
11 Owners of shares have no liability for anything so to speak of limited liability is misleading. What is known as "limited liability" is actually "limited risk" where the maximum risk of loss is the market value of the shares they own.
12 An oxymoron is "a combination of contradictory or incongruous words," such as "cold fire." www.merriam-webster.com/dictionary/oxymoron.

Bibliography

Alchian, A.A., & Demsetz, H. (1972). Production, information costs, and economic organization. *American Economic Review*, 62 (5), 777–795. Retrieved from www.jstor.org/stable/181519.
Berle, A.A., & Means, G.C. (1991). *The modern corporation and private property* (2nd ed.). New York: Routledge.
Biondi, Y. (2007). The economic theory of the firm as an entity. In Y. Biondi, A. Canziani, & T. Kirat (Eds.), *The firm as a legal entity: Implications for economics, accounting and the law* (pp. 237–265). London, Routledge.
Biondi, Y., Canziani, A., & Kirat, T. (2007). Coming back to the enterprise. In Y. Biondi, A. Canziani, & T. Kirat (Eds.), *The firm as a legal entity: Implications for economics, accounting and the law* (pp. 3–8). London: Routledge.
Boulding, K. (1942). The theory of the firm in the last ten years. *American Economic Review*, 32 (4), 791–802. Retrieved from www.jstor.org/stable/1816760.
Coase, R.H. (1937). The nature of the firm. *Economica*, 4 (16), 386–405. doi:10.1111/j.1468-0335.1937.tb00002.x.
Coase, R.H. (1990). Accounting and the theory of the firm. *Journal of Accounting and Economics*, 12 (1–3), 3–13. doi:10.1016/0165-4101(90)90038-6.
Cooper, W.W. (1951). A proposal for extending the theory of the firm. *Quarterly Journal of Economics*, 65 (1), 87–109. Retrieved from www.jstor.org/stable/1879501.
Demsetz, H. (1983). The structure of ownership and the theory of the firm. *Journal of Law Economics*, 26 (2), 375–390. Retrieved from www.jstor.org/stable/725108?seq=1.
Easterbrook, F., & Fischel, D.R., (1989). The corporate contract. *Columbia Law Review*, 89, 1416–1448. Retrieved from https://chicagounbound.uchicago.edu/cgi/viewcontent.cgi?article=2163&context=journal_articles.
Fama, E.F. (1980). Agency problems and the theory of the firm. *Journal of Political Economy*, 88 (2), 288–307. doi:10.1086/260866.
Fama, E.F., & Jensen, M.C. (1983). Separation of ownership and control. *Journal of Law and Economics*, 26 (2), 301–325. Retrieved from www.jstor.org/stable/725104?seq=1.
Foss, N.J. (2000). The theory of the firm: An introduction to themes and contributions. In N. Foss (Ed.), *The theory of the firm: Critical perspectives on business and management*, Vol. 1 (pp. xv–lxi). London: Routledge.

Grossman, S.J. & Hart, O.D. (1986). The costs and benefits of ownership: A theory of vertical and lateral integration. *Journal of Political Economy*, 94 (4), 691–719. doi:10.1086/261404..

Hart, O.D. (1989). An economist's perspective on the theory of the firm. *Columbia Law Review*, 89 (7), 1757–1774. Retrieved from www.jstor.org/stable/1122818.

Hart, O.D. (1995). *Firms, contracts and financial structure*. Oxford: Oxford University Press.

Hart O.D., & Moore, J. (1990). Property rights and the nature of the firm. *Journal of Political Economy*, 98 (6), 1119–1158. doi:10.1086/261729.

Hart O.D., & Moore, J. (1998). Foundations of incomplete contracts. *Review of Economic Studies*, 66 (1), 115–138. Retrieved from http://www.nber.org/papers/w6726.

Hayden, G.M., & Bodie, M.T. (2011). The uncorporation and the unraveling of 'nexus of contracts' theory. *Michigan Law Review*, 109 (6), 1127–1144. Retrieved from https://repository.law.umich.edu/mlr/vol109/iss6/16.

Huber, W.D. (2020). *Corporate law and the theory of the firm: Reconstructing corporations, shareholders, directors, owners, and investors*. London: Routledge.

Jensen, M.C., & Meckling, W.H. (1976). Theory of the firm: Managerial behavior, agency costs and ownership structure. *Journal of Financial Economics*, 3, 305–360. doi:10.1016/0304-405X(76)90026-X.

Kornhauser, L.A. (1989). The nexus of contracts approach to corporations: A comment on Easterbrook and Fischel. *Columbia Law Review*, 89 (7), 1449–1460. doi:10.2307/1122808.

Masten, S.E. (1993). A legal basis for the firm. In O.E. Williamson & S.G. Winter (Eds.), *The nature of the firm: Origins, evolution, and development* (pp. 196–212). London: Oxford University Press.

Meurer, M.J. (2004). Law, economics, and the theory of the firm. *Buffalo Law Review*, 52 (3), 727–755. Retrieved from https://digitalcommons.law.buffalo.edu/buffalolawreview/vol52/iss3/8.

Milhaupt, C.J. (1998). Property rights in firms. *Virginia Law Review*, 84 (6), 1145–1194. Retrieved from www.jstor.org/stable/1073696.

Orts, E.W. (2013). *Business persons: A legal theory of the firm*. London: Oxford University Press.

Scott, R.E. (2006). The law and economics of incomplete contracts. *Annual Review of Law and Society*, 2, 279–297. doi:10.1146/annurev.lawsocsci.2.081805.105913.

Smith, A. (1776). *The wealth of nations* (Cannan Edition). New York: Modern Library.

Ulen, T.S. (1993). The Coasean firm in law and economics. *Journal of Corporation Law*, 18(2), 301–331.

Walker, P. (2016). *The theory of the firm: An overview of the economic mainstream*. London: Routledge.

Weber, M. (1978). *Economy and society: An outline of interpretive sociology*. Trans. E. Fischoff et al., ed. G. Roth & C. Wittich. Berkeley, CA: University of California Press.

Weinstein, O. (2007). The current state of the economic theory of the firm: Contractual, competence-based, and beyond. In Y. Biondi, A. Canziani, & T. Kirat (Eds.), *The firm as a legal entity: Implications for economics, accounting and the law* (pp. 21–53). London: Routledge.

Williamson, O.E. (1987). *Economic institutions of capitalism*. New York: Free Press.

Part III

Capital, capitalism, and the Communist Manifesto

"I don't know what you mean by 'glory'," Alice said.

Humpty Dumpty smiled contemptuously. "Of course you don't—till I tell you. I meant 'there's a nice knock-down argument for you!'"

"But 'glory' doesn't mean 'a nice knock-down argument'," Alice objected.

"When I use a word," Humpty Dumpty said, in rather a scornful tone, "it means just what I choose it to mean—neither more nor less."

"The question is," said Alice, "whether you can make words mean so many different things."

"The question is," said Humpty Dumpty, "which is to be master—that's all."

Alice was too much puzzled to say anything, so after a minute Humpty Dumpty began again:

"They've a temper, some of them—particularly verbs, they're the proudest—adjectives you can do anything with, but not verbs—however, I can manage the whole lot! Impenetrability! That's what I say!"

The above passage was written by mathematician Charles Lutwidge Dodgson, aka Lewis Carroll, in 1871 in his classic *Through the Looking-Glass*, a sequel to *Alice in Wonderland*. The passage was quoted in hundreds of judicial opinions in Britain and the United States including, as of 2008, two United States Supreme Court cases.[1] (Humpty should have included nouns in his assessment of words with tempers!) We shall encounter this several times in the three chapters in this part.

"Capital" is of course the root and source of "capitalist" and "capitalism." It is thus important to understand "capital" in order to understand "capitalist" and "capitalism." But arriving at an understanding of "capital" and therefore "capitalist" and "capitalism," has proved elusive.

The word "capital" has multiple meanings. Absent a preceding adjective or following noun (in English), its meaning must be drawn from the context, which is more easily said than done. In 1906 Fisher wrote, "Capital has been so variously defined, that it may be doubtful whether it have any generally received meaning. In consequence, almost every year there appears some new attempt to settle the disputed conception, but, unfortunately, no authoritative result has as yet followed these attempts."

Grassby (1999) notes that as of 1918 there were at least 111 definitions of "capitalism." According to Grassby, "capitalism" has been used primarily, but not exclusively, by socialists, sociologist, and historians rather than economists, and when economists such as Keynes or Friedman use it, they use it mostly as a polemic rather than analytical tool.

To illustrate the irrationality to which we are subjected, when I submitted my paper *The FASB Conceptual Framework: A Case of the Emperor's New Clothes*[2] to a journal to be considered for publication, one of the reviewers made the following comments:

> the author seems to take the use of the English language in an accounting context at face value. The use of language can be context-sensitive. Accounting language is different from Finance language and from Economic language. The author appears to think that terms should be used consistently across the three. It is true that the fields are all related but to try to use terms that are 'loaded' to mean different (albeit similar ideas) in different disciplines in the same way across those disciplines is to create a language that no one understands or is unnecessarily complex.
>
> [...]
>
> Virtually all accounting and finance professionals (and academics) know (or should know) that when we say "capital" in accounting or finance, we are referring to Stockholders' Equity and Debt ("the right side of the balance sheet"). It is this capital that is used to acquire the buildings, machinery, inventory, etc. (the assets or the "left side of the balance sheet") with which to run the business. The author is trying to force the language of finance and economics onto accounting.[3]

The absurdity is readily apparent. (I withdrew the paper from that journal.) But, not only did the reviewer claim that I was "trying to force the language of finance and economics onto accounting," it was in fact the reviewer who is forcing an entire cadre of researchers to accept his or her meaning—a prime example of the Humpty Dumpty principle which we will encounter throughout the next few chapters. Using words (capital) to mean different things in different contexts and disciplines (accounting, finance, economics) is precisely why it is confusing and precisely why it is unnecessarily complex.

It would be foolish and futile, not to mention arrogant, to attempt to define "capital" here or attempt to settle any arguments or disputes and I make no such attempt. Rather, I endeavor to find a common denominator, i.e., a definition or concept of "capital" common to corporate law, economics, finance, accounting, and the theory of the firm.

In chapter 8 I review various definitions and concepts of "capital," meaning the different ways in which the term "capital" is used, misused, and abused. It is perhaps strange to think of a word being misused or abused, but that is exactly what frequently occurs in economics, sociology, history, and accounting research. Researchers in accounting, sociology, history, and economics, including Nobel prize-winners in economics, talk past each other, frequently using the term "capital" carelessly to mean one thing when they actually mean something else, and Marx and Weber are no exceptions. This in turn leads to confusion in what is meant not only by capital, but also by capitalist and capitalism.

In chapter 9 I consider the ways in which the (mis)use of capitalism has confused and complicated our understanding of what capitalism means and what it means to be a capitalist.

In chapter 10 I examine Marx's use of "capital" and "capitalist" and how his inconsistent and contradictory use of the terms invalidates his entire theory.

There are certain aspects in the next three chapters that on the surface appear to be repetitious. However, because "capital" and capitalism are multifaceted and multidimensional phenomena like a polyhedron, what may appear to be repetitious is the result of examining each facet from a different perspective. This allows us to comprehend "capital" and capitalism as a whole, rather than just one plane. When "capital" and capitalism are seen as a whole, then the contradictions between economics, accounting, finance, and corporate law are readily apparent.

Notes

1 Humpty Dumpty. https://en.wikipedia.org/wiki/Humpty_Dumpty.
2 Huber (2020). *The FASB Conceptual Framework: A Case of the Emperor's New Clothes.* https://papers.ssrn.com/sol3/papers.cfm?abstract_id=3400769.
3 Review on file with author.

Bibliography

Fisher, I. (1906). *The nature of capital and income.* London: Macmillan.
Grassby, R. (1999). *The idea of capitalism before the Industrial Revolution.* Lanham, MD: Rowman & Littlefield.

8 Capital

Introduction

Capital is of course the root and source of "capitalist" and "capitalism." It is thus important to understand "capital" and the relation of "capital" to "capitalist" and "capitalism." An incorrect understanding of "capital" inevitably leads to an incorrect understanding of "capitalist" and "capitalism." But arriving at an understanding of "capital," and therefore of "capitalist" and "capitalism," has proven to be elusive.

"Capital" is confusing. That is, the word has multiple meanings so that absent a preceding adjective or following noun (in English), its meaning must be drawn from the context. which is more easily said than done. In 1906 Fisher wrote±: "Capital has been so variously defined, that it may be doubtful whether it have any generally received meaning. In consequence, almost every year there appears some new attempt to settle the disputed conception, but, unfortunately, no authoritative result has as yet followed these attempts." Von Mises (2009) adds, "The views of scholars on the definition of capital are more divergent than their views on any other point in economics" (pp. 86–87).

The word "capital" appeared during the reign of Emperor Leo III in the late eighth century and in Muslim writings in the early ninth century (Milios, 2018). But the word "capital" has multiple meanings. "Capital" as a noun without a preceding adjective, or as an adjective without a following noun, has no objective meaning. Any meaning attached by a reader to "capital" alone must be inferred from the context in which the author is using it, which is easier said than done and often not correct. Often the assumption of what an author means by "capital" is the result of preconceived ideas or the personal philosophical beliefs of the reader. For example, a "capitalist" may infer "capital" means one thing (e.g., the right side of a corporate balance sheet, or the private ownership of the means of production in a capitalist economy), while a "Marxist" may assume it means something else (the private ownership of the means of production in a capitalist economy or the exploitation of labor), essentially a reverse Humpty Dumpty where a word means what the reader wants it to mean. To make matters even more confusing, many authors switch meanings without explicitly advising the reader of the change, assuming the reader knows the meaning has been changed or, worse, that the author does not fully understand the distinction in meanings.

To illustrate the truth of Fisher's and von Mises' statements, recall the comments made by the reviewer of my paper referred to in the Introduction to Part III, which can be considered as "Exhibit A":

> the author *seems to take the use of the English language in an accounting context at face value.* The use of *language can be context-sensitive.* Accounting language is different from Finance language and from Economic language. The author appears to think that terms should be used consistently across the three. It is true that the fields are all related but to try to use terms that are 'loaded' to mean different (albeit similar ideas) in different disciplines in the same way across those disciplines is to create a language that no one understands or is unnecessarily complex.
>
> [...]
>
> Virtually all accounting and finance professionals (and academics) know (or should know) that when we say "capital" in accounting or finance, we are referring to Stockholders' Equity and Debt ("the right side of the balance sheet"). It is this capital that is used to acquire the buildings, machinery, inventory, etc. (the assets or the "left side of the balance sheet") with which to run the business. *The author is trying to force the language of finance and economics onto accounting* [emphasis added].[1]

The absurdity is clearly revealed. Not only did the reviewer claim that I was "trying to force the language of finance and economics onto accounting," it was in fact the reviewer who is forcing an entire corps of researchers to accept the reviewer's meaning—an all too unfortunate occurrence and a prime example of the Humpty Dumpty principle which we will encounter throughout this and the next two chapters. Using words such as capital to mean different things in different contexts and disciplines (accounting, finance, economics) is precisely why understanding "capital" is confusing and precisely why it is unnecessarily complex.

Furthermore, the reviewer's statement is completely wrong. A corporation does not use stock or debt to acquire machinery; it uses cash to acquire machinery. Issuing stock and bonds is merely a method to obtain the cash (financial capital) necessary to acquire capital resources of production.

In the previous chapters I examined corporate law, economic, finance, and accounting considerations from the perspective of corporations, owners of shares, and investors in shares. This included a review of securities laws and generally accepted principles of accounting. "Capital" is integral to and inseparable from those considerations.

In this chapter I briefly review various definitions and concepts of "capital," meaning the different ways in which the term "capital" is used, misused, confused, and abused. It is perhaps strange to think of a word being misused or abused, but that is exactly what frequently occurs in economics, sociology, history, and accounting research. Researchers in accounting, sociology, history, and economics, including Nobel prize-winners in economics, talk past each other, frequently using the term "capital" carelessly to mean for one thing, when they actually mean something else, and Marx is no exception. This in turn leads to confusion in what is meant by not only "capital" but consequently also "capitalist" and "capitalism."

It would be foolish and futile, not to mention arrogant, to attempt here an authoritative definition of "capital" or attempt to settle any arguments or disputes concerning the meaning of capital, and I make no such attempt. Rather, I endeavor to find a common denominator, i.e., a definition or concept of "capital," that cuts across the artificial boundaries of the various disciplines that is common to corporate law, economics, finance, and accounting. Finding a common denominator for the meaning of "capital" can then lead to a better understanding of the meaning of "capital" and the nature of "capitalists" and "capitalism."

Types of capital

There are various "types" of capital so the term "capital" without a preceding adjective or following noun is confusing. For example, as a noun there is social capital, cultural capital, financial capital (money), and physical capital (a resource of production). There is constant capital, permanent capital, variable capital, working capital, venture capital, human capital, intellectual capital, imaginary capital, productive capital, industrial capital, paid in capital, and fictitious capital. Marx referred to human capital (labor) as "variable capital," and physical capital, productive, and industrial capital as "constant capital". Fisher used "permanent capital" to mean physical capital. Thus, physical capital, productive capital, constant capital, industrial capital, and permanent capital are merely synonyms for the same thing—the factor of production.

As an adjective there are capital assets and capital equipment (physical assets such as machines), as well as that which is erroneously referred to as capital assets meaning shares of stock traded in the market (as in the Capital Asset Pricing Model), capital markets (for trading shares of stock), capital stock (the shares of a corporation), capital structure (a misnomer, as I explain in this chapter), and capital expenditures (cash used for acquiring physical assets).

Fisher (1906) counsels us that it is important to differentiate capital and income (that distinction is not relevant here). From the context we infer that capital is money. But is it? Capital, according to Fisher, is a fund and income is a flow. Fisher defines a stock of wealth existing at an instant of time as capital and a flow of services through a period of time as income. He defines "fund" as "A stock of wealth or property or its value," but he classifies objects that are owned as land and commodities[2] rather than as a fund. So, we will consider capital as distinguished from income and focus only on capital. However, we are no closer to understanding what is meant by "capital" since Fisher classifies money as well as items that are not money (property rights such as leases and patents) as wealth. Thus, Fisher classifies wealth as land, commodities, and property rights, as well as money, as capital since all are a stock of wealth. But "capital" cannot mean all those things since, as we saw chapter 2, the resources of production are land, labor, and capital. Money is not a resource of production as explained in chapter 2 so therefore Fisher is careless in his classification scheme.

As explained in this chapter, there are two definitions or concepts of capital that are relevant—financial capital and physical capital, but only one that is actually a common denominator. With the myriad of definitions of capital, finding the common denominator is essential while the peripheral definitions can be ignored since they are not pertinent to capital as part of capitalism and do not unite corporate law, property law, economics, finance, investment, and accounting. In the following sections I examine the distinction between financial capital and physical capital in order to relate them to capitalism discussed in the next chapter.

Financial capital

The concept of financial capital is well known. Financial capital is the reason for the existence of capital markets, the place where financial capital (cash) is obtained by corporations when they issue shares in an IPO.

Berle (1954) comments that "When an individual invests capital in the large corporation, he grants to the corporate management all power to use that capital to create, produce and develop, and he abandons all control over the product" (p. 30), but that can only be done when purchasers purchase shares in an IPO. Obviously, from the context, by "capital" Berle is here referring to cash. Nothing else would make sense. This is confirmed by his later statement that "An investor considers an enterprise, decides on its probable usefulness and profitability, and puts down his savings …" (p. 39). Savings here, of course, means cash.

Berle (1954) refers to a 1953 study by the National City Bank of the sources and uses of "capital," which obviously refers to cash, and the amount of cash spent on "capital expenditures," which he equates to physical assets (p. 37). Moreover, since the nineteenth century, "financial capitalism increasingly came to characterize capitalism itself, rather than referring simply to the use of capital provided by the owners of a business or borrowed from their immediate circle of family, friends, and business associates" (Michie, 2014, p. 261). Williamson (1987) concurs:

> One possibility would be for entrepreneurs to supply all their equity financing directly—from their own funds of from friends and family who

know and trust them ... . This would place a severe limit, however, on the amount of equity funding available.

(p. 305)

As the business expands, the capitalist-entrepreneur may also borrow money from a bank.

Related to, but not synonymous with, financial capital is working capital. Working capital is that which is used for day-to-day operations and is defined as current assets (assets that can be turned into cash within a year), which includes cash, accounts receivable, short-term investments, and inventory, while net working capital is defined as current assets minus current liabilities. Note that neither definition is related to equity or shares of stock. Nor is either directly related to cash other than the cash that is a part of working capital. There is no direct correlation between financial capital (money) and working capital.

But what, exactly, does financial capital mean? Money is financial capital if it is intended by its owner to be used to acquire productive capital, but to better understand money as financial capital we will look first at securities laws and then the *Financial Accounting Standards Board's Conceptual Framework*. I begin with a review of chapter 3 and securities laws.

Securities laws

At the height of the Great Depression the U.S. Congress enacted two major securities laws that have impacted the global market for financial capital: the Securities Act of 1933 ('33 Act) and the Securities Exchange Act of 1934 ('34 Act). The '34 Act established the Securities and Exchange Commission (SEC, or Commission). The '33 Act regulates initial issues of securities while the '34 Act regulates securities exchanges and the subsequent trading of securities in the market.

The term "capital" is used 17 times in the '33 Act. While the '33 Act contains a list of 19 definitions as used on the Act, capital is not one of them. The '34 Act uses the term "capital" 57 times, but again there is no definition. It's as if the term "capital" were self-evident. To make matters worse, the securities laws use the term "capital" inconsistently. For example, the '33 Act refers to "capital formation" and "capital stock" while the '34 Act refers to "capital formation," "capital expenditures" and "capital resources," "capital adequacy," "capital requirements," "capital structure," "venture capital funds" "Capital" used alone, i.e., with no preceding adjective or following noun, is also used: "A futures commission merchant, introducing broker, broker, or dealer shall maintain sufficient capital to comply with the stricter of any applicable capital requirements ... ."[3]

In the context, "capital stock" refers to the number of shares issued by a corporation. "Capital adequacy" and "capital requirements," on the other hand, refer to the dollar amount of shares issued by the corporation (along with other components of equity such as preferred stock), while the erroneous term "capital structure" refers to the ratio of corporate debt to corporate equity (the debt/equity ratio) as is taught in every introductory finance course. However, recall the review of my article where the reviewer states the "right hand side" includes debt as part of capital and the capital structure ("when we say 'capital' in accounting or finance, we are referring to Stockholders' Equity and Debt ('the right side of the balance sheet'"), thus exhibiting the confusion in the application of the term "capital."

However, while "capital requirements" refers to the equity section of the balance sheet, the equity section of the balance sheet is not related to the cash of the corporation; i.e., "capital requirements" refers to adequate equity, not adequate cash. "Capital requirements" could not refer to adequate equity if "capital" includes everything on the right side of the balance sheet—debt plus equity—since that would only mean that debt plus equity equals assets which would mean a deb/equity ratio of 99 would satisfy capital requirements. That is untenable and therefore, we can conclude confidently that "capital requirements" refers to equity only. (But that in itself is a problem since equity does not equal cash.) "Capital expenditures" does refer to cash since capital expenditure requires the use of cash to acquire the physical capital to be used in production ("Investment Activities" in the statement of cash flows).

Levy (2014) notes that "Global banks howl against new regulations that would increase *their equity (their capital)*" (p. 213). This raises two issues. One issue is banks' complaints against such regulations show that capital is not the right side of the balance sheet. It would be strange indeed, not to mention illogical, to consider the capital of a bank to be the equity of the bank, but to consider the capital of non-bank corporations to be the entire right side of the balance sheet. So either the entire right side of the balance sheet of a bank is its capital in which case regulators' concerns of a bank's financial structure is unfounded or the entire right side of the balance sheet of a non-bank corporation is not its capital. It cannot be both ways except in Alice's Wonderland where words have no meaning.

Securities Act of 1933

It is widely believed that these two securities laws were enacted to protect the public interest. As I previously explained, that is false (Huber, 2016a). To see why it is a false belief, consider the purpose for enacting the Securities Act of 1933. The '33 Act regulates initial issues of securities. The '33 Act is

> AN ACT To provide full and fair disclosure of the character of securities sold in interstate and foreign commerce and through the mails, and to prevent frauds in the sale thereof, and for other purposes.[4]

But the purpose of the '33 Act must be considered in conjunction with the purposes of the '34 Act, which I will examine next.

Of equal importance is what is *not* the purpose of the Securities Act of 1933. The '33 At does not regulate the "capital formation" of the capital assets of production. The '33 Act is only concerned with how corporations obtain financial capital by issuing stock (actually all securities) to the public and what corporations do with the cash they receive by issuing stock to the public in an IPO, not with the allocation of scarce resources.

Securities Exchange Act of 1934

To see why it is a false belief that the '34 Act was enacted to protect the public interest, consider the purposes for enacting the Securities Exchange Act of 1934. The purposes of the '34 Act rests on the purpose of the '33 Act:

> For the reasons hereinafter enumerated, transactions in securities as commonly conducted upon securities exchanges and over-the-counter markets are effected with a national public interest which makes it necessary to provide for regulation and control of such transactions and of practices and matters related thereto, including transactions by officers, directors, and principal security holders ... *in order to protect interstate commerce, the national credit, the Federal taxing power, to protect and make more effective the national banking system and Federal Reserve System, and to insure the maintenance of fair and honest markets in such transactions* [emphasis added].[5]

The '34 Act does not address financial capital formation other than the requirements for the registration statement for an IPO because it only governs the trading of securities in the market after the initial issue, not the initial issuance of securities by corporations. Trading securities in the market does not provide financial capital to the corporation. But as with the '33 Act, the '34 Act is not concerned with the capital resources of production or the allocation of resources.

Particularly noteworthy is the fact that neither the Securities Act of 1933 nor the Securities Exchange Act of 1934 uses the term "capital asset" in reference to securities issued by a corporation or traded in the market, a point to be remembered when we again consider the financial asset pricing model.

Financial capital and the FASB Conceptual Framework

As I discussed in *FASB Conceptual Framework: A Case of the Emperor's New Clothes*, the *FASB Conceptual Framework* frequently uses "capital" and "cash" interchangeably, with no overt explanation. The *FASB Conceptual Framework* sometimes uses "capital" when it means "cash." For example, "the objective of financial reporting is to provide financial information about the reporting entity that is useful to present and potential investors, lenders, and other creditors in making decisions in their capacity as *capital providers*"

(FASB, 2018, BC1.26, emphasis added). The "capital" that capital providers provide is cash which is provided when investors in shares purchase stock from the corporation in an IPO, which the *FASB* acknowledges elsewhere:

> Business enterprises *raise capital for production* and marketing activities not only from financial institutions and small groups of individuals but *also from the public through issuing equity* and debt securities that are widely traded in highly developed securities markets.
>
> (FASB, 1978, 13, emphasis added)

Obviously, raising capital from the public for production through issuing equity can mean nothing other than raising cash in an IPO pursuant to the '33 Act.

The FASB correctly links financial capital to individual savings: "Production and marketing of goods and services often involve long, continuous, or intricate processes that *require large amounts of capital, which in turn require substantial savings in the economy*" (FASB, 1978, 11, emphasis added), again demonstrating that large amounts of capital come from substantial savings by individuals in the economy. (See chapter 2.)

At other times the *FASB Conceptual Framework* distinguishes "capital" from "cash." For example, *Statement of Financial Accounting Concepts No. 1, Objectives of Financial Reporting by Business Enterprises*, a previous iteration of the *Conceptual Framework*, states, "saving and investing in *productive resources (capital formation)* are generally considered to be prerequisite to increasing the standard of living in an economy" (FASB, 1978, 33, emphasis added).[6] Here, capital formation refers to investing in capital resources of production, not to acquiring cash, as reported in the Investing Activities section of the statement of cash flows, the "I" of C + I + G. The FASB thus adds to the confusion and contradictory use of the term "capital."

So now we are presented with a question. If the Securities Act of 1933 and the Securities Exchange Act of 1934 are both concerned with "capital formation" (acquiring financial capital) in the securities market, exactly what kind of capital can be formed in the securities market? It can mean nothing other than financial capital, i.e., cash. And if the Financial Accounting Standards Board is concerned with the production of goods that require large amounts of financial capital, which in turn require substantial savings, how are large amounts of capital linked to substantial savings? The substantial savings is the cash provided to corporations, i.e., the "capital formation," when corporations issue shares in an IPO that is then used to invest in productive capital resources.

The FASB also links savings to financial capital: "Business enterprises *raise capital for production ... from the public through issuing equity ...* securities that are widely traded in highly developed securities markets" and "production ... involves ... processes that require large amounts of capital, which in turn require substantial savings in the economy." Here, capital is cash. In the same document the FASB recognizes that "saving and *investing in productive resources* (capital formation) are generally considered to be prerequisite to increasing the standard of living in an economy." The FASB is recognizing first that capital used to acquire resources for production is raised in securities markets which can only mean cash that is raised in securities markets, and second that cash is not itself a productive resource. Thus, productive resources are not actually raised in securities markets. Rather, cash is raised in securities markets which is then used by corporations to acquire productive resources, the capital assets on the left side of the firm's balance sheet. Thus, capital formation refers first to raising financial capital, cash, which comes from savings, which is then used to acquire capital assets (productive capital).

The securities market, also called the capital market (Sharpe, 1964), is the forum where financial capital (cash), not productive capital (capital assets) is raised. Corporations do not issue capital assets for cash. The issue financial assets for cash. They might sell capital assets which then appears on the statement of cash flows as an "Investing Activity," but shares of stock are not and do not represent capital assets. Capital assets are only physical assets that are used in production. Yet, a Nobel prize-winning theory has evolved that considers stock to be capital assets.

Financial capital and the Financial Asset Pricing Model

"In corporate capitalism, the company was center stage with everything directed towards furthering its success. In financial capitalism it was the investment that was center stage, with everything directed towards maximizing the returns obtained" (Michie, 2014, p. 236).[7] This reality is reflected in the emphasis of modern portfolio theory (Huber, 2016b). In fact, the concept of financial capital in portfolio theory as discussed in chapter 3 is so embedded in finance and economics research that it earned Harry M. Markowitz, Merton H. Miller, and William F. Sharpe the 1990 Nobel prize in economics for their work in portfolio and capital markets theory.[8] As seen in chapter 3, and presented again here in a different context, is Sharpe's (1964) erroneously named Capital Asset Pricing Model.

What is referred to as the Capital Asset Pricing Model (CAPM) is a rather simple equation built on rather simple assumptions that is used to estimate the price of what he calls a capital asset, i.e., the price of a security traded in the market (not in an IPO). The validity of the assumptions is not considered here. The CAPM states that the expected return of a security is equal to the risk-free return plus a market risk premium multiplied by the a factor that correlates the return of the security to the market rate of return. The equation is:$E_r = R_f + \beta(R_m - R_f)$where E_r is the expected return on a security, R_f is the risk-free rate of return (U.S. Treasury Bills), β (simply referred to as "beta") is the risk of the security as measured by its correlation with the market risk premium, R_m is the market rate of return, and $R_m - R_f$ the market risk premium.

The model presents several critical issues that are contradicted by other principles of economics and finance. First, ignoring the fact that its empirical validity is highly questioned, the model only applies to securities traded in the market, not to securities purchased in an IPO, which is the only concern when examining the relationship between corporations and capital, corporate law, economics, finance, and accounting. The CAPM is used to evaluate the equilibrium prices of securities and how securities' prices relate to each other and to the market by factoring in risk. Thus, it has no relationship to corporations and therefore it has no relationship to corporations issuing securities to the public to raise financial capital in an IPO.

Recall that financial capital is cash. It is not stock, as will be explained more fully in subsequent sections of this chapter. Financial capital is used to acquire physical capital (capital assets) as recognized by the *FASB Conceptual Framework*. Capital assets are the physical assets used in production. If, as Sharpe's model alleges, the securities traded in the market are capital assets, what is it that purchasers of the securities actually own? Since the purchaser is an individual, the securities form part of her portfolio and are a part of her total assets along with bonds, real property, art, jewelry, etc. Individuals do not own capital assets because capital assets are productive assets. Individuals do not produce anything unless they are operating a business; they consume. Securities are, by legal definition, financial assets,[9] not capital assets, and a medium of savings. (Recall from chapter 2 that whatever amount of net income that is not spent on consumption is by definition saved.)

Securities traded on an exchange cannot be capital assets because no capital is involved since no financial capital is transferred to the corporation and the corporation is not acquiring physical capital. Capital can only be either financial capital raised by a corporation from the savings of individuals when the corporation issues securities in an IPO or physical capital acquired by a corporation as a resource of production using the financial capital received from the purchasers of the securities issued in an IPO. The securities traded on an exchange are neither financial capital nor physical capital because no cash is received by the corporation and corporations do not acquire physical capital with cash that is traded for securities in the market.

An important point to understand here is that financial capital, money, as seen in chapter 2 is not a resource of production, which both the FASB and SEC, as well as the Federal Reserve Bank of St. Louis,[10] acknowledge. Labor cannot use financial capital (money) to produce anything. Financial capital (money) cannot be substituted for labor or physical capital in a production function. Nor can financial capital (money) be substituted for land. Money may of course be used to acquire capital resources of production, referred to as capital expenditures and Investment Activities on the statement of cash flows, but money is not itself a resource of production.

A second important point to understand is that shares of stock, whether issued in an IPO or traded in the market as Sharpe's model suggests, are not capital assets and neither the securities laws nor the UCC refer to them as capital assets. While "capital" may be ambiguous and exhibit chameleon-like characteristics, there are only two types of capital—financial capital (cash owned by a corporation) and physical capital (physical resources of production owned by a corporation)—relevant to corporations and purchasers of shares. Purchasers of shares do not own resources of production. They own cash (i.e., their savings) until they purchase the corporation's shares. The corporation, once purchasers purchase the shares in an IPO, own the financial capital (money) and use the financial capital to acquire capital assets (the capital resource of production). Yet, a Nobel prize was basically awarded for something that does not exist. While the model is arithmetically sound (although not empirically validated, but that is beyond the scope of this book), the name of the model is completely specious. Stocks are *financial* assets, not *capital* assets, whether from the corporation's or shareholder's position. Thus, the correct name of the model is the Financial Asset Pricing Model (FAPM).

The FAPM is considered only from the side of the purchasers of securities in the market. Therefore, it cannot be a purchase of a capital asset. When purchasers purchase stock in the market they own the stock, not the corporation. They invest in the stock, not in the corporation. Individuals do not make expenditures constituting investment. Whatever consumers "invest" in—stock, bonds, certificates of deposit, etc.—is actually an instrument of savings. In the FAPM (CAPM) the return is not on the investment in the corporation, it is a return on the shares. The Capital Asset Pricing Model simply has nothing to do with capital assets. It has everything to do with financial assets and thus, to emphasize, is correctly designated as the "Financial Asset Pricing Model" (FAPM).

Weighted average cost of financing

What is called the "weighted average cost of capital" is intricately related to what is erroneously called the Capital Asset Pricing Model, and it is equally erroneous. It is also inseparable from the mislabelled "capital" when referring to the right side of the balance sheet.

As discussed in chapter 3 but reviewed here in a different context, the "weighted average cost of capital" equals the weighted average of the cost of debt plus the cost of equity, conveniently arranged in (very simplified) equation form as $k_a = \%debt * k_d + \%equity * k_e$ where k_d is the cost of debt and k_e is the cost of equity. On the statement of cash flows, issuing debt and stock constitute financing activities, not investing activities. The financing activities are used to finance investment activities; i.e., the acquisition of land and physical capital as a resource of production.

Since the right side of the balance sheet (debt plus equity) is not capital to call the cost of debt plus the cost of equity the weighted average cost of capital is wrong. What is called the "cost of capital" is, in reality, the cost of financing as reported on the statement of cash flows, which shows financing activities are debt (bonds) and stock. Yet, the "cost of financing" has been, for the most part, relegated to the cost of debt to finance the acquisition of assets or services and written into federal and state consumer Truth in Lending Laws and even into the California Commercial Financing Disclosures Law,[11] while the fallacious "cost of capital" has been enshrined in the math taught in every corporate financing course. The accurate and only correct term is the "weighted average cost of financing."

Physical/productive/industrial capital: the resource of production

Capital, with no preceding adjective or following noun, is the term used to describe one of the three resources of production, i.e., land, labor, and capital. Capital as a resource of production is anything created, produced, or manufactured by humans to be used in the production of other goods rather than to be sold for consumption. Traditionally capital is the physical resource used by labor, or to replace labor, to produce goods. As a resource of production, however, capital has acquired non-physical aspects such as computer programs created by humans to use in the production of goods. Capital as a resource of production is referred to herein as physical capital for convenience, even though it may include non-physical capital created by humans.

I begin with the works of Marx taken largely from *Capital*.[12] Marx's theory of labor and surplus value formed a significant part of *Capital*. However, issues concerning labor and surplus value are for the most part not relevant to this chapter, which focuses solely on Marx's concept of financial capital and physical capital and how he distinguished financial capital from capital as a means of production. Whom Marx considered to be capitalists and who owned capital as the means of production are discussed in the next chapter. Capital as a resource of production obviously occupies a significant part of Marx's theories of the capitalist mode of production (discussed in chapters 9 and 10.)

Physical capital is anything created or manufactured that is used in the production of other goods—tools, machines, computers, computer programs—as opposed to goods produced for consumer use (Krugman & Wells, 2008). Capital can be as simple as a stone tool used to plow, or as complex and sophisticated as a machines and equipment in an assembly line in an auto plant. Physical capital includes

> implements of work, which include tools, apparatus, and machines. In some cases only one or another of these means of production may be used, or none. 'Tools' are those aids to labor, the design of which is adapted to the physiological and psychological conditions of manual labor. 'Apparatus' is something which is 'tended' by the worker. 'Machines' are mechanized apparatus. These rather vague distinctions have a certain significance for characterizing epochs in the development of industrial technology.
>
> (Weber, 1978, p. 121)

Tools, apparatus, and machines, i.e., capital resources of production or physical capital, are not land since land exists naturally. Obviously, they are not labor since they are designed to aid, or possibly even replace, labor and are created by labor. Thus, tools, apparatus, and machines (and computer programs) are the capital resources of production made by humans (referred to herein simply as "physical capital" or "productive capital").

Marx links financial capital (money) and physical capital. At times Marx differentiates financial capital and physical capital; at other times, much to his discredit, he confuses the two and uses them interchangeably in a contradictory manner, which will be explained in chapters 9 and 10.

Financial capital is linked to physical capital in two ways. The link between financial capital and physical capital forms the cycle M → C → M → C → … *ad infinitum*, where C is commodities and M is money. Within the cycle is the accumulation of surplus value (profit that Marx considers as the exploitation of wage-labor), which is added to capital. Money is transformed into commodities, which are capital, which in turn are sold for money. But the two— financial capital (money) and physical capital (commodities)—are not, and cannot be, identical.

"Money which describes the latter course in its movement is transformed into capital, becomes capital, and from the point of view of its function, already is capital" (Chiapello, 2007, p. 248). Thus, financial capital "is any money thrown into the sphere of circulation for the purpose of being recovered with a surplus" through the production of commodities (Chiapello, 2007, p. 279).

Marx explains that the capitalist mode of production involves

> the *conversion of a sum of money into means of production* and labour-power, is the first step taken by the quantum of value that is going to function as capital. This conversion takes place in the market, within the sphere of circulation. The second step, the process of production, is complete so soon as the means of production have been converted into commodities whose value exceeds that of their component parts, and, therefore, contains the capital originally advanced, plus a surplus-value. These commodities must then be thrown into circulation. They must be sold, their value realised in money, this money afresh converted into capital, and so over and over again. This circular movement, in which the same phases are continually gone through in succession, forms the circulation of capital.
>
> (*Capital*, vol. I, p. 400, emphasis added)

Importantly, omitted from being classified as a resource used in production is cash as explained in chapter 2. Cash is not a scarce resource.[13] Cash is not a resource of production. Cash is not used in production. Cash cannot be traced to goods, either directly or indirectly. Cash has no production value. While some resources can be substituted for others, e.g., capital for labor, an enterprise cannot substitute cash for labor, cash for capital, or cash for land in order to increase production.

The money-commodity/financial capital-physical capital cycle

Marx employed the concept of the money-commodity cycle, but financial capital-physical capital is more appropriate since there is an essential difference between capital commodities and consumer commodities. Furthermore, by itself the money-commodity cycle, or financial-capital—physical-capital cycle is quite inadequate since it applies only to an individual (or partnership) capitalist/entrepreneur, not to a corporation, and omits important stages.

The capitalist/entrepreneur cycle

The capitalist mode of production is characterized by the circular movement of capital (financial and physical) which Marx classifies into three stages. In Stage One, the capitalist buys commodities (raw materials and capital goods to use in production) and hires labor. His money is transformed into commodities: money (M) → commodities (C). In Stage Two the commodities are consumed by the capitalist in the production process where commodities are capital. His capital passes through the production. In Stage Three the capitalist re-enters the market as a seller of his commodities, which are sold, thereby transforming commodities back into money, C → M thus completing the cycle which begins again.

But Marx is inexcusably careless. First, money is not transformed into commodities directly. To transform money into commodities requires the capitalist first to acquire certain commodities in the market—capital goods and raw materials—and to pay labor to transform those commodities into other commodities to sell in the market, which he does acknowledge elsewhere but omits from his explanation of the cycle. Furthermore, to acquire commodities in order to transform them into other commodities, then transforming those commodities into other commodities merely to keep in the factory or warehouse, would terminate the cycle. Marx seriously de-emphasizes this step. The transformed commodities must be sold in the market to complete the cycle, which he does acknowledge, but there are different types of commodities which significantly impact the cycle that he does not acknowledge, particularly in his explanation of the cycle.

Second, as a result of the first, the cycle can only function on an economy-wide basis, thus requiring capitalists to interact with each other. The reason the cycle can only function on an economy-wide basis is that commodities consist of both consumer goods sold to consumers (the "C" of C + I + G) and capital goods sold to other enterprises to become their capital factor of production (the "I" of C + I + G). Enterprises do not, for the most part, manufacture their own capital resources of production. Commodities can only be transformed back into money if they are sold in the market. Here we see the impact of different commodities on the cycle.

If the capitalist produced only consumer commodities, eventually the capital resource of production would wear out and become useless and there would be no way to replace it. If the capitalist produced only capital commodities then consumers would have no goods available to purchase. Thus, some capitalists produce consumer commodities and others produce capital commodities. Marx neglects to consider this. Thus, C must be broken down into two categories: C_C for consumer goods and C_G for capital goods. The distinction is crucial because the sale of consumer goods terminates the cycle and the cycle never gets started with only the production of capital goods.

Importantly, nowhere in the $M \rightarrow C \rightarrow M \rightarrow C$ transformation cycle is there any place for debt—or stock for that matter. Marx does have much to say about credit and its role in the capitalist mode of production, but not in the context of the "right hand side of the balance sheet." (Scholars agree that Marx had little to say about accounting, e.g., Chiapello, 2007).

An individual capitalist, an entrepreneur, owns the enterprise.[14] In other words, a capitalist is an individual (or partnership) who, according to the laws of private property, has an ownership interest in the firm. To be an entrepreneur requires that the entrepreneur have an ownership interest in the firm. Even Hicks (1939) recognized that "The enterprise is where resources of production are transformed into commodities. The enterprise is a separate economic unit detached from the private account of the entrepreneur" (p. 79).

It is her money (financial capital) that she invested from her savings, or obtained by borrowing to obtain cash to operate and produce in which case the debt is hers. She then uses the financial capital provided by her savings to acquire capital assets of production. Thus, for a capitalist the balance sheet is the same—assets equal liabilities plus equity—where the capitalist owns the assets and owes the liabilities. She does not issue stock to the public. As Michie (2014) notes, "financial capitalism increasingly came to characterize capitalism itself, rather than referring simply to the use of capital provided by the owners of a business or borrowed from their immediate circle of family, friends, and business associates" (p. 261).

Since she owns the assets, it is also her physical capital to be used in production. She owns all the assets.[15] She makes all the decisions on how to allocate the resources. The capitalist uses her money (or borrowed money) to acquire (or rent) land, to acquire raw materials and physical capital, and to pay labor to transform the raw materials into commodities to be sold for money, thus beginning the cycle. It is the money, i.e., the financial capital, not the debt or the stock, that is used to acquire commodities to produce other commodities.

It is here that Marx skipped an important step in the capitalist cycle. Money is not transformed into commodities directly. The capitalist cycle, i.e., the cycle for the individual entrepreneur, is as follows (implicit in profit is depreciation and interest expenses for money borrowed from friends and family or a bank, and taxes):

Money (M_1)	→	Resources:	→	C_C	→	Money (M_2)	→
(provided by	M_1	• Land/Raw	(transformed	C_G	(sold	(profit)	
capitalist or		Materials	into)		for)		
borrowed)	(used to	• Capital					
	acquire)	• Labor					

Figure 8.1

The source of the capitalist's financial capital (M_1) is provided from the savings of the capitalist or obtained by the capitalist by borrowing. If the financial capital is borrowed some of the money (M_2) received from selling the commodities (C)[16] must be used to pay interest to the creditors. (M_1 and M_2 should not be confused with the money supply M1 (cash plus demand deposits) and M2 (M1 plus time deposits). M_1 and M_2 merely designate the source of the money.) M_2 is then used to acquire and pay for more commodities to transform into other commodities. The commodities acquired must be or capital goods produced by other enterprises. Thus, the cycle is theoretically infinite.

The corporate cycle

Turning to corporations, Berle (1954) says, "The capital is there; and so is capitalism. The waning factor is the capitalist. He has somehow vanished ..." (p. 39). By this, Berle is explicitly acknowledging that corporations are not capitalists. (But, as we will see in chapter 9, capitalism is not there either.)

When publicly traded corporations are inserted into the money-commodity cycle, the capitalist-entrepreneur cycle disappears, replaced by the corporate cycle.

A corporation is not a capitalist. Nor is it an entrepreneur. The capitalist-entrepreneur cycle must be modified to account for the fact that no capitalist or entrepreneur is involved. Unlike an individual capitalist or capitalist partnership, a corporation has no financial capital to invest in itself. It must go outside itself to obtain financial capital in order to acquire in the market certain capital commodities to transform into other commodities to sell in the market. A corporation obtains its financial capital through an IPO by issuing stock to the public. (Of course, financial capital may also be obtained by issuing bonds to the public or borrowing from a bank, which is ignored here.)

The corporate cycle is illustrated below.

Shareholders	→	M_1	→	Resources:	→	C_C	→	→
(provide	M_1	(corporate	M_1	• Land/Raw	(transformed	C_G	(sold	M_2
financial		financial	(used to	materials	into)		for	(profit)
capital to		capital)	acquire)	• Capital			money)	
corporation				• Labor				
in IPO)								

Figure 8.2

The financial capital (M_1) comes from shareholders (savings) and is transferred to the corporation in an IPO. Shareholders purchase a set of rights or expectations (e.g., dividends, voting for directors). It is now the corporation that owns the financial capital, not the shareholders. The shareholders own the shares of stock, not the corporation's financial or productive capital.

With the cycle expanded to recognize that it is the *corporation's* financial capital, not the shareholders', and it is the corporation, not the shareholders, that owns all the assets (both cash and physical assets), makes all the decisions on how to allocate resources, and assumes all the risk associated with the allocation of resources, we can now examine the balance sheet of a corporation

A corporation enters the capital market to obtain financial capital in an IPO. According to the FASB,

> Business enterprises *raise capital for production* and marketing activities not only from financial institutions and small groups of individuals but *also from the public through issuing equity* and debt securities that are widely traded in highly developed securities markets.
>
> (FASB, 1978, 13, emphasis added)

In the United States and western societies in general, *"productive resources are generally privately owned rather than government owned"* (FASB, 1978, 14), and "Markets ... are significant factors in *resource allocation* in the economy" (FASB, 1978, 14, emphases added). That means a corporation issues shares in an IPO to obtain funds (money, cash), i.e., financial capital. The shares are not the financial capital (and obviously they are not physical capital), nor are the shares capital assets; they are financial assets. The corporation does not enter the capital market to obtain shares; it issues the shares. Purchasers of shares withdraw their cash from, let us say, a savings account to purchase shares in the IPO. Now, the shareholders no longer own their cash; the corporation owns it.

Now consider the following four scenarios in which a corporation issues shares to the public. (The amount, of course, is irrelevant.) None of the cases is likely, but the scenarios demonstrate that there is no direct

Table 8.1 Corporation A_{t1}

Assets		Liabilities + Equity	
Cash	1,000,000	Liabilities	0
Machinery	0	Total Liabilities	0
Land	0		
		Equity	1,000,000
Total Assets	$1,000,000	Total Liabilities and Equity	$1,000,000

correspondence between corporate equity and either corporate financial capital or the corporation's capital assets of production.

Here, since money is financial capital as explained by Marx, Corporation A has obtained its financial capital in an IPO issued at time 1 (t_1). It issued shares for cash. The right-hand side of the balance sheet, liabilities plus equity, is portrayed (erroneously) as its capital structure. Since the corporation has no debt, the debt/equity ratio of the corporation is 0. But equity is not capital and therefore capital is not the equity. Capital is either financial capital, which is money, or physical capital which is a physical resource of production other than land or labor. (The equity, of course, is the corporation's equity, not the shareholders'. See chapter 1 and *Corporate Law and the Theory of the Firm: Reconstructing Shareholders, Directors, Owners, and Investors.*)

As noted, both the '33 Act and the FASB assert that corporations enter the capital market in order to obtain capital, which can only mean financial capital (funds, cash, money), by issuing stock to the public. Cash is the corporation's financial capital. It is not the corporation's equity, either total or net. To call the right-hand side of the balance sheet "capital" is misleading. Liabilities plus equity is not capital. (But see Cooper, 1949.)

The late Oliver Williamson, another Nobel laureate, got caught up in the error of "equity capital" and owners of shares as owners of the corporation. "'Owner' is usually reserved for stockholders [and] a well-developed market in shares permits individual stockholders to terminate ownership easily" (Williamson, 1987, p. 304). But he did not stop at merely designating stockholders as owners of the corporation. He went on to argue that the board of directors is "a governance structure safeguard between the firm and *owners of equity capital*" (p. 298, emphasis added). His argument has two weakness, however. One, he is obviously referring to shareholders as the "owners of equity capital." But the owner of "equity capital" is the firm itself. Two, there is no such thing as equity capital. There is equity, and there is capital. The two are not identical, or even equivalent.

What can the corporation do with its financial capital? Consider the scenario presented for Corporation A in Table 8.2:

Table 8.2 Corporation A$_{t2}$

Assets		Liabilities + Equity	
Cash	0	Liabilities	0
Machinery	0	Total Liabilities	0
Land	1,000,000		
		Equity	1,000,000
Total Assets	$1,000,000	Total Liabilities and Equity	$1,000,000

Table 8.3 Corporation B

Assets		Liabilities + Equity	
Cash	0	Liabilities	500,000
Machinery	0	Total Liabilities	500,000
Land	1,000,000		
		Equity	500,000
Total Assets	$1,000,000	Total Liabilities and Equity	$1,000,000

Corporation A subsequently used its financial capital at time $_{t2}$ to acquire land. Now, Corporation A has no financial capital (cash). Nor does it have productive capital. It has land.

The financial structure (debt/equity ratio) is still 0, but where is the capital? Again, to call the right-hand side of the balance sheet the "capital structure" is misleading. Liabilities plus equity is not capital. While money was exchanged for land, land is not capital and is not a commodity. Therefore, it does not enter into the M → C → M → C → M cycle. The corporation has neither financial capital nor physical capital.

Does the analysis change with the use of debt? Consider the scenario presented for Corporation B in Table 8.3:

Here, Corporation B had at some time in the past issued shares in an IPO, and also issued bonds. It then used the financial capital it owned (the cash it received from the issuing the bonds and stock) to acquire land. The debt/equity ratio is now 1.0. The financial structure ("capital structure") is $500,000:$500,000. But again, where is the capital? There is neither financial capital nor physical capital.

What happens if the debt/equity ratio approaches infinity? Consider the scenario presented for Corporation C in Table 8.4.

The debt/equity ratio is now a million to 1. If the right side of the balance sheet is its capital, the corporation's liabilities have been wondrously transformed into the corporation's capital, with no financial capital and no physical capital, in another fine example of Humpty Dumpty, or more accurately, something straight out of Wizarding World!

Money of course is not a resource of production. But debt is neither a resource of production nor financial capital because debt is not money even if

Table 8.4 Corporation C

Assets			Liabilities + Equity	
Cash	0		Liabilities	999,999.99
Machinery	0		Total Liabilities	999,999.99
Land		1,000,000		
			Equity	.01
Total Assets		$1,000,000	Total Liabilities and Equity	$1,000,000

cash was received when the debt was incurred. The cash received from selling bonds or borrowing from a bank is, like the money received from issuing stock, financial capital until it is used to acquire resources of production at which time the financial capital ceases to exist.

Chapter summary

This chapter has examined various definitions and concepts of "capital" in a search for a common denominator between corporate law, corporations, economics, finance, and accounting.

Recall Fisher's (1906) observation more than a century ago that

> Capital has been so variously defined, that it may be doubtful whether it have any generally received meaning. In consequence, almost every year there appears some new attempt to settle the disputed conception, but, unfortunately, no authoritative result has as yet followed these attempts.

In this chapter I do not propose an authoritative definition of capital. An authoritative definition is not necessary. What is necessary, and what I propose, is a common denominator of the meaning of "capital" in corporate law, corporations, economics, finance, and accounting. The common denominator can only be capital as a resource of production (i.e., physical capital). All other definitions can be ignored since they are not held in common.

I have also corrected several mislabelled concepts and theories. The capital asset pricing model is not the capital asset pricing model; it is the financial asset pricing model (FAPM). The "capital structure" is not the capital structure; it is the financial structure. The capital structure is the relationship of financial capital to physical capital. The weighted average cost of capital is the weighted average cost of financing. The FAPM and weighted average cost of financing are the only logical labels that are consistent with corporate law, economics, finance, and accounting.

To put the final nail in the coffin, so to speak, consider that in U.S. GAAP the balance sheet is presented as assets (left side) equals liabilities plus corporate equity (right side). The right side of the balance sheet is referred to as the corporation's "capital" and "capital structure." (Of course, it is still a balance sheet if presented as assets minus liabilities equals corporate equity.) The capital as well as the capital structure is actually the left side of the balance sheet where financial capital, working capital, and physical capital are reported; not the right side. The right side does not report capital. It reports liabilities and corporate equity as originally provided by creditors and purchasers of shares (supplemented by subsequently earned profit).

The question is *where* precisely does the right side of the balance sheet reflect the corporation's "capital structure?" The answer is, the right side of the balance sheet is the corporation's "capital structure" only in the U.S. (and countries that follow U.S. GAAP). If the right side of the balance sheet is not the corporation's "capital structure" universally, it is not the corporation's "capital structure" anywhere. The proof is seen in British financial statements. Take, for example, the balance sheet of Rolls-Royce where the condensed consolidated balance sheet as of 31 December 2019 presents the left side (top) of Total Assets of 32,266 €m and Total Liabilities of (35,620) 32,266 €m for a total of Net Liabilities of (3,354) €m and a right side (bottom) of Total Equity of (3,354) €m.[17] (In 2013 Rolls-Royce reported total assets of 23,063 €m and total liabilities of (16,760) €m for a total net assets of 6,303 €m, and total equity of 6,303 €m).[18]

It may seem like a strange question to ask where does the right side of the balance sheet reflect the corporation's "capital structure," but the answer completely destroys any possibility that the right side of the balance sheet is the corporation's "capital structure" and therefore liabilities plus corporate equity is not capital. To carry it to an extreme, Cooper (1949), although he's not the only one, considers equity accounts to consist of both liabilities and net worth: "One of the characteristics that distinguishes top-from lower-echelon management is the problem of administering the *equity accounts*, i.e., *both liabilities and net worth* ..." (p. 1201). Net worth is, of course, net assets or equity. That not only transforms the right side of the balance sheet into pure equity, but now total assets equals equity, and more outrageous still, total assets equals its capital. That is exactly how the reviewer of my paper cast the concept of capital—"when we say 'capital' in accounting or finance, we are referring to ... 'the right side of the balance sheet'" (see Introduction to Part III), giving us total assets equals capital equals equity. But equity is neither financial capital nor physical capital.

But shifting from capitalist-entrepreneurs to corporations, Weber (1978) finds it necessary to ask: "what does it mean when we say that a corporation has a 'basic capital' (*net worth*)?" (p. 95, emphasis added). Weber is equating "basic capital" as the difference between assets and liabilities as shown on the balance sheet, i.e., net worth which is net assets or equity. Thus, he excludes by definition liabilities as part of basic capital.

The development of double-entry bookkeeping introduced the capital account into the accounting system, which allowed the separation of the owner's personal assets from the business assets. Yet, the capital account is not an account of either financial capital or physical capital. It does not record anything actually related to capital.

Eight hundred years later there has been no improvement in the "capital account." That is, there is still no relationship between the "capital account" and either financial capital (money) or physical capital as a means of production. The "capital account" shows equity, not capital. Yet the myth of the equity account as the capital account has persisted for 800 years

The reader should bear in mind that the theory of the nature of the firm fails to incorporate any consideration of capital, an extraordinary omission given that "firms" (corporations) are at the core of both financial capital and capital as a resource of production and the heart of global economic growth.

There cannot be a separation of ownership and control of a corporation and at the same time consider shareholders as capitalist-entrepreneurs since according the theory of the separation of ownership and control, the purported owners of the firm—shareholders—do not make the any decisions on how or where to allocate resources. Nor can there be a separation of ownership and control of a corporation and at the same time consider managers as capitalist-entrepreneurs since according the theory of the separation of ownership and control, managers are not owners and therefore cannot be capitalist-entrepreneurs.

A corporation whose shares are traded in the market cannot be an entrepreneur because it does not invest in a business separate from itself. Nor does it invest in itself. The corporation does not start a business. It is the business. Shareholders are not entrepreneurs because they do not have anything to do with the firm. Directors/officers/managers are not entrepreneurs because they do not own the firm.

Notes

1 Review on file with author.
2 Fisher also includes slaves merely as fact, not with approval.
3 15 U.S.C. § 78o–10(e)(3)(B)(ii).
4 15 U.S.C. § 77.
5 15 U.S.C. § 78(b).
6 The Securities Exchange Act of 1934 also uses the term "capital" to mean "cash." "CONSIDERATION OF PROMOTION OF EFFICIENCY, COMPETITION, AND CAPITAL FORMATION. Whenever pursuant to this title the Commission is engaged in rulemaking, or in the review of a rule of a self-regulatory organization, and is required to consider or determine whether an action is necessary or appropriate in the public interest, the Commission shall also consider, in addition to the protection of investors, whether the action will promote efficiency, competition, and capital formation" (15 U.S.C. § 78(f)).
7 Corporate capitalism and financial capitalism are discussed in chapter 9.
8 The Nobel Prize. www.nobelprize.org/prizes/economic-sciences/1990/press-release/.
9 "Uniform Commercial Code. ARTICLE 8. INVESTMENT SECURITIES. § 8–102 Definitions. § 8–102 Definitions. (a) In this Article …(9) "Financial asset," except as otherwise provided in Section 8–103, means: (i) a security … (15) "Security," except as otherwise provided in Section 8–103, means an obligation of an issuer or a share."
10 Federal Reserve Bank of St. Louis. (n.d.) www.stlouisfed.org/education/economic-lowdown-podcast-series/episode-2-factors-of-production.
11 CALIFORNIA FINANCING LAW: COMMERCIAL FINANCING DISCLOSURES. https://dbo.ca.gov/california-financing-law-commercial-financing-disclosures/.
12 Marx's *Capital* consists of three volumes. For convenience, references will be only to volume and page number.
13 While cash may be scarce, as the author of this article can personally attest to, it is not a "scarce resource."
14 An enterprise may also be owned by partners.
15 An individual may incorporate his business, or a small group of people may incorporate. As a corporation whose shares are not publicly traded, the corporation is merely an "alter ego" of the incorporators.

16 Note that Marx sometimes uses C to represent commodities and at other times as "capital." "The surplus-value generated in the process of production by C, the capital advanced, or in other words, the self-expansion of the value of the capital C, presents itself for our consideration, in the first place, as a surplus, as the amount by which the value of the product exceeds the value of its constituent elements. (Marx here uses C to represent capital advanced. Elsewhere he uses it to represent commodities.) The capital C is made up of two components, one, *the sum of money c laid out upon the means of production* [that] represents the portion that has become constant capital … ." (See chapter 9.)
17 News Release. www.rolls-royce.com/~/media/Files/R/Rolls-Royce/documents/inves tors/2019-fy-press-release.pdf.
18 News Release. www.rolls-royce.com/~/media/Files/R/Rolls-Royce/documents/inves tors/results/archive/2013-prelims-press-release-final-tcm92-54902.pdf.

Bibliography

Berle, A.A., Jr. (1954). *The 20th century capitalist revolution*. New York: Harcourt Brace & World.

Chiapello, E. (2007). Accounting and the birth of the notion of capitalism. *Critical Perspectives on Accounting*, 18 (3), 263–296. doi:10.1016/j.cpa.2005.11.012.

Cooper, W.W. (1949). Theory of the firm: Some suggestions for revision. *American Economic Review*, 39 (6), 1204–1222. Retrieved from www.jstor.org/stable/1816597.

Federal Reserve Bank of St. Louis. (n.d.) Retrieved from www.stlouisfed.org/educa tion/economic-lowdown-podcast-series/episode-2-factors-of-production.

Financial Accounting Standards Board (FASB) (1978). *Statement of Financial Accounting Concepts No. 1, Objectives of Financial Reporting by Business Enterprises*. Norwalk, CT: FASB.

Financial Accounting Standards Board (FASB) (2018). *Statement of Financial Accounting Concepts No. 8, Conceptual Framework for Financial Reporting*. Norwalk, CT: FASB.

Fisher, I. (1906). *The nature of capital and income*. London: Macmillan.

Hicks, JR. (1939). *Value and capital* (2nd ed.). Oxford: Oxford University Press.

Huber, W.D. (2016a). The myth of protecting the public interest: The case of the missing mandate in federal securities laws. *Journal of Business & Securities Law*, 16 (2), 402–423. Retrieved from https://papers.ssrn.com/sol3/papers.cfm?abstract_id=2605301.

Huber, W.D. (2016b). On neo-colonialism and the colonization of accounting research. *International Journal of Critical Accounting*, 9 (1), 18–41. Retrieved from https://pap ers.ssrn.com/sol3/papers.cfm?abstract_id=2548742.

Krugman, P., & Wells, R. (2008). *Microeconomics* (2nd ed.). New York: Worth Publishers.

Levy, J. (2014). Accounting for profit and the history of capital. *Critical Historical Studies*, 1 (2), 171–214. Retrieved from www.jstor.org/stable/10.1086/677977.

Marx, K. (1990). *Capital: A critique of political economy*, 3 vols. London: Penguin Classics.

Michie, R. (2014). The rise of capitalism from ancient origins to 1948. In L. Neal & J. G. Williamson (Eds.), *The Cambridge history of capitalism*, vol. 2, pp. 230–263.

Milios, J. (2018). *The origins of capitalism as a social system: The prevalence of an aleatory encounter*. London: Routledge.

Neal, L. (2016). Introduction. In L. Neal & J.G. Williamson (Eds.), *The Cambridge history of capitalism*, vol. 1, pp. 1–23. Cambridge: Cambridge University Press.

Sharpe, W.F. (1964). Capital asset prices: A theory of market equilibrium under conditions of risk. *Journal of Finance*, 19 (3), 425–442. doi:10.1111/j.1540-626.1964.tb02865.x.

von Mises, L. (2009). *The theory of money and credit*. Tr. J.E. Batson. Auburn, AL: Ludwig von Mises Institute.

Weber, M. (1992). *The protestant ethic and the spirit of capitalism*. Trans. T. Parsons. London: Routledge.

Weber, M. (1978). *Economy and society: An outline of interpretive sociology*. Trans. E. Fischoff et al., ed. G. Roth & C. Wittich. Berkley, CA: University of California Press.

Williamson, O.E. (1987). *Economic institutions of capitalism*. New York: Free Press.

9 Capitalism

Six blind men and capitalism: a parody[1]

A group of blind men heard that a strange animal, called Capitalism, had been brought to the town, but none of them were aware of its shape and form. Out of curiosity, they said: "We must inspect and know it by touch, of which we are capable". So, they sought it out, and when they found it they groped about it. The first person, whose hand landed on the trunk, said, "Capitalism is like a free market." Another, whose hand reached its ear, exclaimed, "Capitalism is like long-term assets used in production." The third blind man, whose hand was upon its leg, declared, "Capitalism is like appropriating wage labor." The fourth blind man, who placed his hand upon its side, said, "Capitalism is like an economic system." One blind man who felt its tail described capitalism as private property. The last man felt its tusk and said, "Capitalism is like a social system."

Introduction

The word "capitalism" was first used in 1850, when it was used to distinguish between capital and capitalism (Chiapello, 2007). Marx rarely used it. It was popularized by Sombart at the beginning of the 20th century in intellectual and political circles and became the natural antonym of socialism (Chiapello, 2007). The term was incorporated into Marxist theory in order to categorize the stages of economic development identified by Marx.

Berle (1954) thinks that scholarly studies of capitalism are mere "descriptive clichés" consisting of "little more than a deposit of the verbiage left over from a previous historical age" (p. 9). Defenders of capitalism against Marx's theories, according to Berle, have been content with "reiterat[ing] theories of and descriptions of capitalism propounded by Adam Smith [and] developed to a high point by Ricardo in 1817" (p. 10). Berle then proceeds to "discard and occasionally treat disrespectfully, some of the hallowed phrases dear to lawyers, economists, businessmen, and the advertising fraternity" (p. 11).

Capitalism is more than an economic system. It is a social construct on which an entire social system was created.[2] But the social system built on the ownership of capital resources of production was built on something that has no basis in law or economics.

Obviously, the root of "capitalism" is "capital." But, as seen in the previous chapter, the term "capital" is ambiguous. The consequence of the ambiguous meaning of "capital" is that the social system created by capitalism was constructed, in large part, on the failure to distinguish financial (money) capital from physical capital as a resource of production[3] and who owns financial capital and physical capital.[4]

Even Marx, as discussed in the next chapter, although he recognized the difference between financial capital and physical capital as a resource of production, failed to understand the important implications of that difference when it came to examining capitalists, the ownership of financial capital, and the ownership of the means of production.

Marx rarely used the term "capitalism" (Chiapello, 2007) but rather the "capitalist mode of production." The fundamental issue, indeed the only issue, in either a "capitalist" or "socialist" economic system is not whether physical capital is used in production, but who owns the capital resources of production and how those resources are allocated—according to the laws of private property, by the government, or the "people?"

Capitalism is almost universally confused with a free-market (free enterprise) economy (Derks, 2008), with some even going so far as to exclaim, "'capitalism' refers to the 'market system' or 'the free enterprise system'" (Bullock, Trombley, & Lawrie, 1999). Weber (1978) defines a free market as "the degree of autonomy enjoyed by the parties to market relationships in the price struggle and in competition" (p. 82). There are of course many other definitions but they are essentially identical in all material aspects.

Free-market economies as defined by Weber existed long before capitalism emerged (Grassby, 1999; Chandler, 1984) either as the ownership of the means of production or as a social system. Nor is capitalism when used to refer to the means of production dependent on a free-market economy since even command economies also use physical capital to produce goods. The question again is, who owns the capital resources of production and how are those resources allocated—through laws of private property or by the government?

Unlike what is now known as Marxism, or Communism, capitalism was not planned. There was no "Capitalist Manifesto" to follow or guide the development of capitalism.[5] Capitalism as it is understood today emerged from the coalescence of several historically independent yet interdependent events. Theories of the origin of capitalism include certain elements of the Christian religion as expressed in the advent of the Protestant Reformation[6]; the "invention" of the capital account and the proliferation of double-entry bookkeeping; the discovery by Europeans of other continents and ways to circumnavigate the globe; colonialism as practiced by European geo-political powers; the invention of the printing press; certain scientific theories and discoveries accompanied by a rational, scientific mindset; population growth; a money-based rather than barter-based economy; technological inventions leading to the "Industrial Revolution" in Britain and the United States; and the rapid expansion of overseas commerce.

These events and processes have of course presented questions in academia of what came first, the chicken or the egg, which preceded the others sequentially, and whether one caused the others. But it is clear first that there were multiple events associated with the transformation of feudal/agrarian society into capitalism. Meticulous details of what constituted feudal/agrarian society and means of production are not relevant to this book.

Many of the events and processes occurred independently but more or less simultaneously (although the arrival of Europeans in the western hemisphere in 1492, and the invention of double entry bookkeeping in the 13th century, occurred prior to almost all other events and processes), and some played a more significant role than others. As expected, proponents of each theory criticize the proponents of other theories (when the chronology enables such criticisms).

This chapter examines very briefly the history, origins, and types of capitalism, capitalists, the ownership of financial capital, the ownership of capital as a resource of production, and the relationship of corporations and capitalism. The reader should bear in mind that the theory of the nature of the firm does not incorporate any consideration of capital, capitalists, or capitalism, an extraordinary omission given that "firms" (corporations) are at the core of both financial capital and capital as a resource of production, and the heart of global economic growth (Neal, 2016).

Since "capital" is the root of "capitalism," there is significant overlap between the concepts of capital discussed in chapter 8, this chapter, and chapter 10. Furthermore, the reader is urged to keep in mind the distinction between financial capital and physical capital as a resource of production. Finally, the reader must bear in mind that financial capital (money) is not a capitalist mode of production because it is not a resource of production, as explained in chapter 2.

As with "capital," "capitalism" requires an adjective and failure to use "capitalism" with an adjective often compounds the confusion in understanding what is meant by "capitalism."

This chapter is not a dissertation in sociology, history, or economics on the history and origin of capitalism. Nor does it propose a new theory on how, when, where, or why capitalism arose. This chapter merely serves the purpose of calling to our attention the issues involved in how the history and origin of capitalism contributed to the modern (mis)understanding of capitalists and capitalism, and facilitates our understanding of the inherent contradictions that are exposed when we cease isolating capital, capitalists, capitalism, accounting, finance, economics, and corporate law.

The origin and history of capitalism

Ignoring momentarily who owns the capital, whether financial or physical, the capitalist mode of production is grounded in the use of productive capital in greater proportion than labor (Giddens, 1971). It need not be proven that there would be no capitalism without capital. There would be no Judaism without Moses, Christianity without Jesus, or Islam without Mohammad. We therefore look for a time when productive capital began to overtake labor as the major part of production; that is, when production became capital intensive vs. labor intensive.

The capitalist mode of production is a function of first the ratio of capital as the mode of production to labor, and second, and more importantly, who owns the capital as a means of production. The basis of the production of goods (that Marx called commodities) on a large scale can only be accomplished in the capitalistic form production. "A certain accumulation of capital, *in the hands of individual producers of commodities*, forms therefore the necessary preliminary of the specifically capitalistic mode of production" (*Capital*, Vol. I, p. 440, emphasis added). It is important to note first, that Marx explicitly equates the accumulation of capital and the capitalist mode of production to individual producers, and second, he does not explain what he means by "capital"—that is, the type of capital that is being accumulated—leaving it to the reader to infer from the context what he means in any particular passage.

Marx assumes that the accumulation of capital occurs during the transition from handicraft to capitalistic industry and refers to it as "primitive accumulation" because it is the historic basis, rather than the historic result, of the capitalist mode of production (*Capital*, Vol. I, p. 440). Primitive accumulation is the historical process of separating the producer from the means of production. However, "The minimum amount of [productive] capital ... which distinguishes a capitalist from a non-capitalist economy, is never stipulated" (Grassby, 1999, p. 64).

The two-volume set *Cambridge History of Capitalism*[7] contemplates the appearance of different stages and types of capitalism in Babylonia, ancient Greece, ancient Rome, ancient China, ancient India, the Middle East 700–1800, and medieval Europe in addition of course to the Industrial Revolution. The emergence of the capitalist mode of production, however, coincided with the decline of European and English feudalism (whether one caused the other is not relevant), among the other things cited in the Introduction, and both Marx and Weber recognized the collapse of feudal society as contributing to the rise of capitalism.

In looking for a time when productive capital began to overtake labor as the predominate means of production, we must keep in mind that

> There has been no single pattern of capitalist development ... capitalism is a vague concept that can be applied to any society that has developed beyond subsistence agriculture into a market economy ... . But most of the characteristics attributed to it ... were clearly a consequence of the Industrial Revolution, which, though battered as a concept and stretched chronologically, still has some merit because it ... transformed the economic basis of society.
>
> (Grassby, 1999, p. 63)

Multiple volumes of books and hundreds of articles in history, economics, and sociology have been written attempting to explain the origin and history of capitalism and it would be foolish and futile, not to mention arrogant, to try to explain either the history or the origin of capitalism here. The title of this section is not intended to convey the impression that the origin and history of capitalism is known, understood, or agreed upon. Nor is it the purpose of this chapter to provide a comprehensive review of those works, and certainly not to resolve the conflicting theories of how, why, or where capitalism originated, or the economic or historical validity of those theories.

The purposes of this section are first, merely to identify in an extremely brief manner some of the more prominent theories of capitalism and its history and origins in order to place capitalism and the types of capitalism in context in order to understand the inherent contradiction between property law, corporate law, the theory of the firm, and capitalism, and to understand Marx's contradictions discussed in the next chapter. A few paragraphs will thus suffice merely to highlight the pertinent issues concerning the economic and social issues of capitalism and their relationship to corporations and the theory of the firm.

A second purpose is to understand another plane of the polyhedron comprising capitalism and how it relates to other planes—capital, accounting, economics, finance, property law, and corporate law.

An examination of the origin and history of capitalism cannot be done without considering the three most important authors on capitalism—Karl Marx, Werner Sombart, and Max Weber. All that follow them are either commentaries, interpretations, or criticisms of their theories. Therefore, I begin with an examination of their works. However, before I review their theories of capitalism and its origins, I will set the stage.

First, capitalism, i.e., the capitalist mode of production, is not a function of the actual use of physical capital as a means of production. The capitalist mode of production requires first a greater ratio of physical capital to labor. As noted in chapter 8, a prehistoric farmer in Mesopotamia who used a stone tool to cultivate the first domesticated crops was using capital, and he owned the tool. Giddens (1971) concludes his analysis of Marx and Weber by noting, "in short, in Marxist socialism, capital does not disappear; it is merely administered by society and not by individuals" (p. 204).

Second, although capitalism is often viewed in favorable terms with respect to improvements in economic growth and overall standard of living (Neal, 2016), not only has capitalism often been portrayed in negative terms, the term "capitalism" itself was "invented and deployed by the critics of capitalists" (p. 2).

But what the critics of capitalism were criticizing was not the actual use of capital as a resource of production, but the ownership of the capital resources of production and the social system constructed based on the ownership of capital resources of production which they attributed, incorrectly as I explain in this chapter, to capitalists. And this is a fundamental error committed by both those who condemn capitalism, and those who extol it—the means of production are not owned by capitalists. By property law and corporate law the means of production (i.e., the physical capital) are owned by corporations, not capitalists and not the owners of the shares of corporations (see chapter 1).

Third,

> Modern economic growth ... began not so very long ago ... . As modern economic growth emerged within a favored few nations and modern capitalism began to take on its distinguishing features, the wealth of nations began to diverge at the same time. Capitalism both shaped and responded to the structural changes required to sustain modern economic growth.
>
> (Neal, 2016, p. 1)

Note that Neal's comments are neither a praise nor a condemnation of capitalism, but merely an observation. It is important here to avoid making moral or ethical judgments in favor of or against capitalism and focus only on what, where, and how capitalism arose and what it means.

So let us begin. Consider that at one time there was no capitalist mode of production (generally thought of as agrarian or feudal). Later, there was a capitalist mode of production. We can conclude that whatever the mode of production was prior to the arrival of the capitalist mode of production, and whenever the arrival of the capitalist mode of production occurred, there was a period of transition—a tipping point or point of no return so to speak, when production became capital intensive vs. labor intensive, and when primitive accumulation became capitalist accumulation. That period of transition encompassed the coalescence of various historically independent yet interdependent events: certain elements of the Christian religion as expressed in the advent of the Protestant Reformation; the "invention" and proliferation of double-entry bookkeeping; the discovery by Europeans of other continents and ways to circumnavigate the globe; colonialism; the invention of the printing press; scientific theories and discoveries accompanied by a rational, scientific mindset; population growth; and technological inventions leading to the "Industrial Revolution" in Britain and the United States.

Therefore, given the occurrence of historically independent and interdependent events we can engage in a "but for" analysis. In other words, could the capitalist mode of production, i.e., capitalism, not have developed "but for" any one particular historical event or process? Can any one historical event or process be identified as a tipping point or point of no return in which society was transformed from a non-capitalist mode of production into a capitalist mode of production? The most persuasive argument favors technological inventions leading to the "Industrial Revolution" in Britain and the United States as the tipping point or point of no return since all the other events and processes could have staggered ahead historically without the technological inventions that precipitated the Industrial Revolution, and without capitalism becoming the dominant mode of production. To see this, I first review the three most prominent writers concerning the origin and evolution of the capitalist mode of production: Karl Marx, Werner Sombart, and Max Weber.

Karl Marx

Scholars agree that Marx rarely used the term "capitalism" (e.g., Chiapello, 2007). He uses the term twice in Volume I, First, he explains the period of capitalism as the time "when social wealth becomes to an ever-increasing degree the property of those who are in a position to appropriate continually and ever afresh the unpaid labour of others" (*Capital*, Vol. I, p. 414). Second, he states, "the constant tendency of capital is to force the cost of labour back towards this zero ... [which] betrays the innermost secret soul of English capitalism" (*Capital*, Vol. I, p. 421).

He uses the term four times in Volume II, twice in connection with its abolishment. He uses the term three times in Volume III, mostly in relation to profit and surplus value. The first is, "the rise in the rate of surplus-value and the fall in the rate of profit are but specific forms through which growing productivity of labour is expressed under capitalism" (*Capital*, Vol. III, p. 169).

Continuing,

> Since the aim of capital is not to minister to certain wants, but to produce profit ... a rift must continually ensue between the limited dimensions of consumption under *capitalism* and a production which forever tends to exceed this immanent barrier. Furthermore, *capital consists of commodities*, and therefore over-production of capital implies over-production of commodities.
>
> (*Capital*, Vol. III, p. 180, emphasis added)

Marx refers here to productive capital not financial capital. Financial capital is not produced.

Rather than "capitalism," Marx prefers to use the term "capitalist mode of production" or "capitalist production." He uses "capitalist mode of production" 44 times in Volume I, 22 times in Volume II, and 184 times in Volume III. A few examples serve to illustrate his use and meaning of the capitalist mode of production. Not surprisingly, much of his exposition of the capitalist mode of production deals with labor vs. machines, as reflected in the section entitled *The Strife Between Workman and Machine*.

> The wealth of those societies in which the capitalist mode of production prevails, presents itself as 'an immense accumulation of commodities ... .'
>
> (*Capital*, Vol. I, p. 27)

This point [the simultaneous employment of a large number of wage-labourers] coincides with the birth of capital itself...on the one hand, the capitalist mode of production presents itself to us historically, as a necessary condition to the transformation of the labour-process into a social process ... .

(Capital, Vol. I, p. 233)

The production and the circulation of commodities are the general pre-requisites of the capitalist mode of production ... .

(Capital, Vol. I, p. 245)

[S]ince machinery is continually seizing upon new fields of production, its temporary effect is really permanent. Hence, the character of independence and estrangement which the capitalist mode of production as a whole gives to the instruments of labour ... is developed by means of machinery ... .

(Capital, Vol. I, p. 289)

Marx was of course wrong that "this point coincides with the birth of capital itself" since capital as a resource of production is anything made, created, manufactured, or produced by humans and is therefore thousands of years old. However, Marx is not considering capital merely as a resource of production, but capital as machines replacing labor as a means of production rather than aiding labor. He was therefore very imprecise in the use of his language. It is clear that Marx regarded the British Industrial Revolution as the actual birth of capitalism:

The basis of the production of commodities can admit of production on a large scale in the capitalistic form alone. A certain accumulation of capital, in *the hands of individual producers of commodities*, forms therefore the necessary preliminary of the specifically capitalistic mode of production.

(Capital, Vol. I, p. 440)

With the accumulation of capital, therefore, the specifically capitalistic mode of production develops, and with the capitalist mode of production the accumulation of capital. Both these economic factors bring about ... change in the technical composition of capital by which the variable constituent [variable capital, i.e., labor] becomes always smaller and smaller as compared with the constant [i.e., physical capital].

(Capital, Vol. I, p. 440)

According to Marx, the prelude that laid the foundation of the capitalist mode of production occurred in the last third of the 15th century and the first decade of the 16th century (*Capital*, Vol. I, p. 510). "The capitalist mode of production ... can assume greater dimensions and achieve greater perfection only where there is available in the country a quantity of money sufficient for circulation" (*Capital*, Vol. II, p. 220).

Granted that early agrarian societies (meaning the advent of cultivation generally understood to have originated in Mesopotamia) may have used capital in the form of stone tools to plow and reap, such societies were not capitalist, although Marx and others do consider a type of agrarian capitalism. The capital (tools) was owned by the laborers themselves.

Thus, early agrarian societies were laborist,[8] not capitalist, in spite of their use of capital resources of production such as stone tools due to the high ratio of labor to capital (labor intensive vs. capital intensive) and the absence of the other necessary elements identified in the Introduction. The means of production in a society characterized by the capitalist mode of production explained by Marx are the use of machines, whether automated or manually operated:

> If in consequence of a new invention, machinery of a particular kind can be produced by a diminished expenditure of labour, the old machinery becomes depreciated more or less, and consequently transfers so much less value to the product. But here again, the change in value originates outside the process in which *the machine is acting as a means of production.*
>
> (*Capital*, Vol. I, p. 147, emphasis added)

Werner Sombart

Sombart is regarded as responsible for originating the thesis that the system of double-entry bookkeeping, first disseminated by Luca Pacioli in 1494, "played an important part in releasing, activating, stimulating or accentuating the 'rationalistic pursuit of unlimited profits,' an essential element in the capitalistic spirit" (Yamey, 1949, p. 99).

Sombart argued that the system of double-entry bookkeeping "was an active catalyst in the economic expansion that occurred in Europe following the close of the Middle Ages ... and in the role that it played in transforming medieval man's attitude toward economic life" (Yamey, 1949, p. 333). The development of double-entry bookkeeping introduced the capital account into the accounting system (Winjum, 1971).[9] Sombart (1902) attempted to synthesize the economic history of Europe, and emphasized the role and significance of the "spirit of capitalism," later adopted by Max Weber, and how the spirit of capitalism and double-entry bookkeeping influenced the evolution of modern capitalism (Winjum, 1971):

> (1) Double entry contributed to a *new attitude toward economic life* ... . The goals of the enterprise could be placed in a specific form and the concept of capital was made possible. (2) This new spirit of acquisition

was aided and propelled by the refinement of economic calculations [which] made it possible for the entrepreneur to pursue profits rationally … .

(pp. 335–336, emphasis added)

Double-entry bookkeeping allowed profit to be put into the specific form of a definite sum of money. It was this abstraction of profit that made the concept of capital possible (Yamey, 1949) because the invention of double-entry bookkeeping was accompanied by the introduction of the "capital" account. Double-entry bookkeeping was used by individual merchants and partnerships to reflect the "capital" contributed to (invested in) the firm by the owner(s). But the capital account was nothing other than an account to show the initial investment, i.e., amount of money the merchant contributed to the firm. Thus, it is not the invention of double-entry per se, but the invention of the "capital account" as an integral part of double entry bookkeeping. But referring to the equity account as the capital account is an error that has persisted for some 600 years or more.

Sombart differentiated tools from machines. A tool is used by labor. A machine, whether manual or automated, replaces labor (Sombart, 2019, p. 36). Work that was previously done by humans is now done by machines (Sombart, 2015, p. 61). Thus, Sombart agrees with Marx regarding the use of automated machines as the dawn of the capitalist mode of production, but emphasized double-entry bookkeeping rather than machines as the ultimate stimulus for the development of capitalism.

Presaging Berle and Means (1991), Sombart (2015) misinterpreted capitalism and the replacement of capitalists by corporations: "A business becomes standardized, i.e., a corporation, when the head of the firm is replaced by a board of directors" (p. 62). With corporations whose shares are publicly traded, the capitalist has disappeared and is replaced by a corporation. But like Marx, he fails to follow through and integrate the impact of that difference into his conclusion.

If one insists that the equity account is the capital account, it must be understood (1) that it is the corporation's capital account, not the capital account of the owners of the shares, and (2) that it would at best report only the financial capital that was originally acquired by the corporation when it issued shares in an IPO, not the financial capital that now exists, since immediately following the inflow of financial capital into the corporation from an IPO the financial capital is used to acquire physical capital. Thus, to continue to call the equity account the capital account is misleading. To refer to the equity section of the balance sheet, not to mention the entire right side, as capital is misleading.

As previously noted, the "capital account" shows equity, not capital. But now we encounter conceptual as well as terminological problems. Both the entire right side of the balance sheet and the equity are referred to as the firm's capital, even though neither are related either to financial capital or physical capital. But now what happens when we consider assets minus liabilities equals corporate equity? The balance sheet still balances, but the firm's capital (right-hand side of the balance sheet) has been shattered by simple arithmetic. A further twist is seen in that if the firm's assets are entirely physical capital, then subtracting part of the firm's "capital" (liabilities) from the total assets (physical capital) still leaves capital (equity). Thus, to link "capital" with either the right side of the balance sheet or the equity account cannot be justified. Sombart's thesis is misguided.

The notion of capitalism has been built on the equity (capital account) of individual owners and transferred into the equity (capital account) of the corporation without questioning whether the capital account of individuals can be equated to the capital account of corporations. It cannot be.

Max Weber

Weber is probably best known for his 1904 *The Protestant Ethic and the Spirit of Capitalism*. For Sombart, capitalism developed primarily as a result of double-entry bookkeeping. For Weber, who borrowed from Sombart the importance of double-entry bookkeeping as well as the "spirit of capitalism," the development of the spirit capitalism was more the result of the Protestant Reformation, especially Calvinism, than of double-entry bookkeeping. In other words, both Weber and Sombart agree that the development of double-entry bookkeeping was essential for the emergence of capitalism but differ over how essential.

However, Aho (2005) argues that double-entry bookkeeping was not a product of Calvinism, but originated from the culture of the High Middle Ages (ca. 1,000–1,250 CE). Double-entry bookkeeping appeared in several Italian cities simultaneously dating from at least 1327 and spread as the result of Pacioli's (1494) *Summa* and the invention of the printing press. If Aho is correct, double-entry bookkeeping appeared before capitalism and there is no reason to believe its use would not have continued and expanded without the development of capitalism.

Weber (1978) defines "capital goods" as "goods that are administered on the basis of capital accounting" which excludes households (budgetary units) (p. 94). "Capital accounting" then is

> the valuation and verification of opportunities for profit … by means of a valuation of the total assets (goods and money) of the enterprise at the beginning of a profitmaking venture, and the comparison of this with a similar valuation of the assets still present and newly acquired. at the end of the process … .

> (p. 91)

This leads to his definition of "capital" as the

> balance [that] is drawn between the initial and final states of the assets. 'Capital' is the money value of the means of profit-making available to

the enterprise at the balancing of the books; 'profit' and correspondingly 'loss,' the difference between the initial balance and that drawn at the conclusion of the period.

(p. 91)

and "the means of profit-making ... are those goods and other economic advantages which are used in the interests of economic profit-making" (p. 91).

Since "capital accounting" can only be done in the "capital account," by inference, Weber is equating capital both to physical assets of production and to equity since the money value of the assets are the means of profit making (production), i.e., capital as conceived by Marx.

Weber (1978) admits that his "concept of capital has been defined strictly with reference to the individual private enterprise and in accordance with private business-accounting practice" (p. 94) and acknowledges that his definition conflicts with how the term is used in the social sciences, where it has been used inconsistently. But shifting from the individual capitalists to corporations, Weber finds it necessary to ask, "what does it mean when we say that a corporation has a 'basic capital' (net worth)?" Weber is equating "basic capital" with the difference between assets and liabilities as shown on the balance sheet, i.e., net worth, which is net assets or equity. Thus, he excludes by definition liabilities as part of "basic capital."

Weber explains the necessity of separating the business from the individual owner of the business for the development of capitalism, which is of course only possible with the invention of the capital account:

> The tendency to separate the sphere of private affairs from the business *is* thus not fortuitous. It is a consequence of the fact that, from the point of view of business interest, the interest in maintaining the private wealth of the *owner* [of the business] is often irrational.
>
> (p. 98, emphasis added)

But he clarifies this distinction:

> The sharp distinction between the budgetary unit (the household) and the profit-making enterprise should also be clearly brought out in the terminology. The purchase of securities on the part of a private investor who wishes to consume the proceeds is not a 'capital-investment,' but a '*wealth*-investment' ... . A money loan made ... to a consumer and one to an entrepreneur for business purposes are quite different ... . The bank is investing capital [cash] and the entrepreneur is borrowing capital [cash] ... .
>
> (p. 99, emphasis in original)

The factory today is a category of the capitalistic economy. Hence in the present discussion the concept 'factory' will be confined to a type of establishment which is at least potentially under the control of a profit-making firm with fixed capital ... with a high degree of mechanization of the work process by the use of mechanical power and machinery ... the concept 'factory' will ... be limited to organized workshops where the material means of production are fully appropriated by *an owner*... .

(p. 135, emphasis added)

Having reviewed the three major contributors to the history and origin of capitalism, I will now examine other contributors. Much of what they have to say is either a commentary, interpretation, or criticism of their theories.

Weber uses the expression spirit of modern capitalism to describe that attitude which seeks profit rationally and systematically (Giddens, 1971): "attitude of mind has on the one hand found its most suitable expression in capitalistic enterprise, while on the other the enterprise has derived its most suitable motive force from the spirit of capitalism" (Weber, 1978, p. 28). But the "capitalist spirit" or "spirit of capitalism," which Weber also calls an "attitude," is nothing more than a social construct: "Any and every 'economic' phenomenon is at the same time always a social phenomenon, and existence of a particular kind of 'economy' presupposes a definite kind of society" (Giddens, 1971, pp. 120–121)—which is, of course the social construct of capitalism erected on the capitalist mode of production. Capitalism is not just a system or means of production using capital resources of production: "Capitalism is a concept that comes from the social sciences, used to refer to a certain perceived way of thinking in an economic system ... . It is not a concept that originated in the world of business, as accounting did" (Chiapello, 2007, p. 276). Economics historian T.S. Ashton reminds us that the changes from a feudal system to a capitalist system were not industrial only; they were also social and intellectual (Ashton, 1968).

Elsewhere, Weber (1978) outlines the stages of the development of capitalism. In the final stage;

All material means of production become fixed or working capital ... . As a result of the transformation of enterprises into associations of stock holders, the manager himself becomes expropriated and assumes the formal status of an 'official.' Even the owner becomes effectively a trustee of the suppliers of credit, the banks.

(p. 148)

In other words, a firm that was once owned by a capitalist is now no longer owned by a capitalist, as later noted by Berle (1954). But it is not owned by stockholders either, as I established in chapter 1 and in greater detail in *Corporate Law and the Theory of the Firm.*

Mechanization dominates the capitalist mode of production. There is set in motion the constant impetus towards technological modification which becomes the hallmark of capitalism [i.e., long-term assets]. The development of increasingly more complicated and expensive machinery is a primary factor in the centralisation of the capitalist economy upon which Marx lays so much stress in *Capital* … .

(Giddens, 1971, p. 34)

Berle (1954) summarizes his previous thesis regarding the separation of ownership and control of corporations (Berle & Means, 1991). The corporation is "incapable of being owned by any individual or small group of individuals" (p. 30), thereby implicitly negating here the idea of the capitalist-entrepreneur. He goes on to explain, partly right and partly wrong, that "when an individual invests capital in the large corporation, he grants to the corporate management all power to use that capital to create, produce, and develop …" (p. 30). It is partly right because it again recognizes, although not explicitly, that there are no longer capitalist-entrepreneurs. It is partly wrong because, as I previously established, individuals do not invest in corporations; they invest in the shares of the corporation which then become the financial capital of the corporations.

Berle correctly recognizes that a corporation obtains it financial capital in the market: "the corporate entrepreneur from time to time had to go into the markets seeking funds: to add this plant, to increase the size of his existing business …" (p. 36). However, while it is true the corporations must obtain their financial capital in the market, it is not the "corporate entrepreneur" who does so, but the corporation. There is, in every legal, economic, finance, or accounting respect, no such thing as a "corporate entrepreneur" when dealing with corporations whose stock is traded in the market. An entrepreneur is an individual, not a corporation.[10] This is strange wording for Berle because he is fully aware that capitalist-entrepreneurs are individuals and that corporations are not capitalist-entrepreneurs: "The capital is there; and so is capitalism. The waning factor is the capitalist. He has somehow vanished … . He is not extinct; roughly a billion dollars a year … is invested by him …" (p. 39). But Berle was again partly wrong because, as I show in this chapter, capitalism is not there either.

Thus, the conclusion must be that Berle was referring to the capitalist-entrepreneur who transforms her solely owned, alter-ego corporation into a corporation whose stock is traded in the market. This conclusion is supported by his statement that seeking financial capital in the market meant "he had to submit the enterprise operation to the scrutiny and judgment of investors …" (p. 36).

While physical capital actually existed since the first stone-made tools, the concept of capital was non-existent prior to double entry bookkeeping and could not have come into existence without it (Sombart, 2019; Chiapello, 2007). But capital as a stone tool and capital introduced by double-entry bookkeeping are not the same. The former is productive capital; the latter financial capital, though it ceased to be financial capital when the owner used it to acquire productive capital.

Nevertheless, with the introduction of the capital account, and hence the concept of capital, rational accounting, the separation of the business from the individual's personal life and the spirit (attitude, construct) of capitalism were born. The spirit of capitalism, i.e., the social construct of capitalism as the ownership of productive capital by capitalists, was based only and entirely based on the ownership and use of productive capital by individual capitalist-entrepreneurs separate and apart from the individual's ownership and use of his personal assets.

Types of capitalism

Types of capitalism are naturally related and correspond to types of capital and the origin and history of capitalism. But there are actually no "types" of capitalism, contrary to what other authors suggest. For example, Chandler (1984):

> In the late nineteenth and early twentieth centuries, a *new type of capitalism* emerged. It differed from traditional *personal capitalism* in that basic decisions concerning the production and distribution of goods and services were made by ... managers who had little or no equity ownership in the enterprises they operated.
>
> (p. 473, emphases added)

Neal (2016) asks, "What are the salient features of modern capitalism?" He identifies four elements common to all types of capitalism: private property, enforceable contracts, markets with responsive prices (presumably "free markets" and including capital markets), and supportive governments. He recognizes that capital as a resource of production is embodied in each of the four elements and goes on to explain that capital must be long-lived (what in accounting is referred to as "long-term assets") and productive (p. 2) By definition that excludes financial capital (money) since financial capital is not a long-lived asset and is not productive (see chapter 2).

Neal notes that scholarly literature has described several types of capitalism, including agrarian capitalism, industrial capitalism, financial capitalism, monopoly capitalism, state capitalism, and crony capitalism. One important type of capitalism omitted by Neal is welfare capitalism that Hicks and Kenworthy (2003) and Esping-Andersen (1999) categorize as socialist (social democratic), liberal (residual), and conservative (corporatist). Another type of capitalism that Neal omits is corporate capitalism (Smith, 1965), although it can be considered as subsumed under industrial capitalism or conservative/corporatist capitalism. Amin (2013) refers to "contemporary capitalism," "historic capitalism," and "abstract capitalism." Chandler (1984) refers to personal capitalism, family capitalism, group enterprise capitalism, and managerial capitalism.

Weber (1978) refers to political capitalism, trade capitalism, rational capitalism, market capitalism, industrial capitalism, colonial capitalism, early, ancient, modern, slave capitalism, bourgeois capitalism, mercantilistic capitalism, imperialist capitalism, patrimonial capitalism, which had existed everywhere in Antiquity and the Middle Ages of east and west with only a few interruptions, robber capitalism, and routinized capitalism.

While one may find justification for detecting, in one context or another, all the types and forms of capitalism discussed in the previous paragraphs, only two types of capitalism correspond to the types of capital identified in chapter 8, and only one type of capitalism can be said correspond to the common denominator of capitalism, economics, finance, investment, accounting, property law, and corporate law—the physical capital as the resource of production.

I have previously alluded to financial capitalism and industrial capitalism. Relevant to the purposes of this book and consistent with financial (money) capital and industrial (physical) capital as a resource of production are financial capitalism and industrial capitalism which is what most people think of when they hear the term "capitalism" as it refers to privately owned capital as a resource of production. Yet, there is only one type of capitalism. While "capitalism" has acquired many adjectives on its journey to the present, thus requiring frequent clarification in this book, those adjectives serve only to detract from a full understanding of capitalism as found in history, sociology, corporate law, economics, finance, and accounting.

Financial capitalism

Financial capitalism is a function of financial capital. But does financial capitalism actually exist? Is financial capitalism actually a social and economic system constructed from the private ownership of the means of production?

Financial capital is important, but its importance should not be mistaken for capital. As seen in chapters 3 and 8, securities laws are concerned with financial capital, the funds that corporations raise when they issue securities to the public in an IPO. The entire intent of the securities laws is to keep the capital markets functioning efficiently, thus reflecting the importance of financial capital.

Michie (2014) considers financial capitalism as the dominant economic system in the nineteenth century: "What made securities central to financial capitalism was the growing importance of joint-stock companies … . It was in the nineteenth century that joint-stock companies began go play a central role in economic activity" (p. 235), which Marx was well aware of.

Importantly, "In financial capitalism the investment became center stage, with everything directed towards maximizing the returns obtained from the security" (p. 236). But the return from the security is not directly correlated to the performance of the company, but to the movement of the price of the security in the market according to the Financial Asset Pricing Model. (See chapter 8.) Thus, "financial capitalism increasingly came to characterize capitalism itself, rather than referring simply to the use of [money] capital provided by the owners of a business or borrowed from their immediate circle of family, friends, and business associates" (p. 261).

Financial capitalism is not capitalism regardless of its label. Capitalism is the use of the capital resource of production and the social construct built on the private ownership of those resources of production by capitalist who are individual capitalist-entrepreneurs. Financial capital is not a resource of production. It produces nothing. Financial capital is not owned by individual capitalist-entrepreneurs. It is owned by corporations.

Productive/industrial capitalism

Just as financial capitalism is a function of financial capital, productive capitalism is a function of productive capital; i.e. capital resources of production. Productive capital has existed for thousands of years, beginning with simple stone tools. Then, with the advent of factories, mere productive capital was transformed into industrial capital by capitalists, and thus into industrial capitalism. However, the industrial capitalists were individual capitalist-entrepreneurs.

Industrial capitalism is what most people think of when they think of capitalism, the heart and soul of Marx's capitalistic mode of production, with the United States as the penultimate standard of the capitalist spirit even though it first appeared in England. The roots of industrial capitalism had its beginnings in the Industrial Revolution.

Industrial enterprise requires, among other things, an organization of wage-labor and which depends upon the possibility of correct calculations. Industrial capitalism requires "the continuity, trustworthiness and objectivity of the legal order, and on the rational, predictable functioning of legal and administrative agencies" (Weber, 1978, p. 1095), in other words, industrial capitalism requires a concomitant supporting social structure.

Industrial or productive capitalism consists first and foremost of physical capital in the form of machines in factories as the means of production. Second, industrial capitalism requires private ownership of the capital as the means of production and the use of wage-labor. Third, related to the second, it requires ownership of the financial capital by the same owners as the means of capital as a means of production in order to acquire productive capital. Corporations fail this test.

"Industrial" and "productive" capitalism are legitimate adjectives provided that individual capitalist-entrepreneurs are the owners of the industrial and productive capital. The adjectives cease to be legitimate when corporations are the owners of the industrial and productive capital.

Corporate capitalism

"Corporate capitalism" has become a popular term in the literature. It is included here only for the purpose of proving there is no such thing as corporate capitalism.

Marx admits that he is well aware not only of the relationship of corporations to the capitalist mode of production, but also of the nature and role of stock exchanges:

> *The stock-company business*, which *represents the abolition of capitalist private industry* on the basis of the capitalist system itself *and destroys private industry* as it expands and invades new spheres of production ... . Since property here exists in the form of stock, its movement and transfer become purely a result of gambling on the stock exchange, where the little fish are swallowed by the sharks and the lambs by the stock-exchange wolves. There is antagonism against the old form in the stock companies, in which social means of production appear as private property; but the conversion to the form of stock still remains ensnared in the trammels of *capitalism*; hence, instead of overcoming the antithesis between the character of wealth as social and as private wealth, *the stock companies merely develop it in a new form*.
>
> (*Capital*, Vol. III, p. 317, emphases added)

Unfortunately, he stops short of following his awareness that corporations represent the abolition of capitalist private industry that destroy private industry to its obvious and logical conclusion. His failure thus undermines his entire thesis.

"Corporate capitalism" as developed in the United States encompassed the "private ownership of the means of production, increased participation of the state in the political economy, centralizaton of the major institutions, imperialism, efficiency, and functionalism" and was a transition from traditional *laissez-faire* between 1870 and 1900 (Smith, 1965, p. 401). But all of this could be, and has been, done without corporations, in particular corporations whose shares are traded on an exchange.

Perrow (2002) traces the beginning of corporate capitalism back to 1837 when Connecticut became the first state to allow incorporation by registration rather than by special charter. Johnson (2010), on the other hand, suggests the foundations of corporate capitalism are found in 19th-century Britain.

The key to corporate capitalism is what Johnson calls "companification," which is "the substitution of an impersonal corporate legal entity for the sole proprietorship or partnership [which] has long been seen by economic analysts and commentators as *the* defining element of modern capitalism" (p. 106, emphasis in original). While it is true that impersonal corporate legal entities have been substituted for the sole proprietorship or partnership capitalist-entrepreneur, that substitution destroys the concept and meaning of capitalist and capitalism.

According to Smith (1965), "corporate capitalism" was the progeny of American ideological sociologists. Charter members and presidents of the American Sociological Association were "dedicated capitalists in their ideologies" who "recommended capitalism, but the corporate form" (p. 402). Noteworthy is Smith's assessment that

> The impending and imminent threats to the essential nature of the capitalist system served as a very strong impetus to the development of

sociology. Sociology as part of the general movement endeavoring to reform and maintain capitalism provided an ideological justification for the corporate form of capitalism.

(p. 415)

Furthermore,

> Sociology, serving from its inception as the *avant garde* of the corporate reality, prepared the sketchy and rough blueprint for the total transformation of man into an extension of that system if and when corporate capitalism became the established reality.

(p. 416)

Once the term "corporate capitalism" was created it was assumed that corporate capitalism actually exists. It was (and is) accepted as a given, with no regard to corporate law or property law, propagated through the decades with no critical analysis of the legitimacy of the underlying assumptions. However, there are several insurmountable problems inherent in the theory of corporate capitalism.

The first and most important problem is that there is no such thing as "corporate capitalism." Financial capitalism is a function of financial capital. Productive capitalism is a function of productive capital. But "corporate capitalism" would make corporate capitalism a function of corporate capital, which does not make sense.

A second problem which infects almost every work addressing corporation and shareholder relationships which has been referred to several times in this book and explained more fully in *Corporate Law and the Theory of the Firm: Reconstructing Corporations, Shareholders, Directors, Owners, and Investors*, is the mistaken assumption that owners of the shares of a corporation own the corporation, extending into the even more egregiously mistaken assumptions that shareholders own the assets of the corporation (including either as beneficial owners or residual owners), and directors are agents of shareholders.

Regardless whether "corporate capitalism" originated in the U.S. or Britain, what all who adhere to the notion of corporate capitalism have in common is their substitution of capitalist- entrepreneurs with corporations. But if we attempt to substitute capitalist/-entrepreneurs with corporations we are confronted with the Humpty Dumpty problem, which brings us no closer to understanding capitalism.[11] "Corporate capitalism" simply has no meaning.

Capitalism is a social system consisting of capital as the means of production and the ownership of capital by individual capitalist-entrepreneurs. There simply is no such thing as "corporate capitalism," which Marx himself concedes: "To be a capitalist, is to have not only a *purely personal*, but a social status in production" (*Manifesto*, p. 23). Corporations can have no "spirit of capitalism," no "attitude," a necessary element of the social system of capitalism. Corporations can have no ideologies.

Capitalism, corporations, and the theory of the firm

The theory of the nature of the firm does not incorporate any consideration of capital, capitalists, or capitalism. The theory of the firm is based principally on the separation of ownership and control and directors as agents of shareholders. If shareholders own, but do not control, the corporation, they cannot be capitalists because they do not direct the allocation of capital resources. It is the corporation that owns the capital resources of production, not shareholders. Neither shareholders nor directors/officers/managers are capitalist-entrepreneurs. Therefore, the theory of the firm cannot accommodate capital, capitalists, or capitalism.

Even the new entrant into the theory of the firm—incomplete contracts—avoids capitalism. Incomplete contracts cannot be reconciled with the existence of enforceable contracts which is a pre- and co-requisite of capitalism (Neal, 2016).

Chapter summary

In this chapter I reviewed theories of the origins and history of capitalism and the types of capitalism and concluded that there is only one type of capitalism.

Recall from the discussion in this chapter that capitalists are entrepreneurs. The entrepreneur-capitalist owns the firm and all the assets, specifically the financial capital and the capital resources of production, and hires all the wage-labor. However, now it is the corporation whose shares are traded in the market that owns all the assets, the financial capital and the physical capital as a resource of production, and that hires the wage-labor.

Berle (1954) said, "The capital is there; and so is capitalism. The waning factor is the capitalist. He has somehow vanished … ." Some fifty years later, Levy (2014) claimed, "Today the capitalist is there, and so is capitalism. The waning factor is the capital" (pp. 212–213). But contrary to both Berle and Levy, the capital is there, but there is neither capitalist nor capitalism.

There would be no spirit of capitalism, no industrial capitalism, absent capital resources of production. There would be no social construct of a capitalist society. It is capital as a resource of production that is the common denominator between corporate law, economics, finance, investment, and accounting.

Both Marx and Sombart were well aware of corporations and the stock market, and their role in economic activity. Writing in 1913 Sombart warns us that

it is a matter of common knowledge that the Stock Exchange in Modern time is becoming more and more the heart of all economic activities.

With the fuller development of capitalism this was only to be expected ... . From the 19th century to the present the stock market dominates all economic activities.

(Sombart, 2015, pp. 61, 83)

Corporations whose stock is traded publicly rendered capitalism extinct. Once a corporation issues stock to the public, even if originally the corporation was owned by a single person or small group of people, the individual capitalist-entrepreneur ceases to exist.

Capitalists are extinct, and thus, so is capitalism. Perhaps, to paraphrase Prince, it should be called "the system formerly known as capitalism."[12]

Notes

1 *Six Blind Men and an Elephant.* https://en.wikipedia.org/wiki/Blind_men_and_an_elephant.
2 See *Corporate Law and the Theory of the Firm: Reconstructing Corporations, Directors, Owners, and Investors.*
3 Since "capital" by itself is ambiguous, I will use "physical capital" to mean the long-term assets created by humans (machines, tools) to be used by labor to produce goods. For convenience, "physical capital" includes intangible assets such as computer programs. See chapter 2.
4 The social system constructed by capitalism is also the result of the contradictions of property law, agency law, contract law, and corporate law as explained in *Corporate Law and the Theory of the Firm: Reconstructing Corporations, Directors, Owners, and Investors.*
5 Recently, two publications have appeared purporting to be "capitalist manifestos" which are nothing more than an apology (in the theological sense) for capitalism.
6 Aho (2005) presents a compelling argument that elements of capitalism existed in Italian (and therefore Catholic) cities prior to the Protestant Reformation.
7 *Cambridge History of Capitalism*, Vols. I and II, Ed. Larry Neal and Jeffrey G. Williamson. Cambridge: Cambridge University Press.
8 Socialism (or Marxism) is only on the other side of the continuum of capitalism when social constructs and who owns the means of production are considered. When considering the actual means of production the ends of the continuum are "laborist" and capitalist.
9 Obviously, there is more than one capital account—common stock, preferred stock, etc. For convenience all capital accounts are simply referred to as "the capital account."
10 See any standard English dictionary; e.g., Oxford Reference. www.oxfordreference.com/view/10.1093/oi/authority.20110803095753147.
11 If one insists that the corporation has replaced the capitalist/entrepreneur, then it must be conceded that shareholders do not own the corporation or its resources. That would then render void the argument of separation of ownership and control and directors as agents of shareholders. Corporate capitalism and the separation of ownership and control are mutually exclusive.
12 Prince Rogers Nelson was an American musician who went by the stage name of "Prince." In a contract dispute with Warner Bros. he changed his stage name to "The Artist Formerly Known As Prince." Prince. https://en.wikipedia.org/wiki/Prince_(musician).

Bibliography

Aho, J. (2005). *Confession and bookkeeping.* Albany, NY: State University of New York Press.

Amin, S. (2013). *The implosion of contemporary capitalism.* New York: Monthly Review Press.

Ashton, T.S. (1968). *The Industrial Revolution: 1760–1830.* Oxford: Oxford University Press.

Berle, A.A., Jr. (1954). *The 20th century capitalist revolution.* New York: Harcourt Brace & World.

Berle, A.A., & Means, G.C. (1991). *The modern corporation and private property* (2nd ed.). New York: Routledge.

Bullock, A., Trombley, S., & Lawrie, A. (Eds.). (1999). *The new Fontana dictionary of modern thought.* London: HarperCollins.

Chandler, A.D., Jr. (1984). The emergence of managerial capitalism. *Business History Review,* 58 (4), 473–503. doi:10.2307/3114162.

Chiapello, E. (2007). Accounting and the birth of the notion of capitalism. *Critical Perspectives on Accounting,* 18, 263–296. doi:10.1016/j.cpa.2005.11.012.

Derks, H. (2008). Religion, capitalism and the rise of double-entry bookkeeping. *Accounting, Business & Financial History,* 18 (2), 187–213. doi:10.1080/09585200802058735.

Esping-Andersen, G. (1990). *The three worlds of welfare capitalism.* Cambridge: Polity Press.

Giddens, A. (1970). Marx, Weber, and the development of capitalism. *Sociology,* 4 (3), 289–310. doi:10.1177/003803857000400301.

Giddens, A. (1971). *Capitalism and modern social theory: An analysis of the writings of Marx, Durkheim, and Max Weber.* Cambridge: Cambridge University Press.

Grassby, R. (1999). *The idea of capitalism before the Industrial Revolution.* New York: Rohman & Littlefield.

Hicks, A. & Kenworthy, L. (2003). Varieties of welfare capitalism. *Socio-Economic Review,* 1 (1), 27–61. doi:10.1093/soceco/1.1.27.

Huber, W.D. (2020). *Corporate law and the theory of the firm: Reconstructing shareholders, directors, owners, and investors.* London: Routledge.

Johnson, P. (2010). *Making the market: Victorian origins of corporate capitalism.* Cambridge: Cambridge University Press.

Levy, J. (2014). Accounting for profit and the history of capital. *Critical Historical Studies,* 1 (2), 171–214. Retrieved from www.jstor.org/stable/10.1086/677977.

Marx, K. (1990). *Capital: A critique of political economy,* 3 volumes. London: Penguin Classics.

Milios, J. (2018). *The origins of capitalism as a social system: the prevalence of an aleatory encounter.* London: Routledge.

Michie, R. (2014). The rise of capitalism from ancient origins to 1948. In L. Neal & J. G. Williamson (Eds.), *The Cambridge history of capitalism,* Vol. 2, pp. 230–263. Cambridge: Cambridge University Press.

Neal, L. (2016). Introduction. In L. Neal & J.G. Williamson (Eds.), *The Cambridge history of capitalism,* Vol. 1, pp. 1–23. Cambridge: Cambridge University Press.

Pacioli, L. (1494, 1989). *Summa de arithmetica geometria proportioni et proportionalita.* Tokyo: Yushodo Co.

Perrow, C. (2002). *Organizing America: Wealth, power, and the origins of corporate capitalism.* New Haven, CT: Princeton University Press.

Smith, D.L. (1965). Sociology and the rise of corporate capitalism. *Science & Society*, 29 (4), 401–418. Retrieved from www.jstor.org/stable/40401148.

Sombart, W. (2015). *The Jews and modern capitalism*. Transl. M. Epstein. Mansfield Center, CT: Martino Publishing.

Sombart, W. (2019). *Modern capitalism*, Vol. 1. Transl. K. Alistair Nitz. Wellington, NZ: K.A. Nitz.

von Mises, L. (2009). *The theory of money & credit*. Transl. J.E. Batson. Auburn, AL: Ludwig von Mises Institute.

Weber, M. (1992). *The protestant ethic and the spirit of capitalism*. Transl. T. Parsons. London: Routledge.

Weber, M. (1978). *Economy and society: An outline of interpretive sociology*. Trans. E. Fischoff et al., ed. G. Roth & C. Wittich. Berkley: University of California Press.

Winjum, J.O. (1971). Accounting and the rise of capitalism: An accountant's view. *Journal of Accounting Research*, 9 (2), 333–350. Retrieved from www.jstor.org/stable/2489937.

Yamey, B.S. (1949). Scientific bookkeeping and the rise of capitalism. *Economic History Review*, 1 (2–3), 99–113. doi:10.2307/2589824.

10 Marx, capital, capitalists, and capitalism

Introduction

Marx's theories of capital and the capitalist mode of production are so important in economics, sociology, and geopolitics that they deserve a separate chapter.

As is well known, Marx was vehemently opposed to private property (private ownership of the means of production by capitalists), capitalism (at least his construction of capitalism and the capitalist mode of production), and capitalists (at least who he considered to be capitalists). It is also generally accepted that the implementation of his theories (and perversions thereof) caused the death of millions and extreme economic hardships such as shortages of essential goods and services for millions more.

In the previous chapter we saw how carelessly and recklessly "capital," "capitalism," and "capitalist" have been used, misused, abused, and confused—and Marx was no exception. This chapter focuses solely on Marx's theories.

This chapter examines Marx's theories of capital, capitalists, and capitalism, as expressed in the *Manifesto of the Communist Party*. But this chapter is not a discussion of politics, political science, political theory, sociology, or sociological theory, although some aspects of sociology are necessary. It is not concerned with the political, social, or economic implications of Marx's theories. It does not discuss motivations or behavior of capitalists and labor, or bourgeoisie and proletariat. Nor is it concerned with Marx's rhetoric regarding labor vs. capital, surplus value, or the exploitation of labor.

The subject of this chapter focuses exclusively on Marx's conceptualization of capital, capitalists, and capitalism as revealed in *Capital* and the *Communist Manifesto*.[1] The concern here is limited to Marx's inconsistent and confusing use of "capital," "capitalism," and "capitalist" and his confusion and contradictions of financial capital and physical capital and who owns the means of production, which, in spite of his otherwise perceptive observations of society and economics, transforms *Capital* and the *Communist Manifesto* into incoherent, confusing, and contradictory ramblings.

The contradictions discussed in this chapter are the inherent contradictions of his use of the terms "capital" and "capitalist," and the relationship of capital to capitalism and capitalists. Therefore, very few of the hundreds of books and articles written either praising or condemning his theories are relevant.

There is naturally inescapable overlap between capital, capitalism, and capitalists, as well as with private property. Nevertheless, it will aid our understanding of Marx's contradictions to consider each separately. Even though the faithful disciples of Marx resent "cutting Marx's work into pieces and discussing them one by one ... [because] it displays the incapacity of the bourgeois to grasp the resplendent whole ..." (Schumpeter, 2012, p. 20), it is necessary to do so here (although for reasons different from his other critics). Marx's "resplendent whole" is constructed on contradictions and false assumptions. There is, in effect, no "resplendent whole." As Schumpeter (2012) remarks, "a long list of conclusions that do not follow or are downright wrong; mistakes which if corrected change essential inferences, sometimes into their opposites—all this can be charged against Marx" (p. 56).

As a reminder to the reader, when I use "capital" with no preceding adjective or following noun I am referring to physical or productive capital, the capital resource of production.

Marx and capital

Marx and private property

The ownership of capital, whether financial or physical, is obviously insepar-able from the laws of property. Since Marx was obsessed with the ownership of capital as a function of private property, I will first summarize in a few sentences private property law and corporate law to determine who, by law, owns capital. Private property law and corporate law dictate that shareholders own the shares of the corporation as personal property and financial assets, not as capital assets. Shareholders do not own either the corporation or the corporation's assets. The corporation owns all the assets—both financial capital and physical capital. Therefore, the corporation owns the net assets, i.e., the corporate equity. (See chapter 1 and *Corporate Law and the Theory of the Firm: Reconstructing Corporations, Shareholders, Directors, Owners, and Investors* for a more in-depth explanation of property law and corporate law.)

Although writing in Germany in the mid-19th century, corporation laws were not radically different from the laws that exist today regarding owner-ship of shares vs. ownership of the corporation. Marx not only ignored property law and corporate law, but explicitly misinterpreted them, whether intentionally or carelessly.

Marx's polemic against capitalists and capitalism emphatically declares "the theory of the Communists may be summed up in the single sentence: Abolition of private property" (*Manifesto*, p. 22). But Engels explains that by the "abolition of private property" he means property owned by the bour-geoisie (ruling class, or middle class): "By bourgeoisie is meant the class of modern capitalists, owners of the means of social production and employers of wage labour" (p. 14). The bourgeoisie consists of individuals who are "the middle-class owner of property" (p. 24).

Marx devotes an inordinate amount of time in *Capital* to explaining his concept of the bourgeoisie and their ownership of private property. Engels clarifies in a footnote that "By bourgeoisie is meant the class of modern capitalists, owners of the means of social production and employers of wage labour" (*Manifesto*, p. 14).[2] "Modern bourgeois private property is the final and most complete expression of the system of producing and appropriating products [commodities] ..." (*Manifesto*, p. 22). Thus, it is the bourgeoisie who are the capitalists, and it is the capitalists who own the means of production as private property. His entire theory rests on those assumptions.

But what is the private property that the bourgeois capitalists own? Marx holds that bourgeois capitalists own the capital resources of production (*Capital*, Vol. I) and capital is commodities. But we cannot stop there. We must consider what are commodities.

"On the basis of the production of commodities, where *the means of production are the property of private persons* ..." (*Capital*, Vol. I, p. 439). The commodities that are produced by wage-labor are also capital, which thus become the property of private persons. It is extremely important to understand here that by "capital" Marx is referring to physical capital, not financial capital, although he does not explain what he means. This is not the only time he is careless in his use of the term "capital." It is also necessary to recall from chapter 8 that Marx failed to distinguish between the production of consumer commodities and the production of capital commodities.

But Marx's greatest mistake is his failure to understand that by property law and corporate law individuals—i.e., private persons—do not own capital, either financial capital or physical capital. They do not purchase, sell or own capital commodities. They consume, and they save. All capital, whether financial or physical, is owned by the corporation.

Marx and financial capital

What others called financial capital, Marx called "money capital," money intended to be transformed into productive capital (commodities).[3]

In explaining "The Circuit of Money Capital" (what he calls "the circular movement of capital"), Marx describes three stages of the movement (discussed more fully in chapter 8). Briefly, in the first stage the capitalist is a buyer on the commodity and labor markets. In the second stage "his capital passes through the process of production" into other commodities using wage-labor. In the third stage the capitalist returns to the market to sell the commodities, which are then turned back into money (*Capital*, Vol. I, p. 15). In other words, the third stage is "the conversion of commodity-capital into money-capital" (*Capital*, Vol. III, p. 190). As previously noted in chapter 8, Marx failed to distinguish consumer commodities from capital commodities.

Financial capital is necessary to acquire productive capital. But money capital is not always transformed into industrial capital. "The money capital formed by means of usury and commerce was prevented from turning into industrial [productive] capital, in the country by the feudal constitution, in the towns by the guild organisation" (*Capital*, Vol. I, p. 518). Still, where money capital can be transformed into productive capital, Marx neglects to identify who has the money capital, merely referring to the provider/owner of money capital as the capitalist. The validity of Marx's theories turn on who provides/owns the money capital, as well as who owns the productive capital. As we have seen, it is the corporation that owns all capital.

Marx and productive capital

Marx does not always use an adjective when discussing capital. Its meaning must be gleaned from the context. However, he does refer to the capital resource of production variously as "industrial capital, "real capital" (to distinguish it from "fictitious capital"), "productive capital" (to distinguish it from money or financial capital), and sometimes "commodity capital" or just "commodities." He does not use the term "physical capital."

Capital is one of the three scarce resources of production, along with land and labor. Capital is anything created, produced, or manufactured by humans the use of which increase the productivity of labor—from stone tools used in farming to robotic assembly lines. But Marx is not concerned with stone tools. He is only concerned with capital as it appeared in the factories beginning with the Industrial Revolution where it was not used to increase the productivity of labor, but to replace it.

The distinguishing feature of a capitalist society for Marx was not the actual use of capital, but who owned it. Marx attributed the ownership of capital to capitalists. Capital, however, is owned by corporations.

Marx and capitalists

For Marx, a capitalist is an individual, an entrepreneur. He describes capitalists as follows:

> a capitalist building contractor builds only in exceptional cases on the order of private individuals. His business nowadays is to build whole rows of houses and entire sections of cities for the market, just as it is the business of *individual capitalists to build railways as contractors.*
>
> (*Capital*, Vol. II, p. 140, emphasis added)

But elsewhere, Marx declares individual capitalists do *not* build railways: "long-drawn out enterprises, such as are *undertaken by stock companies, etc., for instance the construction of railways ...*" (*Capital*, Vol. II, p. 290, emphasis added). He is thus inconsistent in both the terms he uses and the meaning of the terms. But this is not the end of his inconsistency: "in the advanced capitalist era, when *on the one hand huge capitals are concentrated in the hands of single individuals, while on the other the associated capitalist (joint-stock companies) appears side by side with the individual capitalist ...*" (*Capital*, Vol. II, p. 140, emphasis added).

There is no bourgeoisie, which is the class that owns the capital, since there are no individuals who own either the financial capital or the physical capital. Only corporations own both the financial capital and the physical capital. Furthermore, owners of shares do not own the corporation that owns the financial capital and the physical capital.

Marx and capitalism

Marx rarely used the term "capitalism." Marx preferred to use the term "capitalist mode of production":

> The wealth of those societies in which the capitalist mode of production prevails, presents itself as 'an immense accumulation of commodities,' its unit being a single commodity. Our investigation must therefore begin with the analysis of a commodity. A commodity is, in the first place, an object outside us, a thing that by its properties satisfies human wants of some sort or another.
>
> (*Capital*, Vol. I, p. 27)

Marx is quite inconsistent in his use of the term "commodity," referring sometimes to an object that satisfies human wants such as food (consumer goods, the "C" of C + I + G) and at other times to productive capital (the "I" of C + I + G) without explicitly identifying its meaning. Whether a commodity is a consumer commodity or an investment commodity significantly affects the financial capital-productive capital cycle, as explained in chapter 8. For example, Marx states, "the production and the circulation of commodities are the general pre-requisites of the capitalist mode of production" (*Capital*, Vol. I, p. 245), but there can be no cycle of circulation of money and consumer commodities, as explained in chapter 8.

The capitalist mode of production requires the accumulation of capital. With the accumulation of capital the capitalistic mode of production develops. With the capitalist mode of production the accumulation of capital develops. Then, "with the development of the capitalist mode of production, there is an increase in the minimum amount of individual capital necessary to carry on a business under its normal conditions" (*Capital*, Vol. I, pp. 440–441), again referring to productive capital.

There is a direct correspondence between Marx's use of the term "capitalist mode of production" and his perception that capitalists own the productive capital, i.e., the means of production. The means of production can only refer to the actual capital resource of production; i.e., capital. The capitalist mode of production can only refer to production with capital owned by capitalists, not with the actual use of capital in production which even socialist and "communist" systems use. That is, one of the "cardinal facts of *capitalist production*" is the "Concentration of *means of production in few hands*" (*Capital*, Vol. III, p. 185, emphasis added). He further explains:

> In order that a man may be able to sell commodities other than labour-power, he must of course have the *means of production*, as raw material, implements, &c ... . The labourer works under the control of the capitalist to whom his labour belongs; the capitalist taking good care ... that the *means of production* are used with intelligence, so that there is no unnecessary waste of raw material, and no wear and tear of the implements beyond what is necessarily caused by the work.
>
> (*Capital*, Vol. I, pp. 120, 131, emphasis added)[4]

The capitalist mode of production is thus distinguished not by the actual means of production, i.e., the particular factors of production used to produce, but by the ownership of the means of production, which can only mean ownership of productive capital since labor cannot be owned. Thus, "the mode of production determines the character of the social, political, and intellectual life" (*Capital*, Vol. I, 58).

In discussing the circulation of money and commodities (M → C → M), Marx notes that

> some circulations of money may be entirely eliminated, as for instance where the agriculturist is himself a landowner, there is 7 – no circulation of money between the farmer and the landlord; where the industrial capitalist is himself the owner of the capital.
>
> (*Capital*, Vol. II, p. 210)

Here we see another problem with his use and application of terms. There is as much difference between capital and land as there is between capital and labor. But here, Marx, in referring to the farmer as the landlord, also refers to the farmer as an industrial capitalist, thereby equating land with capital and owners of land with owners of capital. But land is not capital and owning land does not make farmers owners of capital. The landlord farmer cannot be an industrial capitalist because he owns the land, but because he owns the productive capital—which he could do regardless of whether or not he owns the land.

Marx and corporations

For Marx a capitalist is an individual. To review:

> a capitalist building contractor builds only in exceptional cases on the order of private individuals. His business nowadays is to build whole rows

of houses and entire sections of cities for the market, just as it is the business of *individual capitalists to build railways as contractors.*

(*Capital*, Vol. II, p. 140, emphasis added)

But, elsewhere Marx contradicts himself. Individual capitalists do *not* build railways: "long-drawn out enterprises, such as are *undertaken by stock companies, etc., for instance the construction of railways ...*" (*Capital*, Vol. II, p. 290, emphasis added).

Marx is inconsistent in both the terms he uses and the meaning of the terms: "in the advanced capitalist era, when *on the one hand huge capitals are concentrated in the hands of single individuals, while on the other the associated capitalist (joint-stock companies) appears side by side with the individual capitalist ...*" (*Capital*, Vol. II, p. 140, emphasis added).

Marx first states, "the various *capitalists are just so many stockholders* in a stock company" (*Capital*, Vol. III, p. 121, emphasis added). But in another egregious contradiction Marx acknowledges that it is corporations that own the "real capital": "latent money-capital, which is accumulated for future use, consists ... [o]f stocks [which] are titles of ownership of some corporative *real capital ...*" (*Capital*, Vol. II, p. 212,). This is not an isolated occurrence. Foreshadowing Berle and Means some ninety years later, Marx states, "The capitalist mode of production has brought matters to a point where the work of supervision, *entirely divorced from the ownership of capital*" (*Capital*, Vol. II, p. 263, emphasis added) and, "this function in the person of the manager is *divorced from ownership of capital*" (*Capital*, Vol. II, p. 315, emphases added).

He unfortunately considers share of stock to be titles of ownership of the corporation thereby making the owners of the shares owners of the corporation and thus the corporation's "real capital." But then he again contradicts himself by considering a corporation ("joint-stock company") to be an "associated capitalist" that appears side by side with the individual capitalist. But according to Marx, it is the individual who is the capitalist that owns the means of production. These cannot be reconciled. There is no such thing as an "associated capitalist" and he offers neither proof nor explanation for how corporations can be "associated capitalist." Corporations cannot be capitalists, associated or otherwise.

Although Marx wrote in the mid-19th century, corporations at the time did issue shares publicly traded in the market and ownership of the shares did not constitute ownership of the corporation by shareholders then any more than it does now. Ownership of the assets of the corporation by shareholders was prohibited then just as it is now, something Marx was well aware of ("the capitalist mode of production has brought matters to a point where the work of supervision, entirely divorced from the ownership of capital"). But even though Marx was in fact also well aware of stock exchanges and stockbrokers (calling them "stock-exchange wolves"), he nevertheless "had no theory of the enterprise and failed to distinguish the enterprise from the capitalist" (Schumpeter, 2012, p. 45).

Marx and the Communist Manifesto

Marx was not concerned with the actual use of productive capital, but with its ownership. In the *Manifesto* he writes:

> The bourgeoisie [middle-class owners of capital] cannot exist without constantly revolutionising the instruments of production [productive capital], and thereby the relations of production, and with them the whole relations of society ... . Constant revolutionising of production, uninterrupted disturbance of all social conditions, everlasting uncertainty and agitation distinguish the bourgeois epoch from all earlier ones.
>
> *(Manifesto*, p. 16)

Bourgeois society emerged from feudalism and in doing so established new classes. The feudal system of industry was pushed aside by the machinery that revolutionized industrial production. In its place appeared giant modern industry led by the modern bourgeoisie (owners of capital). As the bourgeoisie developed, the capitalist mode of production developed, as did the modern proletariat working class (wage-labor). Modern industry converted little workshops into "the great factory of the *industrial capitalist*" (*Manifesto*, p. 16). "*To be a capitalist, is to have not only a purely personal, but a social status in production ... . Capital is therefore not only personal; it is a social power*" (*Manifesto*, p. 23, emphases added).

What we see here is Marx's inability to distinguish the personal private ownership of capital by members of the capitalist bourgeoisie, giant modern industry, and ownership of capital by giant modern industry. In the *Manifesto*, Marx wanted to put an end to the private ownership of capital by individual members of the capitalist bourgeoisie. But capital is not owned by capitalist bourgeois individuals. It is owned by giant modern industry.

Chapter summary

This chapter examined Marx's theories of capital, capitalists, and capitalism, as expressed in *Capital* and the *Manifesto of the Communist Party*. According to Marx, capitalists are those individuals who own the capital means of production, which is limited to modern industrial capital—machinery invented in and since the Industrial Revolution. The capitalist mode of production consists of the use of wage-labor using industrial capital in production and the social system that evolved from the ownership of industrial capital by capitalists.

This chapter concluded that Marx's theories are contradicted by property law and corporate law. Property law and corporate law make corporations the owners of industrial/productive capital, not capitalists and not shareholders. Corporations are not capitalists. Property law and corporate law do not enable owners of shares to be either owners of the corporation or capitalists since they own no capital. It is the corporations that own the capital.

In this chapter we discovered that Marx contradicted himself innumerable times with regard to what capital consists of and who owns the capital. Thus, this is little need for others to criticize Marx's theories. He did it to himself much better than anyone else. For all his years of writing and thousands of pages, Marx's contradictions rendered them all meaningless.

Notes

1 The *Manifesto of the Communist Party*, written by Marx and Engels over a period of 6–7 weeks, is commonly referred to as the *Communist Manifesto*. The final version was written exclusively by Marx (see https://en.wikipedia.org/wiki/The_Comm unist_Manifesto) and thus references are attributed only to Marx. For brevity, it is referred to herein simply as *Manifesto*.
2 Neither Marx nor Engels explain explicitly either in Capital or in the *Manifesto* what Marx meant by "social production."
3 Marx inserts an intermediate stage of converting money, or money capital, into loan capital before it is transformed into productive capital. This does not alter the analysis.
4 Land is not a means of production.

Bibliography

Marx, K. (1976). *Capital: A critique of political economy* (Vols. 1–3). Ed. B. Fowkes & D. Fernbach. New York: Penguin Classics.

Marx, K., & Engels, F. (1848). *Manifesto of the Communist Party*. Transl. S. Moore & F. Engels. Moscow: Progress Publishers. Retrieved from www.marxists.org/archi ve/marx/works/1848/communist-manifesto/.

Schumpeter, J.A. (2012). *Capitalism, Socialism, and Democracy* (2nd ed.). Floyd, VA: Wilder Publications.

Part IV

Economics and corporate law

In chapter 11 I summarize the contradictions of corporate law, property law, agency law, and trust law which is from chapter 1 and abbreviated from *Corporate Law and the Theory of the Firm: Reconstructing Corporations, Shareholders, Directors, Owners, and Investors.*

In chapter 12 I summarize the contradictions identified in chapters 2 through 10 in economics, finance, investment, and accounting, and look at how those contradictions are found in theories of capital, capitalists, and capitalism, including those of Marx.

11 Review of the contradictions of corporate law[1]

Introduction

Corporate law is rife with contradictions. The contradictions of corporate law are evident in state supreme court rulings up to the United States Supreme Court in a kind of "trickle up" manner since federal courts, including the United States Supreme Court, must follow state law and state supreme court rulings of state law regarding corporations and corporate law. Then, once the United States Supreme Court has ruled, state courts must follow the United States Supreme Court's ruling. The contradictions were then woven into the theory of the firm and then incorporated into subsequent judicial decisions, a cycle that has endured for decades and has to this point been impervious to the few, weak attempts to rectify them.

Some of the contradictions in corporate law were alluded to in previous chapters but readers may not have realized the breadth, depth, and scope of how pervasive the contradictions are. Other contradictions were implicit, which some readers may not have identified. Both the explicit and implicit contradictions are brought together and organized in this chapter to provide perspective and demonstrate the chaotic and confused state of corporate law. These contradictions are then replicated in economics, thereby creating contradictions between corporate law and economics.

I begin by first examining the contradictions between property law and corporate law, followed by an examination of the contradictions between agency law and corporate law, and between trust law and corporate law.

There are more contradictions than those that are summarized in this chapter, but the contradictions summarized here are sufficient to alert the reader to the lamentable state of affairs in judicial rulings and legal research.

The contradictions of property law and corporate law

Shareholders are owners of corporations

Shareholders have been cast in judicial decisions as owners of the corporation. For example, in *Malone v. Brincat*,[2] the Delaware Supreme Court ruled:

> One of the fundamental tenets of Delaware corporate law provides for a separation of control and ownership. The board of directors has the legal responsibility to manage the business of a corporation *for the benefit of its shareholder owners* [emphasis added].

Rulings such as these are harmful, not to mention embarrassing to the courts issuing those rulings. They transform corporations into property, which—according to property law and statutory corporate law—cannot be owned by shareholders.

No corporate statutory law makes shareholders owners of corporations. But what corporate statutory laws do not do is overshadowed by what corporate statutory laws actually do. The Delaware General Corporation Law explicitly makes shares the personal property of the shareholder subject to the provisions of the Uniform Commercial Code. The Uniform Commercial Code makes shares financial assets. A shareholder cannot both own shares as their financial assets as personal property and also own the corporation that issued the shares. Shareholders as owners of shares excludes shareholders as owners of the corporation.

Shareholders are beneficial owners of corporations

State courts have ruled that shareholders are beneficial owners of corporations, although it is not clear exactly what they are beneficial owners of. If shareholders are beneficial owners then trust law must be applied. Shareholders as beneficial owners of either corporations or corporate property is related to the contradictions of trust law and corporate law, discussed below. This section views the contradictions from the shareholders' side.

In *Malone v. Brincat*,[3] the Delaware Supreme Court ruled: "The board of directors has the legal responsibility to manage the business of a corporation *for the benefit of its shareholder owners*" (emphasis added). As seen in chapter 1, beneficial owners of property have an absolute right to receive the income earned from the property. Beneficial owners have no control, rights or influence over the trustee of the property who invests the property solely for the benefit of the beneficial owner, not for the benefit of the trust. Beneficial owners of trusts property do not elect trustees. Yet, directors' primary duty is to the corporation:

> the fact of insolvency does not change *the primary object of the director's duties, which is the firm itself* ... . Put simply, when a director of an insolvent corporation, through a breach of fiduciary duty, injures the firm itself, the claim against the director is still one belonging to the corporation [emphasis added].[4]

The corporation-shareholder relationship is formed by contract with the corporation when the corporation makes an offer to the public to sell the shares and the public accepts the offer by purchasing shares. The purchase of shares from the corporation cannot and does not make the shareholder a beneficial owner of the corporation or the corporation's property.

The Delaware General Corporation Law is very explicit in explaining the ownership rights of a corporation: "Every corporation created under this chapter shall have power to ... [*p*]*urchase* ... *own* ... and to *sell* ... or otherwise dispose of ... *all or any of its property and ass*ets, or any interest therein, wherever situated" (emphasis added).[5]

The New York Business Corporation Law provides that "Each corporation ... shall have power in furtherance of its corporate purposes ... (4) To *purchase* ... *own* ... [and] *sell* ... all or any of its property [and] ... To *make contracts*, give guarantees and incur liabilities ..." (emphasis added).[6]

According to the law of trusts, in order to create a beneficial owner property must be delivered to the trustee. In the case of corporations, property is delivered to the corporation when shares are purchased in an IPO. That makes the corporation the trustee by the law of trusts. Yet, the corporation has never been ruled to be the trustee of shareholders' property. It is the directors who are referred to as trustees.

Shareholders cannot be an owner of shares as personal property, an owner of the corporation, and a beneficial owner of the corporation at the same time. They are mutually exclusive.

Furthermore, if directors were trustees of shareholders' property (however defined), trust law requires that directors have legal title to shareholders' property. Directors do not have legal title to any property.

Shareholders are residual claimants/residual owners of corporations

Shareholders have been ruled to be residual claimants/residual owners although courts have not definitively ruled on what shareholders are residual claimants/residual owners of. The corporation's property (assets)? Its earnings? Its equity (net assets)? The corporation itself? But putting that ambiguity aside for the moment, consider what it actually means to be a residual claimant.

In *Prod. Res. Group, L.L.C. v. NCT Group, Inc.*,[7] the court ruled:

> The reality that *creditors become the residual claimants* of a corporation when the equity of the corporation has no value does not justify expanding the types of claims that the corporation itself has against its directors ... . In insolvency, creditors, as *residual claimants* to a definitionally inadequate pool of assets, become exposed to substantial risk as the entity goes forward ... the transformation of a creditor into a *residual owner* does not change the nature of the harm in a typical claim for breach of fiduciary duty by corporate directors [emphasis added].

If creditors "become the residual *claimants*" and at the same time a creditor is "transform[ed]... into a residual *owner*," the logic is undeniable and inescapable. By the law of the transitive property of equality, residual claimants are residual owners.[8]

It matters not whether the residual claimant/residual owner is a creditor or a shareholder. Residual claimants are residual owners. If creditors became residual owners and shareholders remained beneficial owners, then creditors rights would be subordinated to shareholder's rights since a beneficial owner takes precedence over a residual owner.

If shareholders are residual claimants they are residual owners, and if they are residual owners, they cannot be either owners or beneficial owners. State courts ruling that shareholders are beneficial owners and at the same time ruling that shareholders are residual claimants/residual owners is contradictory and mutually exclusive.

Shareholders are investors in the corporation

It is commonly accepted that shareholders are investors in corporations.

An investment is something you expect to receive a return from. But to be an investor requires an ownership interest in what you invest in. Beneficial owners cannot be investors because beneficial owners have no ownership rights. An investor can only invest in property to which ownership rights are attached.

As shown in chapters 2 and 4, from the perspective of individuals, investments are savings. Shares of stock are defined by the UCC as financial assets and investment securities. Furthermore,

> An investment is an asset or item acquired with the goal of generating income or appreciation ... an investment is a monetary asset purchased with the idea that the asset will provide income in the future or will later be sold at a higher price for a profit.[9]

If a shareholder is an investor in the corporation, she cannot be a beneficial owner, thus negating any ruling that holds shareholders are beneficial owners. If a shareholder is a beneficial owner, she cannot be an investor, thus negating any ruling that holds shareholders are investors. The two rulings are contradictory. It is not that if one is true, then the other is not true. It is not that they are just mutually exclusive. They actually cancel each other out so that neither one is true, much like matter and anti-matter.

Corporate statutory law is emphatic that corporations own the assets (property) as seen in, e.g., the Delaware General Corporation Law and the New York Business Corporation Law. It is also quite clear that corporations can incur liabilities. Finally, the most well-known characteristic of corporations is what is known as shareholders' "limited liability," which means shareholders are not liable for the liabilities (debt) of the corporation.

The corporation owns the assets and owes the liabilities. Therefore, the corporation owns the net assets (assets − liabilities = net assets). Since the net assets are the equity, the corporation, not shareholders and not investors in shares, also owns the equity,. If the corporation owns the equity, the shareholders cannot own the equity. Thus, the shareholders have no ownership interest in the corporation or its equity and are not investors in the corporation.

The contradictions of agency law and corporate law, and the contradictions of trust law and corporate law

The contradictions of agency law and corporate law, and the contradictions of trust law and corporate law are considered together here to demonstrate the blatant and inexcusable contradictions of court rulings.

Directors are agents of shareholders

Corporate statutory law does not make directors agents of shareholders. Yet, state courts have ruled that directors are agents of shareholders. If directors are agents, then agency law must be applied.

An agency relationship requires, and is limited to, two parties. In order to create an agency relationship both parties—the principal and the agent—must exist. In order to create the agency relationship, the principal hires the agent to act on his or her behalf. An agent does not hire a principal. If any one of the requirements is absent there can be no principal-agent relationship.

In Delaware, once the certificate of incorporation is filed in accordance with the Delaware General Corporation Law, the corporation begins its existence:

> Upon the filing with the Secretary of State of the certificate of incorporation, executed and acknowledged in accordance with § 103 of this title, the incorporator or incorporators who signed the certificate, and such incorporator's or incorporators' successors and assigns, shall, from the date of such filing, be and constitute a body corporate, by the name set forth in the certificate, subject to § 103(d) of this title and subject to dissolution or other termination of its existence as provided in this chapter.[10]

The New York Business Corporation Law is more emphatic: "Upon the filing of the certificate of incorporation by the department of state, the corporate existence shall begin ... ."[11]

The corporation begins its existence and the governance structure is in place prior to the election of the directors by the shareholders. There are in fact no shares outstanding at this time so there are no shareholders to elect the directors.[12] The duties of directors to the corporation begin when the certificate of incorporation is filed if the directors are named in the certificate of incorporation, or when the incorporators meet and name the directors.

Either way, directors exist prior to shareholders existing and thus directors cannot be agents of shareholders. This presents a conundrum that judges and those who promote the theory that directors are agents of shareholders, upon which the entire economic "theory of the firm" is built, cannot resolve.

First, corporate directors exist before shareholders exist. If directors are agents of shareholders, they are agents of non-existent principals, which is not allowed under agency law. Second, only directors can issue shares. When a corporation is formed, there are no shareholders, only directors. Directors then issue the shares creating shareholders. Thus, agents are creating the principals! This is, of course, contrary to agency law and nullifies the theory that directors are agents of shareholders, which also undermines the economic theory of the firm.

For example, in Delaware,

> If the persons who are to serve as directors until the first annual meeting of stockholders have not been named in the certificate of incorporation, the incorporator or incorporators, until the directors are elected, shall manage the affairs of the corporation and may do whatever is necessary and proper to perfect the organization of the corporation, including the adoption of the original bylaws of the corporation and the election of directors.[13]

If directors are agents of shareholders, then shareholders are the principals of the directors, and as principals, shareholders would be liable for the acts of the directors. If shareholders are principals of directors they cannot be beneficial owners of the corporation. Finally, if directors are the agents of shareholders, then every time the corporation issues shares, new principals would be created and agents do not create principals.

Courts' rulings that directors are agents of shareholders contradict property law, agency law, and corporate statutory law.

Directors are trustees of shareholders

Corporate statutory law does not make directors trustees of shareholders. Yet, courts have ruled that directors are trustees of shareholders. (See, e.g., SEC v. Chenery Corp., 318 U.S. 80.)

If directors are trustees, then trust law must be applied. A trust relationship requires three parties: the trustor, the trustee, and the beneficiary. There are no two-party trusts. The trustor transfers property to the trustee, who is then the legal owner of the property and who manages the property for the benefit of the beneficiary. The beneficiary is a beneficial owner of the property.

Trust law requires that the trustee has legal title to the trust property. But directors do not have legal title to any property. It is the corporation that owns all the property.

Furthermore, if directors are the trustees of beneficial owner shareholders, then every time the directors issues new shares on behalf of the corporation, new beneficial owners owners are created.. But beneficial owners can only be created by a trustor who transfers property to the trustee for the benefit of the beneficial owner. That would make the directors both the trustor and the trustee, even though the trustor-directors have not transferred any property to the trustee-directors (themselves) on behalf of the shareholders. It is the shareholders who transfer property (cash) to the corporation when they purchase shares from the corporation in an IPO. But the corporation is not a party to any kind of trust arrangement.

Finally, agency law and trust law are mutually exclusive. It is legally impossible for one to be both an agent and a trustee. Directors are not permitted by law to be both agents and trustees.

Court rulings that directors are trustees of shareholders contradict property law, trust law, and corporate statutory law.

Directors owe a fiduciary duty to shareholders

As a result of state courts ruling that directors are either agents or trustees of shareholders, state courts have ruled that directors owe a fiduciary duty to shareholders.

For example, in *Loft v. Guth*[14] the Delaware Court of Chancery stated,

> It has frequently been said by this court and clearly enunciated by the Supreme Court of this State in *Lofland et al. v. Cahall, Rec'r.*,[15] that the directors of a corporation stand in a fiduciary relation to the corporation *and its stockholders* [emphasis added].

In *Lofland et al. v. Cahall, Rec'r* the Supreme Court of Delaware held that there are "well settled *principles of equity applicable to trustees* and ... the *fiduciary relation existing between directors and stockholders*" (emphasis added).

Directors cannot be trustees of shareholders under "well settled principles of equity applicable to trustees" because that would be contrary to the laws of trusts. Trust law requires that the property be delivered to the trustee who then takes legal title to the property. Shareholders do not deliver property to the directors. They deliver property (cash) to the corporation when they purchase the shares in an IPO. As seen in chapters 5 and 8, it is even (erroneously) called "shareholders' equity."

The Delaware Supreme Court revisited the issue in 1998. In *Malone v. Brincat*,[16] the Court ruled:

> An underlying premise for the imposition of fiduciary duties is a separation of legal control from beneficial ownership. Equitable principles act in those circumstances to protect the beneficiaries who are not in a position to protect themselves. One of the fundamental tenets of Delaware corporate law provides for a separation of control and ownership. The board of

directors has the legal responsibility to manage the business of a corporation *for the benefit of its shareholder owners*. Accordingly, fiduciary duties are imposed on the directors of Delaware corporations to regulate their conduct when they discharge that function.

The directors of Delaware corporations stand in a fiduciary relationship not only to the stockholders but also to the corporations upon whose boards they serve. The director's *fiduciary duty to both* the corporation and its shareholders has been characterized by this Court as a triad: due care, good faith, and loyalty [emphasis added].

But the court erroneously interpreted fiduciary duty as characterized by the duty of loyalty even though they are not the same under the Delaware General Corporation Law since shareholders have the option to eliminate fiduciary duty but not duty of loyalty. Note also that fiduciary duties to shareholders are imposed on directors by the courts because shareholders are owners of the corporation: "The board of directors has the legal responsibility to manage the business of a corporation *for the benefit of its shareholder owners. Accordingly*, fiduciary duties are imposed on the directors" (emphasis added).

By "beneficial owners" the Delaware Supreme Court meant that shareholders are owners of the corporation which is made explicit by its statement that

One of the fundamental tenets of Delaware corporate law provides for a separation of control and ownership. The board of directors has the legal responsibility to manage the business of a corporation for the *benefit of its shareholder owners*. Accordingly, fiduciary duties are *imposed* on the directors of Delaware corporations ... [emphasis added].

The court did not say how fiduciary duties are imposed on the directors of Delaware corporations. It is certainly not by the Delaware General Corporation Law, which must mean it is imposed by the court. But the court is not empowered to create such a duty contrary to unambiguous statutory law. The Delaware Supreme Court was, simply, wrong.

Another problem with the *Malone* ruling is that Delaware corporate law does not make shareholders the owners of the corporation. It is simply not true that "Delaware corporate law provides for a separation of control and ownership," and nowhere in Delaware General Corporation Law is there any section or paragraph that "provides for a separation of control and ownership." Ownership of the corporation does not even exist in the Delaware General Corporation Law. It is an unjustifiable construct created with smoke and mirrors.

Delaware Supreme Court decisions that hold Delaware corporate law makes shareholders the owners of a corporation, that Delaware corporate law provides for the separation of ownership and control, or that Delaware corporate law makes directors trustees have no foundation in the Delaware General Corporation law and are contradicted by property law and agency law. If, as Robé (2011) and others have concluded, shareholders do not own the corporation, the Delaware Supreme Court was wrong. The Delaware Supreme Court expanded and interpreted Delaware corporate law well beyond the plain language of the statute. Can there be any question why corporate law is in such a state of confusion when courts cannot make up their minds and their rulings conflict with statutory law?

Several things must be noted here. First and foremost, this section of the Delaware General Corporation Law does not impose on directors a fiduciary duty to stockholders. Contrary to the court's ruling, nowhere in the entire in the statute is a fiduciary duty to stockholders imposed on directors.

The astute reader can no doubt immediately see the problem, a direct result of the director-as-agent-of-shareholders theory. The problem is whether the initial directors are named in the certificate of incorporation or are elected by the incorporators at the organization meeting, there are directors prior to shares being issued and prior to there being any shareholders. One might ask, therefore, how can directors be agents of shareholders when shareholders do not exist? How can directors owe a fiduciary duty to shareholders or a duty of loyalty to shareholders when shareholders do not exist?

A fiduciary duty is created when a principal appoints an agent or when a trustor creates a trust. But if it is the corporation that issues the shares, then issuing shares that create shareholders is tantamount to the corporation appointing directors as agents or creating trustees.

Chapter summary

This chapter summarized and organized the contradictions between property law and corporate law, between agency law and corporate law, and between trust law and corporate law. There are more contradictions than those presented in this chapter, but the contradictions presented here are sufficient to alert the reader to the lamentable state of affairs in judicial rulings and legal research.

Notes

1 Adapted and summarized from Wm. Dennis Huber, *Corporate Law and the Theory of the Firm: Reconstructing Corporations, Shareholders, Directors, Owners, and Investors*, Routledge, 2020, with permission.
2 Malone v. Brincat, 722 A.2d 5, 8 (DE, 1998).
3 Malone v. Brincat, 722 A.2d 5, 8 (DE, 1998).
4 Prod. Res. Group, L.L.C. v. NCT Group, Inc., 863 A.2d 772 (DE, 2004).
5 Delaware General Corporation Law § 122(4).
6 New York Business Corporation Law Sec. 202.
7 Prod. Res. Group, L.L.C. v. NCT Group, Inc., 863 A.2d 772 (DE, 2004).
8 The transitive property of equality says that if a = b and b = c, then a = c.

9　Investment. www.investopedia.com/terms/i/investment.asp.

10　Delaware General Corporation Law § 106.

11　New York Business Corporation Law Sec. 403.

12　Delaware General Corporation Law § 106. "Commencement of corporate existence. Upon the filing with the Secretary of State of the certificate of incorporation, executed and acknowledged in accordance with § 103 of this title, the incorporator or incorporators who signed the certificate, and such incorporator's or incorporators' successors and assigns, shall, from the date of such filing, be and constitute a body corporate, by the name set forth in the certificate, subject to § 103(d) of this title and subject to dissolution or other termination of its existence as provided in this chapter."

13　Delaware General Corporation Law § 107.

14　Loft v. Guth, 2 A.2d 225 (Del. Ch. 1938).

15　Lofland et al. v. Cahall, Rec'r., 13 Del. Ch. 384 (DE, 1922).

16　Malone v. Brincat, 722 A.2d 5, 8 (DE, 1998).

Bibliography

Cases

Lofland et al. v. Cahall, Rec'r., 13 Del. Ch. 384, 118 A. 1 (Del. Ch. 1922).

Loft v. Guth, 2 A.2d 225 (Del. Ch. 1938).

Malone v. Brincat, 722 A.2d 5 (Del. 1998).

Prod. Res. Group, L.L.C. v. NCT Group, Inc., 863 A.2d 772 (DE, 2004).

SEC v. Chenery Corp., 318 U.S. 80 (1943).

Authors

Robé, J.-P. (2011). The legal structure of the firm. *Accounting, Economics, and Law: A Convivium*, 1 (1), 1–85. doi:10.2202/2152-2820.1001.

12 The contradictions of corporate law, economics, finance, investment, accounting, and the theory of the firm

Introduction

Although, as expected, there is vigorous disagreement among academics, legal scholars, and lawyers regarding the interpretation of corporate law and its relation and application to economics, finance, investment, and accounting, the disagreements are quite insignificant compared to the two things they have in common, to wit, assumptions, and therefore conclusions, contrary to law—the equivalent to the assumption of the can opener in the desert and the Humpty Dumpty principle where the terms they use mean what they want them to mean, regardless what they actually mean.

In the previous chapter we saw how contradictions in court rulings, from state supreme courts to the United States Supreme Court, permeate the field of corporate law. Judicial rulings contradict contract law, property law, agency law, trust law, and corporate statutory law. The contradictory court rulings are fed by, and in turn feed, economic, finance, investment, and accounting research, and research in corporate law.

To review, much of the economic and social structure of society includes corporations and therefore corporate law. Corporate law is an amalgamation of contract law, property law, and agency law. Economics is the science of the allocation of scarce resources. Property constitutes resources to the owner of the property. Property law determines who owns the property (government, private persons, or "the people"), which scarce resources are allocated to production (labor or capital), and how scarce resources are allocated and controlled—by the market or centrally planned by the government within society, or by and within the corporation, and how the allocation of scarce resources by and within the corporation is related to the owners of shares of the corporation.

Baird and Henderson (2008), both of the University of Chicago School of Law, are insistent that

> *Legal principles that are almost right are often more mischievous than those that are completely wrong* ... . An almost-right principle invites sloppy thinking, vague generalities, and a general distortion of the

otherwise sound ideas that lie close by. An example of *an almost-right principle that has distorted much of the thinking about corporate law in recent decades is the oft-repeated maxim that directors of a corporation owe a fiduciary duty to the shareholders* ... . People who should know better paint themselves into embarrassing corners trying to reaffirm the principle.

(pp. 1309, 1312, emphasis added)

Chassagnon and Hollandts (2014) concur that economists have distorted the legal nature of the firm.

Of course, there are other "almost right" principles such as directors are agents or trustees of shareholders, which gives rise to the oft-repeated maxim that directors of a corporation owe a fiduciary duty to the shareholders, or the more scandalous "almost right" principle that shareholders own corporations.

Ignoring the basic precepts of western common and statutory property law and the legal boundaries between corporations and shareholders determined by corporate law and property law judges, economists, legal scholars, and researchers in finance, investment, and accounting have been indoctrinated, one might even say brainwashed, into accepting as gospel the "almost right" principles that shareholders own corporations and directors are the agents of shareholders.

This chapter summarizes the more blatant contradictions found in economics, finance, investment, accounting, and corporate law discussed in Parts I, II, and III. The contradictions are woven within, between, and across fields and disciplines in law, economics, finance, investment, and accounting research, thereby amplifying the contradictions. The contradictions have, in fact, become the habitus of modern legal, finance, investment, accounting, and economic research and theory.

The contradictions of corporate law and economics

The most significant contradiction between corporate law and economics concerns the ownership and control not just of corporations but also of the ownership and control of scarce resources of production. Like the proverbial elephant in the room, little attention has been given by either economists or legal scholars to the analysis of who owns the resources of production. The analysis of who owns resources of production is important since the ownership of resources of production is related to the mode of production and the production of commodities and thus to the economic and social system.[1]

Much of the responsibility for the contradiction between corporate law and economics lies principally and originally with Berle and Means and with Jensen and Meckling, who, together with their followers, erected an impenetrable social and economic system based on the separation of ownership and control and the agency theory of the firm. Separate from, but related to, the economic and social system that arose from the capitalist mode of production, the social and legal construction inaugurated by Berle and Means, and

Jensen and Meckling, infiltrated court rulings, which reinforced the already unconvincing logic that shareholders owned corporations and therefore directors were agents of shareholders, and therefore directors owe a fiduciary duty to shareholders.

Directors cannot be agents of shareholders because to be an agent requires that the agent act on behalf of the principal with respect to the principal's property, contracts, or property rights; for example, a real estate agent, or an agent for an athlete or an actor. Directors of corporations do not act on behalf of shareholders with respect to shareholders' property, contract, or property rights. The agency theory of the firm is contradicted by agency law.

Marx and Sombart, along with their followers. also bear considerable responsibility for the contradictions between corporate law and economics as a result of how they framed their theories of capital and capitalism. Their theories, although quite contradictory themselves, share the same common erroneous assumption as Berle and Means, and Jensen and Meckling—that shareholders own corporations—but in a somewhat different manner. That is, their assumption that shareholders own corporations is implicit in their ignoring it. By ignoring the question of ownership of the corporation, they bypass the question entirely and thereby attribute the ownership of capital, whether financial capital or productive capital, to the shareholders, thereby transforming shareholders into capitalist-entrepreneurs.

Marx considered productive capital to be owned by capitalists who were individuals. While he was cognizant of the existence of corporations whose shares were publicly owned and traded on a stock exchange, his theories of the ownership of capital and thus of the capitalist mode of production are contradicted by both property law and corporate statutory law. Both financial and productive are owned by corporations, not individuals. Since shareholders do not own the corporation, they do not own the capital regardless of how capital is defined.

Sombart credits the invention of the capital account for the rise of capitalism, which allowed for the business to be separated from the personal finances of the owner. The capital account was originally merely a record of the investment in the firm by the individual owner or partners in a partnership, but which was actually the equity account. This poses few problems with respect to individual or partnership enterprises but creates an insurmountable contradiction when extended to corporations whose shares are publicly traded since it is now the corporation that owns the equity, not the shareholders. Furthermore, the equity is not the capital of the corporation and therefore the equity account is not the capital account. The capital is the financial and productive capital and the corporation is the owner of both financial and productive capital.

Capitalist-entrepreneurs are capitalist-entrepreneurs in part because they are willing to take risks with their investment in their enterprises. In trust law, the trustee is prohibited from taking risks. If the relationship of shareholders to corporations is such that shareholders entrusted their money to directors and directors are trustees of shareholders, then according to trust law directors would be precluded from taking risks. However, shareholders do not entrust their money to trustees. They provide financial capital to the corporation when the purchase shares in an IPO which, were it not for the fact that the purchase of shares in an IPO is a matter of contract, would make the corporation the trustee of shareholders' property since shareholders are transferring legal title of their money to the corporation. The contradictions between economics, specifically the capitalist mode of production and the ownership of the means of production, and corporate law, property law, and trust law are readily apparent. Furthermore, shareholders want directors to take risks.

The contradictions of corporate law, finance, investment, and accounting

The social and economic system erected on the foundation established by Berle and Means, Jensen and Meckling, and Marx, Weber, Sombart and others became intertwined with finance, investment, and accounting research and with generally accepted accounting principles when they accepted without question that shareholders own corporations, that directors are agents of shareholders, that the corporation's equity was shareholders' equity, and that the corporation's equity (or its equity plus liabilities) was its capital.

Friedman's (1970) dictum that "the social responsibility of business is to increase its profits" is based on his erroneous belief that shareholders own corporations and directors are the agents of shareholders. "In a free-enterprise, private-property system, a corporate executive is an employee of the owners of the business. He has direct responsibility to his employers." His belief is contradicted by property law, agency law, and corporate statutory law.

Sharpe's (1964) Capital Asset Pricing Model followed the party line not only by treating the corporation's equity as capital but also by representing share of stock as capital assets of shareholders. However, property law, contract law, and corporate statutory law contradict the assertion that shares of stock are capital assets of shareholders. Shares of stock are defined by statutory law as financial assets, not capital assets. Furthermore, shares of stock are not corporate capital since capital owned by the corporation is either financial capital or productive capital.

In addition, when shareholders purchase stock, they are actually saving. As defined by economics, whatever individuals do not spend on consumption they are saving. By purchasing the stock in an IPO they provide financial capital to the corporation, but they are not investing in the corporation; they are saving by investing in the stock that they purchase.

> All definitions vary slightly, but most are along the same lines. An investment is an asset or item acquired with the goal of generating income or appreciation in the future ... . Examples of well-known and popular investments include the stock market, bonds, U.S. Treasuries and mutual funds.
>
> (Holmes, 2018)

Since a shareholder is not acquiring an ownership interest in the corporation, she is not investing in the corporation.

> In place of actual physical properties over which the owner could exercise direction and for which he was responsible, the owner now holds a piece of paper representing a set of rights and expectations with respect to an enterprise ... the shareholder in the modern corporate situation has surrendered a set of definite rights for certain indefinite expectations.
>
> (Berle and Means, 1992, pp. 64, 244)

Generally accepted accounting principles, that corporations are required by securities laws to comply with, require that corporations issue financial statements that report their assets, liabilities, and equity and their sources and uses of cash. The balance sheet reports the assets owned by the corporation according to property law and corporate law, i.e., the financial and productive capital. The balance sheet reports the liabilities of the corporation, which by contract law and corporate law are owed by the corporation. The equity reports the net assets, i.e., the assets owned by the corporation minus the liabilities owed by the corporation. Therefore, the equity, the net assets, is also owned by the corporation, not the shareholders. Corporate financial statements that report corporate equity as shareholders' equity are contradicted by property law and corporate statutory law.

The contradictions of corporate law and the theory of the firm

The agency theory of the firm is an extension of Berle and Means' theory of the separation of ownership and control. Since I have established that by property law and corporate statutory law shareholders do not own corporations, there is no separation of ownership and control because there is no ownership of a corporation and therefore the agency theory falls apart. Furthermore, the agency theory of the firm and the attendant agency costs[2] is contradicted by the fact that agency law and corporate law preclude directors from being agents of shareholders.

A subset of the agency theory of the firm is the nexus of contracts/ incomplete contract theory of the firm. Elaborate, sophisticated, Nobel prize-winning mathematical models were then created to explain corporations as a nexus of incomplete contracts and how ownership of corporate assets are decided vertically and horizontally. But the theory of incomplete contracts is contradicted by contract law which holds that the omission of any one material factor required to form a contract renders the contract unenforceable. Furthermore, an essential factor for the capitalist mode of production is the enforceability of contracts. Therefore, the very existence of the capitalist mode of production contradicts the incomplete contracts theory.

Chapter summary

This chapter summarized the more blatant contradictions found in economics, finance, investment, accounting and corporate law discussed in Parts I, II, and III. The contradictions are woven within, between, and across fields and disciplines in law, economics, finance, investment, and accounting research, thereby amplifying the contradictions. The contradictions have, in fact, become the habitus of modern legal, finance, investment, accounting, and economic research and theory.

It is incredible that economists and legal scholars, not to mention the judiciary, continue to maintain any legal or economic theory of the firm that is a product of the theory that shareholders own corporations and directors are the agents of shareholders. Such legal or economic theories of the firm have no legal or logical basis, being contradicted by property law, agency law, and corporate statutory law.

Notes

1 There is much research regarding industry structure (e.g., monopoly vs. oligopoly) that necessarily requires considering corporations, but not in the context of who actually owns the resources of production.
2 I do not address the here the faulty proposition advanced by Coase that the reason people create corporations is to reduce agency costs. People create corporations in order to accumulate large amounts of financial capital and to reduce individual risk to a maximum of losing the market value of their shares.

Bibliography

Baird, D.G., & Henderson, M. (2008). Other people's money. *Stanford Law Review*, 60 (5), 1309–1344. Retrieved from https://chicagounbound.uchicago.edu/cgi/view content.cgi?article=8043&context=journal_articles.

Berle, A.A., & Means, G.C. (1992). *The modern corporation and private property* (2nd ed.). New York: Routledge.

Chassagnon, V., & Hollandts, X. (2014). Who are the owners of the firm: Shareholders, employees or no one? *Journal of Institutional Economics*, 10 (1), 47–69. doi:10.1017/ S1744137413000301.

Friedman, M. (1970). The social responsibility of business is to increase its profits. *New York Times Magazine*, Sept. 13, p. 2.

Holmes, F. (2018). Investing vs. speculating: Why knowing the difference is key. *Forbes*, Oct. 31. Retrieved from www.forbes.com/sites/greatspeculations/2018/10/31/investing-vs-speculating-why-knowing-the-difference-is-key/#4e0c584538b1.

Sharpe, W.F. (1964). Capital asset prices: A theory of market equilibrium under conditions of risk. *Journal of Finance*, 19 (3), 425–442. doi:10.1111/j.1540-626.1964.tb02865.x.

Epilogue

The purposes of this book were first to identify the more outrageous invalid assumptions and conclusions of the theory of the firm as substantiated by contract law, corporate law, property law, agency law, and trust law and how the outrageous invalid assumptions and conclusions related to economics, finance, investment, and accounting.

Second, it was to expose the blatant contradictions concerning the use of the terms "capital" and as a consequence "capitalist" and "capitalism" by examining the underlying theories and concepts of what constitutes capital, who capitalists are, and how capital and capitalist are related to capitalism.

Third, it was to reveal the discrepancies between judicial opinions and corporate law, economics, finance, investment, and accounting. The discrepancies were shown to be the result of failing to use terms consistently across fields and disciplines thus isolating each field and discipline from other fields and disciplines. "Capital," for example, is used inconsistently, and therefore contradictorily, in economics, finance, and accounting.

Fourth, it was to discover a common denominator between economics, finance, investment, and accounting that will serve to dismantle the artificial boundaries established by decades of research founded on indefensible assumptions and fallacious conclusions. That common denominator was shown to be capital as one of the three resources of production.

In furtherance of the purposes of the book, I have highlighted the disjointed, fragmented, disorganized, and disconnected judicial opinions and state of research in corporate law (including securities laws), theories and principles of corporations and economics, theories and principles of corporations and finance, theories and principles of corporations and accounting, and the misuse of concepts of capital, capitalists, and capitalism. The book has revealed contradictions in the use and meaning of terms, theories, and applications in corporate law, economics, finance, investment, and accounting.

As pointed out in the Prologue, there is significant overlap between and among the fields and disciplines of corporate law, economics, finance, accounting, history, and sociology. There has been, therefore, a significant amount of cross-referencing within and between the chapters in this book. What appeared as repetition was not actually repetition but an examination of theories and principles from different perspectives that was necessary in order to examine each factor not only in isolation but also in relation to all the others, like a polygon. Oddly, in spite of the overlap, the fields and disciplines remain essentially isolated, with no attempt to find a common denominator that cuts across fields and disciplines. I have endeavored to find that common denominator, and I think I have succeeded.

A summary of the previous chapters follows.

Summary of chapters

Chapter 1 reviewed the basics of contract law, property law, agency law, trust law, and corporate law. This review included the creation, governance and operations of corporations, and the ownership and control of corporations. Chapter 1 demonstrated that contract law, property law, agency law, and trust law do not permit shareholders to own corporations or directors to be their agents or trustees. It showed that corporations own the total assets, owe the liabilities, and therefore own the net assets, which is the equity, erroneously referred to as capital.

Chapter 2 reviewed basic macro- and microeconomic considerations with respect to corporations and shareholders. Scarce resources of production are land, labor, and capital. As owners of resources of production—except for labor, which cannot be owned—corporations decide how to allocate scarce resources to production. The acquisition of capital by corporations constitutes investment as part of GDP. Corporations acquire capital with the savings obtained from shareholders when they purchase shares in an IPO. The funds obtained by corporations from shareholders who purchase shares in an IPO, along with the funds obtained from the sale of bonds in an IPO, are the corporation's financial capital, which it then uses to acquire productive capital.

Chapter 3 reviewed finance considerations with respect to corporations, owners of shares, and investors in shares. Federal securities laws dictate what is required by corporations in order to raise financial capital from the public. In order to issue stock to the public, corporations must file a registration statement with the Securities and Exchange Commission. The registration statement requires corporations to provide audited financial statements that comply with generally accepted accounting principles (GAAP). The registration statement must disclose what the corporation intends to do with the financial capital it receives from purchasers of shares, which in general, depending on the type of business, includes the acquisition of capital resources of production. The price of stock issued in an IPO is generally determined by the corporation and not a function of supply and demand determined by trading in the market since the stock is not traded in the market until after it is issued.[1]

Chapter 4 reviewed basic investment considerations with respect to corporations, owners of shares, and investors in shares. While owners of share

are investors in shares, I segregated the terms to emphasize the fact that owners of shares are not investors in the corporation. Investment from the corporation's perspective is the acquisition of capital resources of production, the "I" of GDP (C + I + G). Investment from the shareholders' perspective is not actually investment although it is called investment in both popular and scholarly literature. By definition, funds not used by individuals for consumption is savings so when individuals purchase shares they use their savings in one type of savings (e.g., a savings account) to purchase shares which is just another type of savings. The money in individual savings accounts is used by the financial intermediary (bank) to lend to corporations (which includes purchasing bonds), giving rise to the equation savings by individuals equals investment by corporations.

The corporation's assets are financed by debt (bonds) and the equity created when it issued stock, which together constitute its weighted average cost of financing (erroneously called its weighted average cost of capital).

The Financial Asset Pricing Model (erroneously called its Capital Asset Pricing Model) relates the price of stock traded in the market to risk as a function of the market. Stock is neither a capital asset of the owners of shares, not a capital asset of the corporation. Shares of stock are defined by the Delaware General Corporation Law as personal property and by the Uniform Commercial Code as financial assets.

Chapter 5 reviewed accounting considerations from the perspective of both corporations and owners of, and investors in, shares. Corporations whose share are publicly traded must provide audited financial statements that comply with GAAP to accompany the registration statement filed with the SEC and thereafter must issue on an annual basis general purpose financial reports also audited by an independent public accounting firm. The financial reports include the balance sheet, which reports the financial and productive capital owned by the corporation (the left side of the balance sheet), as well as the liabilities owed by the corporation and the net assets (equity) owned by the corporation (the right side of the balance sheet). The corporation's equity is erroneously reported as the shareholders' equity. It is, according to property law and corporate law, the corporation's equity. The corporation's equity, erroneously referred to historically as the "capital account," or the entire right side of the balance sheet, is erroneously called the corporation's capital.

The financial statements also include the statement of cash flows that reports how the corporation financed its acquisition of productive capital and how it obtained its financial capital. In other words, it reports how the corporation invested its newly obtained financial capital.

Chapter 6 reviewed the nature of the firm as expounded by Coase (1937). The nature of the firm attempts to explain what is a firm and why firms come into existence. According to Coase, the distinguishing mark of the firm is the suppression of the price mechanism. It attempts to bridge the gap in economic theory between the assumption that resources are allocated by the price mechanism in the market and the assumption that the allocation depends on the entrepreneur. The use of the price mechanism in the market has costs, and according to Coase reducing transaction costs explain why firms come into existence.

While transactions costs may be reduced within a firm, reducing transactions costs is not the reason why corporations are created. Corporations are created in order to acquire large amounts of financial capital and to reduce risk. But Coase makes a fatal error in assuming that the allocation of resources depends on the entrepreneur when in fact the allocation of resources depends on the corporation that owns the resources.

Chapter 7 reviewed the multifaceted theory of the firm. The theory of the firm was originally based on agency theory and its concomitant agency costs and transaction costs. The agency theory of the firm posits that directors are agents of shareholders. I have proven that to be false according to agency law. The theory of the firm was then extended into the nexus of contracts, property rights, and incomplete contracts theories. The nexus of contracts contends that a corporation is a nexus of contracts. But since everything is a nexus of contracts the theory does nothing to advance our understanding of corporations. Property rights theory is based on the mistaken principle that shareholders have property rights in the corporation or the corporation's assets which I have shown is precluded by property law and corporate law. The latest development in the theory of the firm is the incomplete contracts theory which argues that a corporation consists of a series of incomplete contracts. However, contract law requires contracts to be complete in all essential elements. If any one essential element is absent, there is no enforceable contract. If there is provision in a contract that is missing but not essential, then whether a corporation consists of incomplete contracts adds little to our understanding of corporations or capitalism.

The theory of the firm cannot accommodate capitalists or capitalism because it depends entirely on the separation of ownership and control. If shareholders are separated from controlling corporations, as the theory holds, then shareholders are separated from the ownership of capital and they therefore cannot direct the allocation and use of capital. Thus, if they cannot own capital, they cannot be capitalists. If there are no capitalists, there is no capitalism.

Chapter 8 reviewed various aspects of capital and how the failure to use the term "capital" consistently has led to a distortion of the meaning and significance of capital. Financial capital (money, cash) is not a scarce resource of production. It is used to acquire capital resources of production. Productive capital is the resource of production which, along with land and labor, is a scarce resource. Both financial capital and productive capital are owned by corporations, not individuals.[2]

Productive capital, or capital, is nothing more than something made, created, produced, or manufactured by labor to use in production and ranges from stone implements to automated machinery. Marx mischaracterized the ownership of capital, asserting capital is owned by individual capitalist-entrepreneurs when it is, by property law and corporate law, owned by corporations. His mischaracterization of capital led him to misinterpret the money-commodity cycle. The ownership of capital by corporations is not the ownership of capital by shareholders by proxy. Shareholders do not own corporations. Furthermore, Marx was not consistent in distinguishing financial capital from productive capital, compounding his misinterpretation of the capitalist mode of production.

Chapter 9 reviewed the notion of capitalism, or what Marx called the capitalist mode of production. Capitalism is both an economic and a social system. The chapter reviewed Marx, Sombart, and Weber's theories of capitalism and its origins.

Marx frequently confused financial capital and productive capital. He consistently misinterpreted capitalism by attributing the ownership of capital to individual capitalist-entrepreneurs, which may have been true prior to the advent of corporations whose shares are traded in the market, but was not true in Marx's time. Attributing the ownership of capital to individuals was also an error committed by Sombart and Weber.

Chapter 10 continued with the review of capital with an emphasis on Marx's mischaracterization of the ownership of capital. Marx's *Manifesto* calling for the abolition of private property and the ownership of capital by capitalists, is an undeniable indication of his failure to understand who owns capital. His tirade against the capital mode of production was not actually against the capital mode of production, but against the social and economic system created by the ownership of capital by capitalists which was no longer true with the advent of corporations whose shares are traded in the public.

Chapter 11 reviewed the contradictions of corporate law. Courts, economists, and legal scholars proclaim that shareholders are owners, residual owners, or beneficial owners of corporations when property law, trust law, and corporate law state otherwise. Courts, economists, and legal scholars declare that directors are agents or trustees of shareholders when agency law and trust law do not permit directors to be agents or trustees of shareholders.

Chapter 12 was a recap of the contradictions of, economics, finance, investment, accounting, and the theory of the firm in relation to corporate law summarized in the Epilogue.

Summary

The discussions in the previous chapters revealed the erroneous assumptions that owners of shares are capitalist-entrepreneurs and that they own the capital resources of production. An entire spirit, attitude, and mindset—indeed, an entire economic and social system—has emanated from these errors.

Ownership of capital, whether financial or physical, as determined by property law and corporate law, is ignored in all theories of the firm and theories of capitalism. Attempts were made to somehow link capitalism and corporations by inventing the term "corporate capitalism," but such attempts were futile from the start. Ownership of capital is still imputed to shareholders rather than the corporation. As a matter of corporate law and private property law, shareholders do not own either the financial capital or the productive capital. Therefore, shareholders cannot be capitalist-entrepreneurs, and corporations (or their directors, officers, or managers) cannot be capitalist-entrepreneurs.

The theories and research in corporate law, economics, finance, investment, and accounting is intent on supporting an agenda designed to maintain the artificial boundaries established by decades of research founded on indefensible assumptions and fallacious conclusions. Maintaining such artificial boundaries is akin to the behavioral traits of certain species marking and defending their territories. They are loath to abandon theories that have proven to be lucrative, including receiving Nobel prizes.

Entire social and economic systems have been constructed on concepts of "capital," "capitalist," and "capitalism" that are not legally, historically, economically, or sociologically valid. Capitalism as a social and economic system is said to be a function of the laws of private property while at the same time it is said to be based on the private, as opposed to government, ownership of the means of production. Refusing to interpret capital, capitalist, and capitalism within the parameters of corporate law and property law, which preclude individuals from owning the means of production, corrupts the meaning of capitalist and capitalism.

What can be said conclusively is first, that the capital is there, but since corporations now own the capital, the capitalist and capitalism have become extinct. The system previously known as capitalism is today merely an artifact of history.

Second, in order to prevent corporate financial statements from being misleading, corporations must cease labelling equity as shareholders' equity when it is in fact the corporation's equity. This also requires a revision in GAAP nomenclature.

Third, economics, finance, investment, and accounting researchers must cease referring to stock as capital assets; they must cease referring to owners of shares as owners, residual owners or claimants, or beneficial owners of corporations; and they must cease referring to directors as agents.

For those who persist in advancing the economic theory of the firm based on shareholders as owners of or investors in the corporation, or directors as agents of shareholders, the burden of proof is now on them to refute the legal proof I have provided herein. I submit that the evidence is incontrovertible.

Notes

1 The corporation will generally set a minimum price, which may be bid up by subscribers to the issue. The corporation may withdraw the offering if there is insufficient demand.
2 Of course, an individual may own productive capital if the individual owns a business and is using that capital in her business.

Bibliography

Coase, R.H. (1937). The nature of the firm. *Economica*, 4 (16), 386–405. Retrieved from www.jstor.org/stable/2626876.

Ulen, T.S. (1993). The Coasean firm in law and economics. *Journal of Corporation Law*. 18, 301–303.

Index of Subjects

Index of Cases and Statutes

Index of Authors